THE DEALER

a novel
By JODI CERALDI

Holly Springs Publishing Company
Holly Springs, GA. USA

THE DEALER

Published in the United States of America
Holly Springs Publishing Company
P. O. Box 23, Holly Springs, Georgia, 30142

Cover and graphic design by Cindy Steele Tucker

Picture by Trisha Lee West

Ceraldi, Jodi.
The Dealer/Jodi Ceraldi

   1. Title   2. Fiction

Holly Springs Publishing Company 2018

ISBN 9781981588381 Trade Paper Back—First Edition
Also available on Amazon Kindle

ACKNOWLEDGMENTS

A special thanks to Commander Geoffrey F. Decker USN Retired for his editing and wise counsel.

And to Cindy Steele Tucker, author, consultant, and award winning graphic designer, who created the perfect cover and designed and formatted The Dealer.

To Debbie Proctor, my friend and neighbor for her undying dedication in helping me get *The Dealer* completed and published.

I am also fortunate to have a wonderful critique group, composed of Gray Bridges, Kathleen Walker, and Jim Roberts who were with me all through the book.

DEDICATION

To my three wonderful children who grew up with a mother who always worked and was rarely home while they struggled through their school years. They all turned out to be exceptional parents, awesome friends, and law-abiding citizens of a country where they can still choose a way of life.

GOD BLESS THE U.S.A.

Man did not weave the web of life, he is merely a strand in it.

Whatever he does to the web, he does to himself – Chief Seattle, Quoted in an undated bulletin from The Association on American Indian Affairs.

It is good to have an end to journey towards, but it is the journey that matters in the end.—Ursula K. LeGuin, The Left hand of darkness.

OTHER BOOKS BY JODI CERALDI

REDESIGNING THE MOB

NICKY-TWO-FISTS

CESSNA DOWN

Prologue

Nick Salvatoro, aka Nicky-Two -Fists, was a big tough kid from the streets of Hoboken, New Jersey. He had a good heart but still got into trouble. He met Joe Gaetano, a whiny kid who got picked on. When Nick stood up for him, they became friends. After high school, Joe became a police officer. Nick, who had a flare for math, began to deal cards in a mob social club before he graduated into petty larceny and hijacking trucks carrying expensive cargo.

When $200,000.00 was robbed from a jewelry store, Joe, now a detective, answered the alarm and chased the criminals. When he tried to force them off the road, a dump truck coming the opposite way smashed his patrol car. Joe suffered a broken leg that never completely healed. Since he thought the criminals were Nick and his sidekick Sledge, he tried to convict Nick for any unsolved case he could get his hands on.

Nick's sister married a loser without a job. Nick refused to support his sister's family, and got her husband, Putsy, a job as a bag boy for a Mafia drug dealer. The mob caught Putsy cutting the drugs and making a hefty profit. They gave Nick an ultimatum. "Get rid of Putsy, or the mob will get rid of both of you."

When Nick gunned down Putsy, the area was under police surveillance. The mob had set him up, so he turned state's evidence and entered the Federal Witness Protection Program under the name of Robert Anderson. Disappointed in the program, Nick went back to dealing cards at a Miami club. After coming close to another scrap with the law, he left the country with his girlfriend. Four years later, the FBI caught up with him in Italy and offered him a deal.

CHAPTER ONE
Italy 2007

Motioning toward a road sign, Angela shouts, "We're almost there!" *Turn up the Music* by Chris Brown is blasting on the CD player and almost drowns out her voice.

I nod and smile. I've never been so happy in all my life.

My girlfriend, Angela, and I are traveling from Florence to Rome in our four-year-old Volkswagen Jetta. The car's remarkably safe on the highways, but well suited to maneuver the winding narrow roads in Europe.

We're celebrating Angela's thirty-ninth birthday. We've made many new friends since we fled from Miami to Italy four years ago, but for this special occasion, we want to be alone.

It's a sunny morning and the windows are wide open. A warm breeze whips through the car and lifts my honey's dark-brown curls. Her sweet, fresh smile reminds me of the actress, Ashley Michele Greene.

We arrive in time for lunch at a small *trattoria*. The restaurant is crowded, but we're in luck. One small table for two is available. I beam as patrons turn and stare at Angela. She's a towering six-foot beauty, has a drop-dead figure and walks with the skill of a Paris model. When the waiter arrives, we order *linguini dé maré* with marinara sauce. The aroma of savory herbs drifts in from the Italian *cucina*. It's like being back in my late mama's kitchen in Jersey.

"Did Galleria Borghese say why they weren't open until one o'clock today?" she asks.

"They had some sort of private showing. The lady said I could pick up our passes at window three."

"At least we won't have to stand in line to pay." Angela stretches her back after driving so long. "I've heard this is one of the most visited museums in Italy."

"Would you like me to drive?" I ask.

"No, I'm fine." She smiles. "We don't have far to go."

"I think it's about fifteen kilometers." I smile. "They did offer free vouchers for the affair if we arrived by ten, but I didn't think we could get to the museum that early. I know you don't like to rush."

"Why didn't you ask me what I wanted to do before you turned down the free passes?" She pouts.

"I'm sorry, darling. I thought I was doing the right thing. You hate parties, and we always arrive late."

Angela giggles and blows me a kiss. "I'm only joking, sweetie. I like the quiet."

She teases me constantly and I never know if she means it or not, but when I'm with her, I feel like a teenager. What difference does it make if I'm fifteen years her senior and sometimes don't know what's going on in that pretty little head of hers? My charming princess is a mature woman with the heart of a child. I love her so much.

After lunch, we wander over to the museum and Angela meets two friendly women.

"I'll catch up with you, Billy." Angela waves me on with the tips of her fingers.

Billy's a pet name she calls me when we're out in public. She started playing this game after I grew a mustache and a mini strap beard to change my appearance, so my old friends in the mob wouldn't recognize me. She said I reminded her of the late Billy Mays, so to complete the picture I now use Grecian Formula to cover the encroaching gray.

Angela's few minutes of chatting often turn into long-term friendships, so I mosey along the portraits until I come to Caravaggio's St Jerome. It piques my interest, but before I have a chance to digest the suggestion that St. Jerome is depicted in the act of translating the *Vulgate, a* young man sidles up behind me.

"Mr. Anderson," he whispers.

I'm stunned when I hear the alias the feds gave me back in Jersey when I first entered the Federal Witness Protection Program.

The young man is dressed in a bright blue jacket with gold epaulets. He smiles and holds out an envelope. "I have dispatch," he says with a thick accent.

At over six feet and an easy two-hundred pounds, I dwarf the messenger. Although I'd called ahead and purchased the tickets under the name of Robert Anderson, I'm curious as to how this young man knows I'm the Mr. Anderson he's looking for. I step away from the painting and hesitate.

"The *signore* says it is important," the messenger tells me. "Would you prefer I leave *messaggio* at information desk?"

Now I get it. A gentleman has pointed me out. "No, give it to me."

He hands me the communiqué, clicks his heels, and leaves. I unfold the note.

Meet me at the information desk, next to the settee. I have urgent intelligence for you. Walter Adonis Cox, III Federal Bureau of Investigation Agent, U.S.A.

Oh, Lord. What now? I knew the FBI would keep me on their radar, but they have no reason to come after me. I've been on the straight and narrow for four years.

Although Angela and I have traveled to many art exhibits, this is our first trip to Galleria Borghese, so I don't know where the exits are—not that I have a reason to run.

When I scan the gallery for Angela, I see she's still at the far end of the room engrossed in conversation with the same two women. She spies me walking toward the doorway. I lift my index finger, signaling I'll only be a minute. Without blinking, she turns back to her new friends.

A man with a military haircut, undoubtedly the agent, stands next to the settee. His feet are spread and his jacket hangs open. His arms dangle and he appears relaxed. He reaches into his jacket pocket, and I spring forward, but all he pulls out is identification.

He steps backward and flashes ID. "You're an untrusting species. However, I don't blame you for being jumpy

4

considering all the news about the recent European museum thefts. You must have noticed that security is tighter than usual." The government man reaches out to shake my hand. "It's nice to meet you, Nick. I apologize for sending my message to Robert Anderson. I didn't know if you would respond to Mr. Salvatoro."

I shake his hand. "You don't expect me to believe you traveled all the way from Arlington, Virginia just to let me know how futile it would be for me to steal a Rembrandt."

"Not at all. I have a much greater reason. Let me introduce myself. I'm Walter Cox, FBI Agent for the United States."

"I gathered that."

Cox shrugs off my remark.

"So what's your problem?" I assume offense is my best defense.

He gives me a surface smile. "I noticed you earlier when you were admiring Caravaggio's St. Jerome. I too, am a patron of the arts, an appreciation I acquired many years ago during my father's European assignments in the diplomatic corps."

"Cut the bullshit. You're not here to discuss paintings. What do you want from me?"

Cox moves away from the information desk and lowers his voice. "The FBI has a serious situation, and they thought they could use a person with your reputation."

"My reputation for what?" I ask. "Dealing cards, or just happening to know a few guys in the mob? I wasn't even in tight enough for you to pin the RICO Act on me, or for the mob to care if I got in or out of a jam. Or maybe you're talking about my reputation of breaking the *Omerta,* and getting a price put on my head in exchange for your lousy Witness Protection Program. The FBI used me. My relationship with the FBI is over, and you need to take a hike."

I expect him to back off, but he gives me an intimidating look. "Speaking of your reputation, I believe your fame as a hit man is well established.

I roll my eyes. "How do you guys come up with this crap? Is this what you're gonna prosecute me for?"

"We're not looking to prosecute you. You're going to take a trip to Belize--courtesy of the FBI."

"What?" I spread my arms.

"I'll get right to the point and save us both time and trouble. We recently added a guy named Ernesto Ramos to our kingpin list. He lives in Belize, and we have his address. He's a no-good drug dealer and needs to be taken out."

"Look, buddy." I tap my finger on his lapel. "You got the wrong guy." I turn away.

"You're the right man, Nick, or would you prefer I call you Nicky-Two-Fists like the mob did? You're a convicted felon with outstanding warrants."

His rapid response stops me dead in my tracks. He thinks he knows all about me, but there's one thing he doesn't know. I'm not stupid. "You need to get your facts straight. I'm not a felon, and I was never convicted."

"There may be some truth in that. However, if this were the United States you'd be on your way to jail for questioning, and the interrogation might very well put you behind bars."

"Well, lucky me." My upper lip curls. "I'm not in the United States."

"In case you've forgotten or obliterated the facts from your brain, I'll bring you up to date. Our records indicate that Nicky-Two-Fists built up a mile-long rap sheet, most notably a possible connection to a couple of homicides in New Jersey and illegal gambling in Florida. If that's not enough, a few years back you were a suspect in a grand theft case. Would you say that's a fair analysis?"

He's gonna try to nail me to the Mafia again. "Those days are over. The nickname was nothing more than a kid's game. It never meant anything." I don't care how much he pushes, he's not gonna get a rise outta me. "You better check your facts before you open your yap. There's a reason for my being put in the Witness Protection Program. All those charges were dropped in exchange for my cooperation."

"So you say."

"It's the same old story with you guys. I paid my dues and now you expect me to pay again. It's not my fault you're unable to do your job."

His expression doesn't change.

"If you had anything on me, you wouldn't be standing here flapping your jowls. You would've had me extradited."

"Good point." Cox's chin stiffens. "We might be able to arrange that."

"Did you travel to Italy looking for trouble or a confession?" I snap.

"Neither. We want your help, and in return, you keep your freedom and operate *laissez faire*. How difficult is that?"

"Nothing is ever that simple." I shake my head. "You have a poor way of requesting a favor. Especially when I already have my emancipation."

"The FBI is agreeing not to prosecute for any crimes committed after you entered the Witness Protection Program like for instance your escapades in Miami." He shrugs. "Besides, we don't need grounds on you. We've located your young friend, Raymond Davis, in New Jersey. Joseph Gaetano, Chief Investigator for the City of Hoboken, New Jersey, recognized him from his picture in the newspaper. We know the young man drove to Florida to help you run an illegal poker operation at a night club on Biscayne Boulevard, in Miami. If you decline to help the FBI, we can and will indict Raymond Davis for collaborating with you to pull off a scam."

Davis? He doesn't even have his correct last name. Davis was a part of his alias in Miami. "Listen, asshole. I'm not going to help you. I didn't swindle anyone and I don't know a Raymond Davis. You can't substantiate the activities you're talking about."

"You need to reevaluate your decision. The bureau has been working with Gaetano,"

Oh, so Cox didn't research anything. He got the name Billy-Bob Davis from that lowlife cop. He must have overheard me accidently call him Ray one day when we were all together. "You say he's chief Investigator. It sounds like my old schoolyard pal, Jogger Joey, has weaseled himself a fancy title. Whose butt did he kiss for that job?"

Our interest is not predicated on how Gaetano obtained his advancement. The information he gave the FBI could cause your friend Raymond considerable grief and ruin the young man's business career. Gaetano also informed us that you are the best man for the job."

"Gaetano recommended me?" I laugh. "That's a joke."

"As a matter of fact, he said you were the mobster's best hit man." Cox looks around the gallery before tossing out the next blow. "Gaetano claims the mob paid you to kill your own brother-in-law."

"I've never been paid to kill anyone."

"The court records indicate you admitted to killing your sister's husband."

"The situation with my sister's husband was a long time ago, and I've paid for that mistake." My mouth is so dry I can barely speak. "If you think Joe is trying to help you, you're sadly mistaken.

"That may or may not be true, but it doesn't negate his giving the FBI incriminating information about Raymond." Cox rubs his chin. "This time we think he got it right."

I contemplate punching this guy out, but that would only give him a reason to arrest me. I can't let him sucker me in. I guess Gaetano doesn't care what happens to me. If he did he would've kept his mouth shut about Miami.

My mind unravels the life I had four years ago. First the mob put me between a rock and a hard spot. They forced me to do a job I didn't want to do. When I got caught, the Mafia threw me under the bus. Then the FBI saw an opportunity to use me. After that, my own sister disowned me, and my old flame, Taffy, dumped me. The only person who stood by me was Raymond.

I wrestle with my temper. "Okay, I did know a young kid called Raymond, but he didn't do anything illegal. If the FBI arrests him, I can assure you they'll lose the case."

Cox sneers. "I don't believe the FBI will have to go to court."

"What makes you say that?" I ask the pompous ass.

"Gaetano says you won't risk letting the boy take the rap."

That's the only part Joe got right. "Raymond was only a pizza delivery boy. He's a good kid and the only person who visited me and brought me cigarettes when I was in jail. After I left Jersey, he drove clear to South Florida just to see me. I promised the kid I'd never let him get into trouble."

"Why would you promise him that if you weren't doing anything illegal?"

I should have kept my mouth shut. There's no beating these guys. They got all the answers.

"Our intelligence service personally told me that when he came to Florida, he got more than a vacation." Cox smirks. "He got an education in racketeering."

"Intelligent service my butt. All you got is what Joe Gaetano told you." This guy is really asking to get his ass kicked.

Cox rolls his tongue around in his mouth as if contemplating his next chess move. "How does a poor kid from Hoboken put himself through college, help raise his younger siblings and start his own business in four years?"

"Raymond was a good Catholic boy. He attended St. Peter and Paul's High School. He told me his family received at lot of help from friends and neighbors, and I know he worked hard to help support the family and pay for his education."

Cox isn't paying any attention to what I'm saying.

"Look, Mr. Cox."

"Agent Cox," he says.

"Agent, whoever—Gaetano and I grew up together. Our dads were alcoholics, so we didn't have anyone in the diplomatic corps to look up to. Despite our differences, we got along. We weren't bad kids."

"I'm not interested in your childhood." Cox picks at his paltry black hair.

This guy's a real dickhead. For a minute I stare out the window. I still think I should deck him, but that would be playing right into his hand.

After I tuck my ego into my pocket, I try again. "Back then, Joe lived close to the police station and he started hanging out with the cops. I lived on the other side of town, so I ended up on a corner of the city where the mob hung out. And life takes you down the road you live on."

"So what does all this have to do with the price of tomatoes?" Cox asks.

"Give me a friggin' break. I'm trying to explain to you where Joe is coming from. The flatfoot became a dick. Years later, he gets into a car chase, which leads to a freak accident, and he blames me, even though I wasn't within a hundred miles of the place. It left Joe with a bad limp and a dismal outlook. Since then, he's tried every thing he can to make my life a living hell."

"None of what you say is relevant to our present situation." Cox puts his hands in his pockets.

Angela is probably getting worried about me and I don't want to ruin her day. This guy might be a chump, but he looks like a reasonable man. I need to stop this developing situation, so I put on my best forced smile and try a different approach.

"Let me tell you something you do have to be concerned about." I lean close to Cox. "Gaetano is not a good cop. I guarantee you, he brown-nosed himself into that position. If you're gonna deal with that double-crossin' anus, you better watch your step. He whines and cries like a baby until you appease him. Then he'll screw up your case, and you'll look like a friggin' idiot. Can't you see what he's doing?"

"I've listened to all your excuses, but my time has run out. I had hoped you would volunteer, but now I'll give it to you straight. Ernesto Ramos is a murderer, a drug dealer and an enemy of the United States. He needs to be taken out, removed from this earth, so that others can live in peace. This time your actions will be sanctified by the FBI and you will get paid. You do the job or the kid goes down. Even if some smart attorney gets him off, we will ruin his life forever."

I try to appear calm, but I'm sweating and my shirt clings to my back. "I need a little time."

10

"Your flight to Belize leaves in three days. If I have to come looking for you again, I'll have you extradited and take you back in shackles." He hands me a card. "Here's my cell number." Agent Cox walks away and exits the building.

I refuse to let this unexpected problem ruin Angela's birthday celebration. Instead I go back to the Caravaggio painting, and for the rest of our museum tour I stay close to Angela.

Late in the day, we leave Galleria Borghese and head out of the city on a different route toward home. There is only a short bit of daylight left to take in the beautiful rolling hills and the olive groves along the way. My mind wanders. I sense the richness in the soil, and wish I had been born here. I think my life would have been quite different. The green heart of Italy is enticing. I smell history at every turn in the road.

We stop at a small idyllic mom and pop restaurant in the Tuscany region to enjoy an invigorating Italian *aperitivo* drink. We are seated at a large round table with other friendly patrons. Two of them are from an area close to our home in Florence. We introduce ourselves, and for the next hour we drink and chat with the good-natured people.

Angela requests a glass of sparkling *prosecco*, and I decide on the trendy *Aperol* spritz, which is *Aperol, prosecco* and gin with soda water. Several of these new friends have spent the day visiting the dazzling *Piazzale Michelangeli,* the *Duomo,* and the *Piazza della Signoria*. All the places are on Angela's favorite list, so she is eager to hear about their observations.

The estate owner, who is also a *sommelier,* suggests three different wines from local vineyards. I order all three for her birthday party, and share them with our new friends.

Before we eat, each couple takes their turn toasting Angela's birthday with much laughter and congratulations.

During dinner, I recount the conversation with the FBI agent in my mind, and decide how I'm going to explain the situation to Angela.

She touches my hand, bringing me back from my thoughts.

"Look, darling." She points to her plate. "Hand rolled spaghetti."

The chef has personally brought the pasta course to our table. We continue to chat during our freshly prepared six-course gourmet meal about the places we visited and our love of Italy. After the plates are taken away and they have crumbed the table, dessert is served. It's a creamy birthday cake I had secretly ordered in advance made from scratch by the estate owner's wife. We all agree to come back again.

We have made reservations for the night at a chateau just a few miles from here, so we say good-bye to our dinner companions. Angela steers me toward the terrace. The moon is full, and we linger to soak up the surroundings, which are heightened by the flowing wine and light background music.

"This is my best birthday ever," Angela tells me.

We drive to the chateau and snuggle into the billowing feather bedding. I hold her in my arms and as usual she falls asleep. However, there is no sleep for me. I plan to tell her the bad news on the way home. I go over every word I'm gonna say, every phrase, thinking the worst, but hoping for the best.

The next morning, we drive back to Florence. I'm watching Angela's smiling face as she follows the curving yellow road lines. She loves to drive and is extremely competent.

I glance at the passing countryside. "It's hard to believe that four years have passed since we high tailed it out of the United States on a plane bound for Edinburgh. We've traveled many of Europe's back roads hoping to get lost in the daily scuffle from the Mafia," I ramble on trying to get my courage up before I spring the bad news.

"Do you miss dealing and hanging out with the mob," she says from out of nowhere.

I can't lie to her. "Sometimes I think about the exciting life that almost got me killed, but I also know that if I returned to my exhilarating past, the peaceful life we have now and the bright future we've planned would be lost forever."

"Does that mean that someday you may go back?" She tilts her head to the side and glances at me out of the corner of her eye.

"Never," I say. "My affiliation with the New Jersey mob ended in a narrow escape with the help of Miami Vice. I learned that gambling, narcotics and murder were part of a vicious, unbreakable spiral. Only luck, timing and desperation saved me from a certain death at the hands of one of many persons who blame me for their downfall."

"And if payback time ever comes?" she asks.

Wow! Why did she say that? Did I talk in my sleep?

"Speaking of payback, I have something to tell you." Then I dropped the whole sad tale about the FBI agent catching up with me at the gallery.

"I knew something was up. You left me for a long time."

"The Fed's have promised me a new beginning in return for going undercover to bust up an international drug and money laundering ring."

I figure Angela will view my acceptance of their proposal as a broken promise to her, and not as the only way to ensure our future together.

"When are you planning on leaving?" she asks.

"My commitment will begin in a couple of days."

Immediately she says we should pack up and leave. "We can go to Switzerland and hide out in the mountains."

"You want to leave our home in Florence after all the work you put into it?"

"I don't care about the house. I care about you." Tears glisten in her eyes.

I would love to do what she has suggested, and maybe a few years ago I might have, but after four years with Angela, I've learned what true love is. As much as I would like to pack up and run, I can't do that to her. She deserves better.

"I won't be gone long. It will only take a few days."

"What do they want you to do?" she asks.

"It's secret government work. I can't tell you."

"Is it dangerous?"

"Nah." I laugh. "You know how they are. The government doesn't tell anyone what they're doing. They don't want people to know how they spend our tax money."

"Are you telling me the truth?"

"I always tell you the truth."

She rolls her eyes, then reaches over and holds my hand. "I'll help you pack. As a matter of fact, instead of staying here by myself, I think I'll go see Mom and Dad. They would love a visit from me."

"That's a good idea," I say. However, I'm amazed at her sudden decision.

"Don't forget to call me if you find the job is going to take longer than you expect," Angela says.

"I will, I promise."

A few hours later, we arrive home. Angela makes several phone calls.

"Always being underfoot is not good, so I made plans to go to my girlfriend's on Monday and stay overnight." Angela giggles. "That will give Mom and Dad a night by themselves."

"Which girlfriend is that?" I ask.

"Helen, I don't think you met her. We worked together at the insurance company. She's several years older than I am, but we get along well."

"Is she married?"

"No, she lives alone. I think she has a cat. Helen has a quilting party at her home on Mondays. I thought this would be the perfect time to see what quilting is all about, and a good place for you to call me and let me know when your coming home."

"A quilting party?" I laugh.

"Do you think I can't sew?" she quips.

That was thoughtless of me. I was only laughing with her, but apparently she didn't see it that way. I shouldn't have laughed at her idea. I'm so wrapped up in my own crap that I didn't think about her feelings. I hope she'll understand if this job takes longer than I planned.

Two days later, I kiss her at security, pass through the turnstile and wave good-bye. I hope this is not our last kiss. I don't trust the FBI any more than I trust the mob. I got a hunch that something is gonna go wrong. I grip the boarding pass and my nails dig into my skin.

CHAPTER TWO
Belize Jungle

I wake to chirping birds and screaming tree monkeys. Water shimmers on the leaves from nightly rain showers. FBI Agent Cox said this would be a one-day event, but I've already spent three days in this self-contained prison. He also told me the DEA surveillance team had taken rides on the jungle tour boats. They reported the kingpin is usually outside, sitting alone each time they pass his palatial house. So how come ever since I got here, he's been dragging out a pissy-ass kid that hangs all over him?

Emotional strain and insufficient rest has left me exhausted. When I attempt to doze on the damp, muggy jungle floor, my back aches and my swollen ankles throb. I jump at the smallest movement, and lately I've had to force myself to concentrate on the mansion.

Ramos's magnificent home is located in the Orange Walk area and sits about two football fields back from New River. I use binoculars to see the architectural paradise that serves as the kingpin's residence. The intricate workmanship must have taken eons to build and cost millions.

Small wildlife has adapted to my squatter rights. Raccoons, field mice and garden lizards run along the ground only a few inches from me, but a tree monkey's feet rarely touch the ground. I notice they feed on specific trees, and consume beautiful yellow flowers for dessert. Sometimes they swing low, beat on their chests and screech at me. However, little by little they pay less attention. Hours pass slowly, and the noon-day sun is a fuckin' scorcher. Even shady areas are suffocatingly hot.

Belize has a huge tourist trade, so the government allowed a hotel to be built in the middle of the jungle. The tropical resort isn't far from my hiding place. Tourists, who go on land safaris and river boat tours, feed the wild animals nourishment provided by the resort owners. They keep the animals so well fed that they seem to be unperturbed by the presence of humans.

I haven't seen a crocodile, but Agent Cox claims they're nocturnal and avoid contact with humans. Like I'd believe a tall tale like that. I pat the forty-four-magnum holstered around my waist and tied to my leg. He did warn me to watch out for the nighttime Bristle worm, a small orange caterpillar with glass-like spikes that lodge under your skin. However, on my way here I met an old native fisherman who said the Bristle worm is mostly found near coral.

Belize's travel literature says there are no poisonous snakes in this country, but due to the geographic closeness to Yucatan, one might expect to find all kinds of snakes. During the night, my skin crawls with anticipation of a boa constrictor slithering close by. One species very much aware of my existence is the mosquito. It's too hot to wear my long sleeve jersey during the day, so I tried the netted shirt that Cox loaned me, but the pests bite right through the spaces. Even after spraying myself with Off. . .Wap. I slap a mosquito the size of Nebraska. Blood splatters on my hand. Regardless of the warnings, I'm more concerned with crocs and snakes than caterpillars and mosquitoes.

My body isn't adapting to this primitive environment, and neither is my brain. I've acquired a third-grade attention span, and I'm squandering time I need to prepare for this assignment. Unless an opportunity presents itself soon, the government will need to force another patsy to play their *Hit Man Game*. I've had enough of this jungle life.

My inattentive mind switches to Angela. She seemed to take my leaving for a few days in stride, but now I wonder if she's sorry she left her nice safe home in Miami to hide-out with me in Europe. Her sudden decision to visit her parents was a good idea, but a bit of a shock. After I left Florence,

Angela packed a few clothes and went to the airport. She took a chance to go standby and managed to get a seat on the next plane to the states. I changed planes in Atlanta, and she called me from Miami before I reached Belize.

She said her father reminded her that this would happen. He's such a jerk. Of course, Angela stood up for me, but I hate to think she has to defend my character.

I close my eyes and picture her waving good-bye when I left Florence. I would love to catch a plane and vacation with her. But I won't. Too many people know me in Miami, I could put her life in jeopardy.

Late in the afternoon, I eat my last can of tuna and wash it down with warm, lemon-lime Gatorade. I have a walkie-talkie, but was told to maintain radio silence. I'm only allowed to use it for my extraction from the jungle. I hope someone is listening for my call.

A slanted path from the drug lord's house leads to a twelve-foot, cement containment wall that stretches along the river as far as I can see. Apparently, it is a barrier to keep out the wild animals that have access to the river. Just inside the barrier, about a hundred feet to the left of the path is a large cement slab. It must be Ramos' helicopter pad that Cox told me about.

On my side of *New River*, the embankment is twenty feet higher and the perfect place for a sniper rifle. From my advantage point I can see over the top of the cement fence. The animals need access to the water, so there is no fence on this side of the river.

I can't ever leave my post. The constant vigil grinds on my nerves. Who knows when my distinguished objective will emerge from his mansion and provide me the precise opportunity to make the kill?

When evening approaches, the monkeys stop their playful antics and settle on branches to rest. Another day is slipping away, and. . .what's that noise?

There's a far-off sound of an engine. As it comes closer, I hear the rhythm of helicopter blades. I see "Longview Banana Corporation" printed on the side as it passes over my jungle bed. They must not be scanning the undergrowth because the aircraft continues across New River, hovers over the concrete slab, and puts down on the landing pad.

Ramos comes outside. Today, for the first time since I've been here, he walks out of the house alone. He climbs into a four-seated golf cart and rumbles along the path toward the river.

"This is it." I snap to attention. I can hardly believe my eyes. Once again, I look at the FBI photograph. The driver has a full head of salt and pepper hair and a thin mustache. His jaw line is narrow, and his eyes are deep set. This is the right man and the opportunity I've been waiting for. I look through the binoculars and transfix my vision on the rolling cart.

An attractive young lady with a long ponytail exits the helicopter. She's smiling and waving to the man in the golf cart. He joyfully waves back. I wonder if she could be his daughter?

She's not far away, and the binoculars make her face clear enough to see her long dark eyelashes. She reminds me of a South American beauty queen I once met.

I didn't think the fatal moment would arrive in this manner. The young woman appears to be quite happy. I begin to have second thoughts about doing the job. Then, I remember the resident of this luxurious house is also one of the largest and most ruthless opium and cocaine distributors in the world. It's because of his political power and financial influence that I have been shanghaied into these sweltering surroundings.

My doubts disappear. I feel my heart skip a beat, my hands grow cold and clammy and my fingertips tingle. Good God-Almighty. I haven't shot a man in years and this seems so impersonal. It's not like when I was fighting for my life.

I lay on the ground beside the FBI's Nemesis Arms Rifle that is set up on a tripod. I lift the stock, raise the gun a fraction and sight my victim in the crosshairs.

Just as I take a deep breath, the cart turns off the path and angles toward the helicopter. My target is now at a ninety-degree angle. "Damn." I should have fired before he turned.

Why did I wait? Sweat drips from my forehead and into my eyes. "Stop it. Don't panic. Make the shot."

The loud crack of gunfire interrupts the normal late afternoon chatter of the jungle and causes a flock of birds to spring into the air. There is a brief instant of dead silence before wildlife begins to stir again.

The golf cart has stopped and the kingpin's face is lying flat against the steering wheel. The young lady's smile has been replaced by fear.

The pilot races from the helicopter. He stops halfway and turns all the way around, as if searching for a shooter. Maybe he has just realized he's out in the open and may also get shot. He waves his arm, motioning the girl toward the house, but the girl does not move.

Ramos struggles to get out of the cart, but he falls to the ground. The pretty girl is flailing her arms and yelling. The pilot lifts the bleeding man into the back seat of the cart. The young lady crawls in beside the drug lord and puts her arms around him. The pilot drives the golf-cart up the path toward the big house as fast as it will go. I watch as Ramos' white shirt turns red.

Several people apparently heard the shot and come out of the house to see what the commotion is all about. They stand at the edge of the veranda. When the drug lord waves his blood-soaked arm, they jump up and down and appear to be cheering.

My feet sink into damp dirt that skirts the river bank. Ernesto Ramos is very much alive. This is not the way I planned it.

I glance at the rifle. I had the kingpin square in the crosshairs. I held the gun steady and, given the accuracy of the Nemesis Arms Vanquish, the bullet couldn't have been off by that much. Caught up in excitement, I didn't even think about a second shot, but it doesn't matter. I wouldn't have taken a chance of hitting the woman.

My mind shifts into high gear. I don't have a second to waste. Ramos' guards will be on their way, and even though there's a narrow river between us, they don't have far to go to cross a bridge.

It's almost a mile to my extraction point. It takes thirty seconds to use the walkie-talkie to send the password to pick me up, break down the rifle, and cram it into my backpack. Then I grab the rest of my shit and leave the jungle.

While I race along the over-grown path, I recalculate a direct route to my pick up spot and take-off through the brush. The dense undergrowth slashes my arms and draws blood, but I forge ahead. The closer I get to my destination, the clearer I see the U.S. government's agenda. There's no military base in Belize. All I've seen is a few FBI and DEA guys operating quietly out of the American Embassy, and they are all trained sharp shooters.

According to local news anchors, The Belize government isn't in favor of the U.S. drug enforcement being stationed on their land. This is understandable, if one listens to the embassy gossip that alleges Belize politicians are paid to turn a blind eye while drug dealers transport opium, cocaine and weed through their country, across Mexico, and into the United States.

"Fuck." The FBI has set me up again. They wanted Ramos assassinated, but they didn't want to be held responsible. They railroaded me into doing this job and plan to walk away clean. I'm the one who's at the mercy of the drug lord's guerrillas and the Belizean government officials.

My short-cut crosses a path often used by jungle species, and twice I pull the revolver from the holster. The animals continue on their way and give me no reason to fire. The last thing I want to do is shoot off a round and reveal my position to the watchdogs. I hear the far-off sound of a helicopter, but it doesn't come close.

Reconnaissance confirms my message, and supposedly is on their way to the appointed pickup spot. I'm making better time than if I had followed the winding path.

Thank God this is over. I wasn't able to do what they wanted, but that's not my problem. These idiots will have to find another guy who had an issue with the law and coerce him into doing their dirty work. My missing the mark has put Ramos on high alert. I doubt anyone will ever be able to get this close to him again.

CHAPTER THREE

Minutes later, I'm at the edge of the jungle and the heavy growth is not as thick. My legs feel like they are about to give out, but I keep moving. When I spot the front end of the fed's Ford Lariat, my strength is renewed. I actually pick up speed. The four-wheel-drive is parked at the end of the dirt road. In the early dusk, tiny yellow running lights give off a faint glow from the top of the truck.

I run toward the exit as fast as my legs will carry me. When the crew spots me, one man jumps out of the truck and windmills his arms for me to hurry. I do my best, but although the rifle is lightweight, the backpack is still heavy.

A brawny guy they call Butch sprints toward me. He grabs my backpack and races ahead of me. "Hurry up. There's a bad storm heading our way."

We race across the last hundred yards, ducking limbs and zigzagging through thorns.

"Help him in, Marco. We gotta get the hell out of here." Butch locks the gate, tosses my backpack into the truck bed and leaps into the front seat beside the driver of the extended cab.

I spring onto a heavy pipe that dresses the truck and doubles as a running board. I grasp the handle that hangs in the doorway, and reach for Marco's outstretched arm. He yanks me into the back seat. He's a slender guy, dressed in green camouflage pants and a black T-shirt like he had on the day they brought me here.

The driver shoves the gearshift into low. I pull my leg inside the truck and close the door a second before he slams his boot on the accelerator. I look back to see if anyone is following, but all I see is brush. Large rain drops pepper the windshield as we careen down the dirt road.

"Buckle your seatbelts." the driver says. "This is a rough road."

We continue to travel alongside the river.

"I can't believe you outran the drug lord's guards," Butch says.

"Me neither," I say. "Maybe his goons weren't able to pick up my trail."

"You mean, like maybe a crocodile ate them." Butch laughs. "You couldn't outrun a tricycle, let alone their four-wheelers. Something must have gone wrong at the mansion."

"So you're surprised I made it?"

"That's not what I said. I just think you're slow."

"I know what you meant," I tell him.

"Shut up," the driver snaps. "Pay attention to the side of the road. Let me know if you see anyone."

"It would have been a lot quicker to pick me up in one of those helicopters I see flying around."

"Those helicopters belong to corporations. They have designated pads they land on," Marco says. "The only time we have a helicopter is when Air Force has approved justification to be here."

"You mean I'm not important enough."

"As a matter of fact, you're not, so stop acting like a big shot," Butch says.

"Knock it off." The driver looks at me in his rear-view mirror. "We have enough problems—no more arguments."

At the end of the dirt road, we make a hard right turn on two wheels. Just as I think the Lariat is gonna roll, it plunks down in an upright position on a scrawny blacktop road.

"Is the backpack still there," I ask. "The rifle's stuffed inside."

Marco turns around and looks into the bed of the truck. "It's still there."

It's late in the day, and in the jungle, darkness comes quick. The driver turns on the high beams. We're now running twenty-miles-an-hour over the speed limit on a winding road that's strewn with pot holes and doesn't have a guard rail. The truck is bouncing all over the place. Every time we go around a sharp bend, I think we're gonna end up in a ditch. This is not the tourist road I came here on.

When we reach a concrete highway, Marco asks, "Did you make the shot? Is Ramos dead?"

I decide it might be better to wait until I talk to Agent Cox. I grin. "Didn't they tell you? All this is hush-hush until the FBI has verifiable proof."

"You can tell us." Butch turns around and smiles at me. "We're DEA,"

"How about him?" I point to the driver. "Is he DEA?"

"Nah, he works at the embassy for Ambassador Logan." Marco says.

"How can I be sure? You all might work for a local contractor that the FBI hired to pick me up."

"Go on. You remember us. We drove you out here," Marco says. "We're all staying at the same hotel. I know you've seen us there."

"Government-men all look alike," I tell them. "You walk the same, you talk the same and you eat the same garbage." I keep a sharp lookout, but except for a few cars going in the opposite direction, the road is deserted. It's a good thing because the driver is now going a hundred miles an hour.

When we reach our destination, I see Agent Cox standing beside a back limo. A dark-skinned man wearing a driver's cap appears to be checking the air in a front tire.

The guy driving the truck looks at his watch. "We're right on time."

I unload the .44, pull the back pack out of the truck bed and tuck the gun inside. When I walk away, the Lariat takes off toward Belize City.

After the dark-skinned man closes Cox's door, he gets in the driver's seat and adjusts his cap. I walk around the limo and crawl in beside the agent. My dirty clothes stink.

He moves away from me. "You need a bath."

"Do I smell that bad?"

"Worse." He pushes the button that closes the heavy, dark-glass partition that separates the driver from the passengers. "This is the ambassador's limo." Cox points toward the front seat. "Jon's the ambassador's driver."

"Why the limo?"

"I use it all the time. Ambassador Logan doesn't care. I like being driven around." Cox smirks. "Don't worry about it."

He touches his finger to his lips.

I guess he doesn't want me to talk.

"What did you do with the puma?" he whispers.

"I wasn't able to get one," I whisper back.

"What?" He turns to face me, "Are you telling me you didn't get a shot?"

My voice is barely audible. "I hit the target, but the puma got away. There's a good chance it's still alive." I tell my story using the codename puma that we had agreed on.

Cox's eyes bug out, but he speaks calmly. "You should've waited until you had a clear view. This is not going to go over well."

"Probably not," I say.

"You know there's a fine for wounding a puma?"

"The ambassador said the fine didn't apply if it was self-defense," I say.

"That's true, but he was planning on sending the stuffed animal home with his wife when she returns to Miami. He's already contacted a taxidermist. He wants to hang it on the family-room wall as a memento of his tour of duty here in Belize." Cox groans.

"When are you planning on telling him?" I ask.

"Tomorrow." Cox sighs. "He'll be disappointed."

"I never professed to be a good shot. Sometimes things don't work out the way you plan."

"Did you see anyone while you were out there?" he asks.

"No." I don't tell him about the old man I met on my way in, who said he had lived in the jungle all his life, and now the jungle resort paid him to work there.

"Good," Cox says. "This country puts a heavy fine on poachers."

"Where are we going now?" I ask.

"Jon is taking us to the hotel beside the embassy. You'll probably get your same room again. It doesn't do a lot of business."

A few minutes later, a police patrol car is riding behind us with flashing lights. The driver pulls the limo onto the side of the road. Cox opens the partition. The officer asks Jon for his credentials and he retrieves them from the glove compartment.

The patrolman shines his flashlight in the back and Cox rolls down the dark window.

"Good evening, Agent Cox. Is everything all right?" the patrolman smiles.

"Yes," Cox says. "Everything is fine. I was just out for a drive."

The beefy officer looks at his watch. "Are you having a bad night?"

"It's the heat. The air-conditioned car soothes my nerves," Cox tells him.

When the patrolman shines his bright light directly into my eyes, I squint and turn away.

"Face this way," the cop barks.

I look into the glaring light.

"Who's your friend?" the officer asks Cox.

Cox doesn't miss a beat. "He's a retired U.S. citizen looking for a warm climate to settle in. He came to the embassy for information on how to acquire citizenship in Belize. I wanted to take a drive to relax before going to bed, and I asked him to accompany me."

The officer grunts and looks at Jon's credentials. He warns Jon to drive safely and not go over the speed limit. The officer returns to his car, and Jon pulls onto the highway. When the officer turns and goes in the other direction, Jon picks up speed.

"What was that all about?" I ask Cox.

Cox pats the seat. "Everything will be okay. The driver's a local and friendly with the chief of police."

"Is that good or bad?" I ask.

"A little of both." Cox doesn't say much during the rest of the ride and when we arrive at the consulate, he tells me to get cleaned up.

"Do I have time for a nap? I've been awake for three days."

"You have several hours before breakfast."

Jon lets us off at the hotel and drives next door to the embassy.

"I'm glad we used the code we made up for our conversation in the car. I don't think Jon could hear us, but I noticed his smug look when we got out of the car," I tell Cox.

I get a room at the hotel. The bed isn't comfortable, but sleep comes quick.

The next morning, I hear a loud knock. I open the door to a tall young man in dress blues. "Briefing room, sir. . .nine thirty sharp." Dress Blues hands me a steaming cup of black coffee. I thank him and he salutes. He must think I'm with the military. Marines always look like they're standing at attention even when they're not.

I dress and walk over to the embassy. Raised voices are coming from the briefing room. "Do you realize what would've happened if he had been caught and they were able to trace that Vanquish back to the FBI?"

"Yes, sir." Agent Cox's voice is shaky.

"If you ever give someone outside the service any kind of weapon registered to the FBI again, I will personally see that your position is terminated."

"An oversight," Cox says. "It won't happen again."

When I walk into the room, Agent Cox and another man in a black suit turn to look at me.

"This is Senior FBI Agent Russell Thompson." Cox points to the man in the black suit.

"Good morning," I say. I reach out to the senior agent to shake his hand.

He ignores my hand and commands, "Sit down."

I wonder if a senior FBI agent could terminate a regular FBI agent, that is, without killing him and hiding the body. It's government work, so I guess anything is possible.

Just as I expected, the shit hits the fan. They drill me over and over about taking the shot. I tell them how I set up the rifle, and then positioned the target in the crosshairs.

"I don't see how I could have missed. I was told the rifle was excellent for at least three-hundred yards, and when I pulled the trigger, my target wasn't even two-hundred yards away. Even though I'm a little slower than I used to be, I still see quite well."

Cox rehashes the firing of the Nemesis rifle until he's interrupted by Thompson.

"Before last night, who was the last man to fire this rifle?" the senior agent asks.

"We haven't used this particular rifle on any job before," Cox says. "When it was shipped to us from the states, we checked it out on a hundred-yard range. It was within specs. All Nick had to do was set the range to three-hundred yards."

"What!" I shout. "I thought the rifle was ready to fire. I could see the house quite clear. No one told me to change any of the settings."

"How the hell would we know how far you were going to have to shoot?" Cox's upper lip rises in disgust.

"How did you expect me to know you didn't have any idea about the domain you were sending me into? You were the guy who told me how far the house was from the river, so I assumed the rifle was good for at least that far."

"Didn't you see the gauges on the scope?" Thompson glares as me.

"Of course I saw them. There was one gauge on the top, and one on the side. They were both set on one. I thought one meant best. The rifle didn't come with directions. Agent Cox showed me how to take it apart and then handed it to me."

"If you didn't know, you should have asked," Cox says between clenched teeth.

"Look, I'm not a country boy. I'm from Jersey. I've never been in the military, and up until this job, I've never fired a rifle."

They look at me skeptically.

So I smart off. "None of the handguns I used in my previous profession had scopes."

"Didn't we give you training on a rifle when you first got here?" Thompson asks.

"Exactly what do you call training?" I ask him. "Marco handed me a loaded M16 and said, 'See if you can hit that target.' I was about a hundred yards away. He didn't mention setting a scope. After the third shot I hit what looked like an outline of a man's shoulder. Then Marco said. "'You're not gonna make it, and I'm not standing out here in the hot sun while you try to learn.'" He took the rifle and left. I figured the lesson was over."

The senior agent shakes his index finger at Cox. "The next time you come up with a grand idea, I want you to check it out with me first. I don't want any more ideas from that guinea detective, Joe Gaetano, in Hoboken. Agent Thompson rises from his chair, marches through the room and out the door.

I grin. I tried to warm Cox about Gaetano, but he wouldn't listen. That's the price you pay for being stupid. I guess it didn't take Gaetano long to get under Agent Thompson's skin.

"When am I getting out of this hell hole?" I ask Cox.

He glares at me and leaves the room without answering.

"Is that it?" It appears the FBI is upset with my performance and wants no part of me, which means I'll soon be on my way home. I can't wait to call Angela.

After spending three days in the jungle, a couple of hours sleep is not enough. I'm still tired from the whole ordeal, so I go back to my room, turn on the television and lay across the bed. I'll let Cox cool down before we talk about my pay and ticket home.

I apparently fall asleep and miss dinner because sometime later, I hear a light knock on my door. It's the lady from the information desk. She's holding a bag from a Mexican restaurant.

"Hi, my name's Iris. I brought your dinner."

"Thank you, Iris. That was nice of you. Is Agent Cox available?" I ask.

"Almost everyone has gone to Belize City. No one is available until morning. Is there anything I can do?" She smiles and edges closer to my doorway.

"No, thank you. I'll check with Agent Cox in the morning. How much do I owe you?" "Nothing, the consulate paid for it." She peeks around me and looks into my room.

"Are you watching television?" She looks at the flat screen hanging on the wall that's been playing all day. "The television in my room doesn't work."

"I, ah, was just going to shut it off. I want to get some sleep tonight."

"Make sure you eat first," she says. "I'll see you tomorrow."

"Yes, thank you again." I close the door.

Whoa, that was close. I open the bag and find a piping hot steak burrito and a container of black beans and rice. The food is good, but I don't have any desire for company. Was she just being nice, or was she offering something else? I swear she gave me a come-on look. Oh well, I hope I didn't hurt her feelings, but I didn't want to get into a conversation about Angela. I don't even want to bring her first name into this crazy environment.

I turn off the television, but I can't fall asleep. My thoughts return to the last time Angela and I went out together. I take her picture out of my wallet, close my eyes and imagine the smell of her perfume. We had a wonderful time. It was her birthday, and I replay every little detail of the celebration over in my mind.

CHAPTER FOUR

So here I am standing at the information desk at the United States Embassy in Belize. My job is over and I'm anxious to get out of here. I ask for Agent Cox. A young man standing next to the desk reaches out and shakes my hand. "I'm DEA Agent Jeff Blackwell." He motions for me to follow him. I assume he is taking me to Agent Cox, but we go into a small empty office. He walks around the desk and stands across from me.

"We're gonna get along just fine, Nick. I look forward to working with you." He hands me a bottle of water from a nearby cooler and opens another for himself.

"Hold on there, buddy." I say. "Cox can't just pass me off to the DEA. I wanna talk to your boss."

"We don't have a military commander here. The only participants are three DEA agents and a couple of FBI men. We've been sent here on special assignment. We report our findings to the FBI and DEA directors in the states." The young agent checks his cell phone.

He's a likable guy, but I don't intend to spend any more time in Belize.

"I only agreed to do the government a favor. I have no real link to the FBI."

"I don't know why the FBI picked you in the first place," Blackwell says.

I remember seeing this guy when I first arrived at the consulate. He's average height, short blond hair, and walks like a body builder. He hangs his jacket on the back of the chair.

"Link or no link, let's get started, we have a lot of material to cover," he says.

I raise the palm of my hand to stop him from beginning what appears to be a training session.

"Hold on. I don't think you understand why I came here."

"I'm listening," the young agent says.

"The FBI asked me to do them a favor. I didn't have to do it, but I agreed, and I did what they asked me to do. It's not my problem that it didn't work. Game over. They need to get someone else for their next maneuver," I tell Blackwell.

Jeff's eyebrows arch as he taps a number on his mobile. "Can you come in here, Cox?" he asks.

Cox charges through the door and walks straight toward me. "What's the problem?"

"You tell me." I shrug. "I did what you wanted, and now I'm gonna go home."

"You were supposed to kill Ramos. You didn't complete your contract."

"I didn't sign a contract. They only paper I signed, and you also put your John Hancock right beside my name, was my safe passage home."

"You're not in Italy now. You're in Belize." Cox sneers.

"Take me to court."

"Maybe I should. According to the newspapers, they don't want you guys here any more than they want me."

"Don't threaten me," Cox snaps. "I could have you put in jail for the attempted murder of Ernesto Ramos. All it takes is one phone call."

"What if I tell them it was your idea?"

"With your fingerprints on the gun, you'd still end up in prison, or worse."

Before I can respond, he plays the Raymond Card, reminding me of our conversation back at the museum in Italy. If I don't cooperate, they'll indict the kid. Our exchange of views escalates, and Jeff leaves the room.

A minute later, the door bursts open. Jeff and a white-haired gentleman enter.

"Ambassador Logan, thank you for coming," Cox says.

Without any hesitation or provocation, the ambassador promptly dismisses the two agents. "I don't believe we've met. I'm Donald Logan, the U.S. Ambassador here in Belize."

"I wish we could have met under different circumstances." I tell the ambassador.

"Please sit down, Mr. Salvatoro. There is no need for anger. I only want to talk to you."

For the next hour, Ambassador Login and I discuss the problem of drugs being transported through Belize and into the United States. We exchange observations on how this affects U.S. families and other countries. He tells me he understands my reluctance to stay on and take this assignment to the next level. Then he says I have a choice, and he will see that my choice is honored.

I sit back in my chair to think about it.

After a couple of minutes, he says. "Now, about your friend, Raymond—I understand he was only seventeen when he met you. Since then, he has put himself through college and became a businessman."

No shit. Most people could have accomplished that with the amount of bread I gave him.

"Gaetano's charges, trumped up or otherwise, would fall on deaf ears in a court of law," he says. "However, if it becomes necessary, I will make sure Raymond has proper legal representation."

"That's not good enough. All that crap Gaetano dreamed up has to be removed from Raymond's records before I agree to help the DEA. I want it in writing that none of the charges regarding anything Raymond did or did not do for me in Florida will not be brought against him now, or at any time in the future."

Our President has determined this mission to be vitally necessary, so I believe I can obtain an affidavit confirming your request." The ambassador lights a Cuban cigar. "I'll make it known to the proper authorities that to charge Raymond with a crime would not serve any real purpose.

"What about me? I want to be sure it'll be worth my while to take on this assignment. Ramos is not going to tell me how he transports drugs from another country into Belize and on to the United States just because we become friends. I'll have to do a whole lot more before he'll confide in me. It could take months."

"We have a lot of people, both here and in other countries working with the logistics. Your job is to get just close enough to get a few details. We'll put it together and we'll have our case."

"You honestly think you can do that?"

"I guarantee it. You'll have a lot of help. The FBI only wanted to get rid of him quickly to save time and manpower. Now they're resigned to doing it properly. It's all part of a big picture."

"Sounds more like a horror movie to me." I tell him.

"I have already suggested that the government pay you level twelve DEA rate plus expenses, with additional hazardous pay and a hefty bonus."

"How much cash do they consider a bonus?" I ask.

He shakes his head. "I don't know."

"Find out before you bring papers for me to sign. Like I told you earlier, if it's not in the neighborhood of the price people get when they do unpredictable, high risk duties, you can count me out," I tell him. "I'm not getting my head blown off for a silver star. I want to know exactly how much money I have coming to me, and if I end up six feet under, I want the money to go to a beneficiary."

"And I want you to promise if I meet your requirements, I can depend on you to keep your word." Ambassador Logan rises from his chair.

After I consider the small amount of cash I have left, I say. "You got a deal."

"You've made a difficult decision. My prayers go with you." Ambassador Logan leaves the room.

I stare at the floor and take a deep breath. I rub the back of my neck while I think about all the bad decisions I've made over the years. I wonder if this will turn out to be another wrong move, not that they left me much of a choice.

A minute later, Jeff Blackwell returns. "I can't believe it. I'm going to be working with the notorious Nicky-Two-Fists."

"One more remark like that and you won't be able to work with anyone again."

"Hey, man. I didn't mean anything. We're cool," Jeff says. "Welcome aboard."

"Not yet. The government has to get their act together first, but until they do, I guess I need a place to stay that's closer to Ramos." I can't believe I've made the decision to stay a little longer in Belize.

Jeff and I sit across the table from each other. He appears excited about the DEA's plans to eradicate the cartels that are moving drugs through Belize and into the United States. He shoves a legal pad and pen toward me.

"You'll need to take notes until you memorize everything. You can't carry any reminders with you."

"That sucks. I don't have a good memory."

"That's exactly what I've been trying to tell you," Jeff says.

"You don't have to agree with me." I glare at him.

He leans back in his chair and crosses his right leg over his left knee. "To begin with, bananas are a big export of Belize. Ernesto Ramos' mansion in Belize is owned by Longview Banana Corporation. So far, we've only found a few banana growers who send their crop to Longview's shipping plant."

"He's evidently making a living or he wouldn't keep the business open," I say.

"We know for a fact there aren't enough bananas being shipped to pay the expenses of the company. However, the plant manager insists they always make a huge profit, and we know they pay a tremendous tax."

"Then they're obviously laundering money, or it's a front for moving contraband." I say.

"All of Ramos' expenses are paid for by Longview Banana Corporation," Jeff continues. "The mansion and the company are held in a trust account in Switzerland, and because of the anonymity, we're unable to determine who the corporation owners are."

"Doesn't the City of Belize know who owns the company?" I ask.

"They say they don't, and as long as the country keeps collecting taxes, they don't seem to care. The corporation is also an unselfish, philanthropic group that gives generously to the needy Belizean people. You can see why not only the authorities, but thousands of poverty stricken residents, are reluctant to talk to us."

"Then why does our government insist on interfering in another country's problems and policies?" I ask.

"Because the drugs Ramos is shipping end up in the United States and people are fighting and killing each other over who is in charge," Jeff replies. "We need to find out who the suppliers are so we can stop the carnage."

"Or maybe our government needs to know who the suppliers are so they can get their cut." I laugh.

"We're risking lives to stop this, and it's not something to joke about," Jeff says.

"You're right. It's not unheard of, but it is odd that Belize is not working with you and the U.S. is not giving you much to work with."

He ignores my input. I don't know if he's naïve, or he just doesn't want to talk about the possibility, so I let it slide. "You may be right about the devastation, but I don't think your logic is a good enough reason to kill a man."

Jeff sighs and looks at me as if I should be thoroughly convinced that the drug problem could have been resolved by killing Ernesto Ramos.

"And of course, if people look like they know how to manage their financial affairs and live a better life than a peasant, the United States assumes they're criminals." I draw clouds on my legal pad. "I've had people say the same thing about me."

"Let's not talk about you." he says.

"Are you accusing me of something, or is it just your adolescent attitude shining through?"

Jeff walks across the room and looks out the window. He shoves his hands into his pants pockets while he taps the toe of his jet black polished shoe. He returns with a good-natured expression on his face, and his shoulders are relaxed. "A large sum of cash is used to run the corporation, and even more is being spent on the mansion. Money is coming from somewhere, and it's not from shipping bananas."

"And where do you think all those funds are coming from?" I ask.

"It's coming from the Punjabi Mafia that uses Ramos' company for a front. We also found out that several Longview employees have previously been indicted for illegal drug trafficking, but they weren't convicted."

"Maybe they weren't guilty." I wait for his point of view.

"Don't pull that bullshit on me," he says. "This place is rooted in more graft than Chicago."

He appears to see only one point of view.

"You shouldn't jump to conclusions," I tell him. "Even if you're right, Belize could be awash with any number of drug smugglers from anywhere in the world."

"That could be, but we haven't been able to get the country's narcotics team to stop and search any Longview trucks. They say they check them while they're being loaded. They claim they're too short-handed to even stop all the known drug smugglers in vans, where they're sure to score a bust." Again, Jeff leaves his chair and walks around the room.

"Do I make you nervous?" I ask.

"No, you aggravate me." Jeff reaches for a cigarette then pushes it back into the pack.

"It doesn't bother me if you smoke."

He jams the wrinkled pack into his shirt pocket. "I'm trying to quit."

"Is there anything else I should know?" I ask.

"Ramos has a lady friend. They're not married, but they have a daughter."

"What does this girlfriend look like?"

"Pretty, long dark hair, about thirty-five. Her name's Daniela Diaz."

"Where does she come into the picture?" I ask.

"She doesn't."

"Are you sure? No matter what, there's always a girl to look out for," I tell him.

"The girlfriend is an international flight attendant and is seldom home. She probably doesn't have any idea about what's happening in Belize."

"Your description sort of describes the woman who got out of the helicopter right before I shot Ramos. I understand flight attendants make good wages. Maybe she's footin' the bills."

He sighs "We're not talking fifty or sixty thousand, or even a hundred thousand. The corporation spends millions on the mansion, entertainment, charity, and who knows what else. They paid cash for their helicopter."

"Let me get this straight. What you're telling me is the DEA knows for a fact Longview is transporting drugs into Mexico, and these drugs are crossing the border into the U.S. If that's the case, sooner or later either the U.S. DEA or Belize Narcotics will find out exactly who the suppliers are and squash distribution into the United States. You never needed a hit man, and you probably don't need me now."

"You still don't understand." Blackwell continues to pace while he talks. "We even tried tracing the narcotics trail backwards. The trail always stops at the Longview plant. There's a big gap of missing information and no one in Belize wants to talk to us. Before we can stop the flow, we need to know who the dealers are, how they get the drugs to Longview and how Ramos hides the drugs from the Belize Narcotic Squad when they check out the plant."

"Maybe he doesn't hide it. Maybe he just makes a payoff to keep them from reporting what they see." I polish off the little bit of warm water that's left in my bottle.

"You always want to blame the hard-working lawmen— never the bad guys." Jeff says. "That's difficult to understand when the same officers risk their lives everyday, stopping vans and arresting drug smugglers."

"If I had killed Ramos, you wouldn't have gotten any answers."

"No, but Cox says with Ramos out of the picture, procedures will shift. He thinks the corporation will close and

38

the drug route will take an alternate course. In all the confusion we'll have a better chance of nabbing the smugglers and stopping most of the trafficking through Belize."

"And you believe that?"

"Well, we should make some headway," Jeff says.

"It sounds to me like you're repeating Cox's words. I don't think you're the type of guy who would have agreed that it's okay to kill a man who might not even be responsible for the problem just to try to make your job easier." I fold my hands on the desk and lean forward. "Putting one trucking company out of business won't stop drug smuggling. Money talks and trucks are cheap."

Blackwell fidgets in his chair, but doesn't say anything.

"Surely the DEA has some kind of electronic surveillance to listen to Ramos' phone calls and find out who he's connected with."

"The Belize government doesn't allow the DEA to monitor any electronics."

"And you follow the rules?" I laugh.

Jeff rolls his eyes. "Not exactly. We've tried, but all we ever hear is an occasional call from their hardwired home phone requesting household supplies to be delivered."

"Did you ever think that maybe there are no messages being sent in or out of the mansion?"

Jeff pushes a blond curl away from his eye. "This is a small country, but if you have cash you can have the best impenetrable system money can buy delivered and installed in ten days. Ramos' place is a fortress. If we don't stop him, the drugs will keep flowing into the U.S."

"Is that why the FBI had me use the rifle?" I ask.

"Just between you and me, the DEA didn't know the FBI was gonna pull that off."

Jeff retrieves *The Belize Times* from his briefcase and tosses it on the table. "The newspaper says Ramos was accidently shot while cleaning a rifle."

I glance at the bogus narrative. "Let me guess. Ramos doesn't want any law enforcement officers snooping around his place."

"I have no idea why Ramos would lie," Jeff says. "All I know is they took him by helicopter to Medical Associates of Belize, and immediately put him on the critical list in intensive care. Soon after, he was moved to a private room. I guess your shot wasn't even close to being fatal. You only wounded him."

When I hear that Ramos is doing okay, I'm relieved. However, I don't tell Jeff how I feel.

"Our strategy now is to go to FBI's plan B. They want someone on the inside, which was the DEA's original intention."

"I've already talked this over with the ambassador. I agreed to try to become his friend, keep my ears open for little bits of information. Your guys need to put this all together with what you already know, and build a case against him. I'm not going to become a partner in this drug smuggling business. You need to know how Ramos operates, so you can arrest him. He's not going to take an unknown person into his association."

"You agreed to help, and the help we need is getting a guy into his circle who knows the ropes, someone with an illegal past, so Ramos can check him out and come up with the right answers."

"If Ramos is smart enough to keep the DEA from compromising his electronic system, you're not gonna get a man with in a mile of his association."

"We have DEA agents that infiltrate underworld organizations all the time," Jeff says.

"So send one of your professionals," I say.

"We can't. We can only observe. If an agent gets caught, they'll trace him to us."

"Is that before or after they kill him?" I ask.

"This isn't something to make fun of."

"I wasn't joking." I tap my fingers on the table while deciding how much of my life I want to reveal. "When I helped put a lot of mob guys in the slammer, the Don put a contract on my head. Then the FBI put me in the Witness Protection Program and renamed me Robert Anderson."

"I know this is hard for you," Jeff says.

"Hard! It's not hard it's impossible. If I tell Ramos I'm Nick Salvatoro and he checks me out, every bounty hunter in the whole world will converge on Belize to collect the contract cash. I'll be dead, and the Mafia won't pay the bounty hunter. They'll have a Mafia soldier knock him off, and Ramos will keep on transporting drugs."

"I see your point, but we still need someone under cover, and they can't be FBI or DEA," Jeff says.

"Let me explain something to you. I only dealt cards, and while I was dealing I got mixed up with a few thugs. When I got the chance, I got out. Even if I didn't have a contract on my head, Ramos won't buy my being a big-time racketeer. I don't have the credentials to pave a road to the inside."

"The government thinks you do."

"Well, they're wrong. This so-called drug lord, or kingpin, is no dummy. I'm not gonna get an invite."

"If you want to renege on helping the DEA, you need to take it up with the ambassador."

"You want me to risk my life before I even start to get any of the information you need. And you don't care if I get killed before I even have a chance to try."

"I don't think about it that way," he tells me. "We do what we have to do."

"So when did our National Security Service turn into the KGB?"

"We put our lives on the line every day," Jeff says. "We're asking you to take that same chance for a short period of time."

"You chose this particular career and get paid well for the chances you take," I tell him.

"You also picked a dangerous lifestyle, and you will get paid, one way or another."

"The government's paying me to get information, not be an idiot. Besides, you got a full-time job with a pension. I'm just a temp."

"So how do we get around this bump in the road? You got any ideas?" he asks.

Leave it to Jeff to put things in perspective. "Not right off-hand. Let's get Cox in here. He's always good for a laugh. Maybe he'll come up with something."

Blackwell puts in a call to Cox. When he hangs up, he tells me, "Cox went out to eat. They said he'd be back in an hour. I don't want anyone to see you hanging out with the DEA or the FBI. There could be a leak, so why don't I go across the street and get us some food?"

"You think someone at the embassy might expose you."

"You never know," he says.

"You only have a few people here. Surely you can determine if and who's a leaker."

"You take everything I say and make it a major issue." Jeff rubs his temple like he's getting a headache.

"No, I just point out your weak spots."

"You probably don't believe it, but working with you puts my life at stake just as much as yours."

"You're right," I say. "I don't buy it."

He smiles. "Let's don't make this job any more difficult than it already is. You haven't worked with the Federal DEA before, and there's no doubt in my mind that you don't have any faith in us. But up to now, I haven't had the privilege of trusting a known criminal."

Now I smile. "You're a pretty gutsy son-of-a-bitch for someone who doesn't know anything about me. Why don't you go across the street and get us that food you were taking about?"

After Blackwell leaves, I look at the chronometer watch that Angela bought me. Today is a Monday and she's probably at her girlfriend's house. I pull out my personal mobile. If these guys can't even smell a rat, they'll not even think about checking to see if I have a personal cell phone to make calls to my girlfriend.

When Helen answers her home telephone, I ask to speak to Angela.

"It's that man you're always talkin' about," I hear her say.

The next voice I hear is Angela's. My heart soars, and I'm sorry I agreed to stay on the case. I miss her so much.

"Nick," she says into the telephone. "How's everything going?"

"Not as good as I would like." When I tell her the circumstances, I expect her to be upset and beg me to come home.

Instead, she says, "I understand. You're such a wonderful person. Even though my parents don't know what you're doing, they're still proud that you're working for the government on something that will make our country a safer place."

"What did you tell them?" I ask quickly, afraid she might have blown my short federal career out of proportion.

"Nothing, darling. I just told Dad that you were investigating a case for the government. He's a smart man. He didn't ask questions."

Relieved, I asked how she was doing in the quilting class.

"It's not a class, silly. It's just friends getting together to quilt." She laughs. "Guess what? I have the first row of a beautiful quilt put together."

"I miss you." I tell her.

"I miss you, too," she says.

"I'm sorry this is taking so long." I hope she asks me to come home.

"Please don't worry about me. I've made some new friends, and we all sit and quilt on Monday nights." She giggles.

"You spend your evenings sewing?"

"Yes. They talk about their children and I tell them about Europe."

Happy voices chatter in the background, and I can tell she's eager to get back to her friends. "Do you have plans for tonight?" I ask.

"Not really. Helen is having a friend over, and after the quilting party we're going to watch a movie. Do whatever you need to do, darling," she tells me. "It's not a problem. If you're gone long enough I might be able to finish my project before we return to Italy. You're going to love cuddling underneath our quilt on cold winter nights."

I've always been afraid of losing her, but I never dreamed it would be to a quilt. We say good-bye and I get this empty feeling. I know she loves me, but how important can a blanket be?

Cox doesn't come back after lunch, so Jeff and I eat the food in my room.

The next morning, I meet with Blackwell and Cox. We're seated around a small table, but Cox stands and walks to the middle of the room.

"What I'm about to tell you can't be repeated. Our lives and other lives depend on it." Cox waits.

He's so theatrical. I can hardly stand to be in the same room with him.

"Cox has another persona for you," Jeff whispers. "If you don't want to use your real name, this one might work."

Cox clears his throat. "There was a young man of Italian descent from Chicago. He had a horrible run-in with the mob over drug territory. They shot and killed his wife and their two small children. A neighbor heard the shots and called the police. Before the police arrived, the young drug dealer returned home and the mobsters were waiting for him. They fired just as he jumped out of a two-story window. The police pulled up and the gangsters fled. They thought the young man was dead."

"Was he?" I ask.

Cox whispers as if someone else might be able to hear him. "Not quite."

I stare at the floor. The man is so full of himself.

"We put him in an ambulance and took him to the hospital. He gave us enough information to put ten drug dealers behind bars. He died soon after, and the city buried him in an unmarked grave away from his family. His family still doesn't know if he died or was placed in the Witness Protection Program."

Cox sits in a chair next to Blackwell. A smile spreads across his face. "His name was Dominic Chelogrino. This all happened a long time ago, when I was a rookie cop. All those mobsters are dead now, but people in Chicago still talk about the killings. If he had lived he'd be about your age. He was close to your height, and didn't look any more Italian than you do. Of course, who knows what he might look like if he was alive today?"

"What do you mean, I don't look Italian?" I ask.

"I just meant you're not dark skinned, and you don't have a big shock of greasy black hair." Cox draws back his lips and exposes a large set of straight, white teeth.

Jeff is also grinning. "Dominic is the perfect gangster for you to pretend to be. He's just what we need."

"How's that sound to you, Nick?" Cox asks.

"It sounds like you're both out of your mind," I growl. "In the first place, you don't have any idea what an Italian looks like."

"That doesn't change the fact that Ramos not only peddles drugs, he's killed people, or had them murdered, and we need someone under his roof to get the evidence to put him behind bars for life." Cox looks at Blackwell for support.

For once, Jeff keeps his mouth shut.

"You don't know if he killed anyone and you have no proof that he had anyone murdered, or you would have already had him arrested." After standing and walking toward the window, I stop and turn to face the agents. "I think the two of you are so far out of line that you make the mob look like nice guys."

"Wait until you're here awhile, you'll change your mind." Cox tells me.

"Have you ever thought about Dominic's family?" I say. "The news would leak out. His relatives would get their hopes up. Do you know or even care how upsetting that would be? When they learn the truth, it would be like going through his funeral all over again." I turn my back and stare out the window. "I won't do it."

"All of a sudden you've got scruples?" Cox says.

I make a fist and start across the room toward Cox.

Blackwell jumps up and grabs my arm. "Nick, please don't." He tries to hold me back.

I drag him along and Cox rushes out the door. Jeff lets go of my arm and I sit on a sofa. Beads of sweat form on my forehead.

"It's all right, Nick," Jeff says. "We'll think of another way. Why don't you take the rest of the day off? Relax and enjoy yourself. You could go to Belize City."

"How could I do that? I don't have a car."

"Jon's picking up supplies. You could go with him, see the town, make arrangements to meet him later and ride back with him."

"That sounds good. How do I set that up?' I ask.

"I'm going over to see Logan now." Jeff looks at his watch. "Jon usually leaves before noon. I'll tell him to come by your room. He won't mind."

"I'll be ready." This is a good day to go to the bank. I can't keep carrying around all my cash in a duffle bag.

Around noon, Jon stops by my room. I sit up front and he tells me a little about Belize. We pass the Alliance Bank and I ask him to drop me off on the next corner.

"I'll pick you up right here in an hour," he says.

I get out of the limo and tuck the paper bag that holds the cash under my arm.

I trek back to the bank and go inside. I open an account with two-thousand dollars and put the rest in a safe deposit box. This is a relief off my mind. I had been hiding it rolled up in my dirty clothes at the bottom of the duffle bag. I hit the nearest bar, talk to the bartender and drink a couple of drafts before it's time to meet Jon.

The next day, while the FBI and the DEA work on a new plan, the DEA puts me through a quickie course in karate. I tell them I prefer a baseball bat. When I spend a few minutes on the shooting range with an M16, and a nine-millimeter handgun, Marco and Butch find out I'm okay with the handgun, but I'm still a poor shot with a rifle.

An admin doubling as a physical education coach joins me on a quarter-mile track with instructions to teach me how to breathe while jogging. At the end of the first lap, he stops to explain breathing in through my nose and out through my mouth. After the second lap I'm happy to be gasping well enough to ask for water.

At the end of the week, Jon drives me to a boarding house in Belize where Jeff has finagled me a roomy bedroom with a bath. It's not much, but it's clean and has air conditioning. I turn on the small television, but I fall asleep before the commercial ends.

The second week, the DEA provides me with an emergency telephone number and a regular call-in number. I'm issued a code number and a protected cell phone, or at least that's what they say it is. All these digits have to be memorized. As usual, nothing can be written down. I run the numbers through my head, along with a few more agency codes, and set up a system to recall them like I used to count cards in blackjack.

When I'm not working for the government, I continue to use the Robert Anderson alias the FBI gave me. I didn't like working with feds then, and I don't like it any better now.

On Friday, I'm taken into what they call an exercising process office. I'm to pretend that the man they're sending into the room to see me is a known hit man for a large drug cartel.

The fake hit man enters the office. I wonder if I'm supposed to be sitting in the chair behind the desk, looking out of the window or something like that. I peer out of the cracked closet door. The fake hit man seems to be confused when I'm not there.

I step out of the closet behind him, grab his right arm and twist it behind his back. Now I'm the one who's dumbfounded. He must be left handed because he pulls a gun from a right shoulder holster. How convenient, they didn't say he would be carrying heat and they didn't loan me a Glock. Good thing—I might have shot him.

My hammerlock won't hold the trained agent for long. I let him spin around toward me and use every inch of my strength to deck him. My fist goes numb, and I think my hand is broken. The sound of a scuffle causes the agents to burst into the room. Their eyes bug out when they see their friend rolling around on the floor. If it had been a real fight, I would've kicked him in the head. "Did I pass?"

The two agents pick up their friend and help him out the door.

After Jeff calms down, he says, "come with me." He heads for the door.

I follow him to Senior FBI Agent Russell Thompson's office. I guess he has heard the outcome of the scrimmage because he does not look happy.

"Sit down, Nick. What in the hell made you hit our guy?" he asks. "They told you it was a simulated objective."

I deliberately remain standing. "If someone told you that a hit man was on his way to see you, acting or real, a man needs to defend himself."

"You were supposed to talk your way out." Agent Thompson leans back in his chair.

"Why didn't someone tell me that?" I ask. "And why did he have a gun?"

"If you don't mind, I'll ask the questions," the processing agent says.

"Oh, but I do mind. Just looking at you, it's obvious that I've been on the street a lot longer than you. I've learned to survive, and hope to continue. I don't mind giving my life for my country for a good cause, but I expect the privilege of trying to stay alive while I'm doing the job. Besides that, I never heard of anyone who talked their way out of hit."

Out of the corner of my eye, I catch a glimpse of a smile on Jeff's lips before he slides his hand over his mouth in an attempt to pretend he's in deep thought.

The agent glares at me, but doesn't comment on my remarks. He completes the processing papers and turns them in my direction. "Sign every highlighted line and date it today. The last page has a list of supplies that are on loan to you."

Oh, crap. This must be my last chance to bail. I sign the papers.

"That's all, Salvatoro."

"Do I get a copy of what I just signed?"

"See that he gets a copy," he tells Jeff before he leaves the room.

"I should walk away from this," I tell Jeff. "But maybe if I do a good job, I might be able to finally clean the slate and start a new life."

"That's possible," he agrees, but he doesn't look convinced. "I'll get that copy for you this afternoon."

Jeff and I walk into the rec area. It has a pool table, large screen television, card tables and a bar.

"It's a man cave." I chuckle.

We each get a beer and sit on a couch in front of a television screen.

"Here's my idea," Jeff says. "We get you into Belize Medical Associates Hospital. It's in Belize City on St. Thomas Street. It's an easy walk from your room and looks like a Miami clinic. The hospital posted a job for a maintenance man online, and I've arranged an interview for you."

"How did you manage that?" I ask.

"I filled out the form online and they sent me an appointment time."

"You said Ramos only had a gun shot wound. How come he's still in the hospital?"

"Apparently, the wound has become infected, and they have him on antibiotics, but his body doesn't seem to be responding," Jeff tells me.

"It's been a while. I'll bet Ramos is upset about that."

Jeff doesn't seem concerned. "It's better for us. Hopefully, you'll get a chance to meet him in the hospital. We first thought we would have to make up some excuse for you to meet up with him."

"How'd you plan on doing that?"

"We hadn't gotten that far."

"Sounds to me like you guys don't have much of plan for anything you do."

"We would've found a way."

I'm amazed at his unwarranted confidence.

"So, what do I have to go through to get this job at the hospital?"

"Not much," Jeff says. "I used your name to apply on line. I wrote down that I had just retired and had no family. I said I was looking for a warm climate to settle in and wanted a part-time job. All you have to do is convince them that you can do the job."

"It seems to me you were pretty sure of yourself to arrange an interview for me before I agreed to stay on."

"Let's just say I was hopeful." Jeff grins.

"How did you know what to use for my resume?"

"I made it up." He winks. I'll give you a copy"

I'm afraid to ask the next question. "What happens if I get the job?"

"You get to know Ramos. He gets to know you, and we see how it goes from there."

"Do you expect one of the richest residents in Belize to make friends with a janitor?" I scoff.

"No," Jeff says, "I expect an international drug lord to make friends with a man from the United States who he thinks he can use to his advantage."

CHAPTER FIVE

The two-story building looks like a small-town American hospital, and I've been told it's a very expensive facility. Jeff said it was the hospital of choice for the local elite because of the high level of care given by doctors and nurses. A large easel at the entrance brags that the hospital has all the latest equipment available.

It doesn't take long to convince human resources that I am the man for the job. The nurse at Medical Associates Hospital smiles when she announces I've passed the pee test. The office clerk types my identification card and the manager tells me to report to the custodian.

"His office is the last door on your right." The lady points down the hallway.

The door is open and a man motions for me to come in. His name tag reads Gerald Flowers, Head Custodian. He's a thin guy with a pot belly and a big rear-end. He reminds me of a shmoo. I hand him my ID.

"Did you ever work in a hospital?" Gerald asks.

"No sir."

"Have you ever done janitor work?"

"No sir."

"Why does the hirin' lady keep sendin' me people who don't know how to clean? Some people who apply for the job have no idea what it takes to clean a room properly."

"I beg your pardon. I've worked before, and I'm quite competent. I'm retired and need a part-time job. Working in the hospital will give me a chance to help people who need care."

"Janitors don't help people. They mop. Can you clean a room, a hallway, and stand on your feet for eight hours?" Gerald puts on his glasses.

"Yes, sir." I choose my words carefully. I don't want to lose this job.

"Pick yourself out a pair of them coveralls, grab a cart with a mop and bucket and go to the second floor. They had an incident in the waitin' area. Clean it up." He picks up his pen and starts to write in a notebook.

The guy's wearing the same crisp tan slacks and navy-blue pullover with a collar like the volunteers at the information desk. I guess he doesn't do much cleaning.

I saunter toward the hanging coveralls.

"When you get done with the waitin' room, I want you to mop all the patient rooms on the second floor. They haven't been cleaned in four days cause we ain't had no help. Don't forget to put out the wet floor signs. Tomorrow you need to set yourself up a schedule to see that every room gets completely scrubbed down.

"Does the hospital supply uniforms?" I ask.

"Not until they decide you're a permanent employee and that takes two months. In the meantime, you have to wear coveralls."

I pick out an extra-large pair. I don't expect to be in Belize long enough to get a uniform.

"You from the states?" he asks.

"Jersey," I say.

"You're a Yankee, huh," he hoots.

"No, I'm a northerner." I place a mop and bucket on the cart.

"Me, I'm from Pascagoula, Mississippi. Been here ten years. Started out just like you and worked my way up."

"What time is lunch?" I ask.

"Twelve noon. Eat in the cafeteria. Show your ID. Lunch is free." He stops writing and looks at me. "Do they call you Robert or Bob?"

"Robert will do just fine."

"You need to be respectful to the patients," he says. "They're all well-to-do and they expect a lot—especially Mr. Ramos. He owns a banana company. When you go into his room, keep your mouth shut and do your job."

52

After pulling on the coveralls, I pick up a bottle of disinfectant and push my cart toward the door.

"Take some of those paper footies, too. If y'all need to step on carpet, put'em over your shoes."

"Where do I get the water?" I ask.

"My God, don't you know nothin'? There's a closet up there that's marked cleanin' supplies." He tosses me a key on a chain. "Most everything you need is in there, includin' a sink. Pay attention when you open the door. If anything's runnin' low, come back here and get replacements." He rattles off a few more instructions. "You got all that?"

"Yes, sir." I wonder if he would have forgotten to give me the key if I hadn't asked where to get the water. I push the cart and plod toward the elevator. It's not a career type job, but it's air conditioned and better than the jungle.

The waiting room is an open area directly in front of the elevator. I clean up the mess and wander down the hallway looking for Ernesto Ramos' room.

You can tell the floors haven't been taken care of lately, but the rest of the hospital looks okay. Flowers told me there were only twenty-five patient beds in the whole building, and fifteen of them are on the second floor. Ramos' room is easy to find. I look for the room with a guard sitting outside the door. The beefy watchman looks like he might be Latino.

I push the cart next to Ramos' door.

"Hey, *Amigo,* where you goin'?" the guard asks.

"In the room," I reply.

"Me no think so," he says. "No one goes in. Only doctor and nurse."

"My job is to mop and disinfect all the rooms and hallways." I shrug.

The short, chubby guard uses his cell phone to call the nurse. She arrives almost immediately, checks my identification, and verifies that I'm the new cleaning man. The guard pats me down and checks my equipment.

"You, go over there." The guard points to the other side of the hallway.

When I move away, he opens the door, but keeps an eye on me.

"Boss man," he calls out. "The janitor, he come to mop floor. I check ID with nurse and pat him down. He clean. You want him to come in?"

Judging by his broken English he's not from here, because Belize is an English-speaking nation. Cox says most residents are trilingual and speak English, Spanish, and Creole fluently.

I hear Ramos say, "okay."

The guard motions for me to walk in with him.

"This new janitor, name's Robert." He looks at my badge again. "And. . .der. . .son."

The kingpin is sitting-up in bed eating a banana, and his guard stands on the left side of Ramos' bed. I start to mop on the right.

Ramos is hooked up to a number of machines, and wires sprawl across the floor. I give the mop a good push under the bed and it comes out on the other side, rolling over the guard's shoes. He jumps back and gets caught in one of the wires. A lightweight pole with a medicine bag attached to Ramos' arm tumbles. The guard catches it at the last moment and sets it upright.

"What are you doing, Javier?" Ramos demands.

I continue to mop around the wires as if I don't hear what's being said.

Javier looks puzzled. "It was the mop. The janitor hit my shoes with the *pinche* mop."

When Javier says janitor, I glance at Ramos, and then stare at the guard.

Ramos waves his hand at the guard. "Move away and stop swearing. Do not wreck my equipment."

Good, he doesn't believe Javier.

"How are you today, Mr. Ramos?" I smile.

"How do you know my name?" he spats at me.

"I know your name because everyone in the hospital is talking about you. They say you're a very kind and generous man."

Ramos sits a little straighter.

I move to the other side of the bed and continue mopping. The guard moves out of my way and on to the wet floor.

"Be careful you don't fall. The disinfectant makes the floor slippery," I tell Javier.

"Don't worry for me. Do your job," he growls, just before his heel slips and he has to grab the bedrail to catch his balance.

"Go outside." Ramos gestures to Javier. "He is only a cleaning man."

"Janitor," Javier mumbles as he leaves the room.

Ernesto Ramos has a slight Latin accent, but speaks excellent English. He's wearing crisp pin-striped pajamas instead of a gown like most of the other patients. He looks to be about my age, but his hair is solid gray. I don't know what I expected, but he doesn't look like a drug lord to me.

A hospital orderly stops by to see how Ramos is doing. They have a pleasant conversation and the orderly leaves the room. I've known a number of high ranking criminals and none of them were as polite and intelligent as Ernesto Ramos.

I finish mopping the floor. "I'll see you tomorrow, Mr. Ramos."

When I leave, Javier is reading the newspaper. I nod and smile when I pass him and he nods back. Good, I needed to see how Ramos would react to Javier's remark when I bumped his shoes, but I don't want the guard to be my enemy. Now that I got my foot in the door, I'll treat Javier better. I need Ramos to trust me in order to get any information.

After mopping a few more patient rooms, I check out the custodian closet. Everything seems to be in good order, so I go downstairs to the cafeteria to collect my free lunch and mull over what I know so far.

The FBI is convinced that I have some kind of clout with the mob and they're dead wrong, so maybe they've made a mistake about Ramos, too. He may not be the King Pin. Just because he's living in a big house doesn't mean he has anything to do with the ownership. He seems to care a lot about the country and its people to be a big-time thug. I'd like to prove to the FBI, the DEA, and the ambassador that they are wrong. If he's not guilty, I'd like to clear the guy's name. That's the least I could do after nearly killing him.

CHAPTER SIX

The boarding house is only a couple of blocks from Medical Associates, so I walk to work. I can do this job in four hours, but I stretch it out. It's better than sitting alone in a room. I would like to phone Angela, but I don't. I have no idea who or how the authorities or anyone else can trace calls made from a cell phone. The FBI and the DEA may not be a threat to me, but I'm not taking any chances. I've decided not to call very often.

On my second day as a janitor, I begin to give each room an exceptionally good cleaning, so I don't get far before noon. After lunch I start on Ernesto's room. I'm amazed that he seems glad to see me after the episode with his guard yesterday.

The wastebaskets are overflowing in every room, and this one is no exception. My big black garbage bag is almost full. I dump in the contents of Ramos' receptacle, tie the top in a knot, and place the bag in the hallway.

"How are you feeling today?" I ask Ramos while I push the mop back and forth across the floor.

"Better than I was yesterday." He releases a thunderous amount of gas and pats his stomach. "Hospital food is not like home."

I hang outside his door for a while, pretending to straighten the cleaning supplies on my cart. When I locate a fresh antibacterial cleaning cloth, I wipe down his room. I move every item and go over the surface several times. He watches each move I make.

Ramos turns the volume down on his small portable radio. "You do not look like a man that cleans up after people." He stares directly into my eyes. "And the coveralls do not hide your expensive shoes or the cuffs of your linen shirt."

"Well, it's probably because I haven't been a janitor before."

"Why did you take this job? You can do better."

"The few good positions available were in the medical field, and that's not my bag, but I like to keep busy. Working keeps me out of trouble, and gives me time to look around Belize to see if this is the place I want to want to settle down in."

"Belize is a poor country and there is little need for large businesses, which makes us susceptible to the whims of the tourists." He finishes the last of his lunch, picks up his napkin and wipes his mouth. "So what kind of work did you do in . . . where did you say you were from?"

"I didn't, but I'm originally from New Jersey, and for the last year or so, I lived in Miami."

"What kind of work did you do in Miami?" he asks again about my employment.

I stop cleaning and hesitate. "You know...a little of this, a little of that."

"When I look at you, I see an educated and clever man who knows his way around. I do not think you are telling me the whole story."

"I'm just an average Joe from Jersey. I think if he feels he has the right to ask me questions, maybe he won't mind answering one of mine. "Are you a native of Belize?"

"No, I was born in Brazil. I come from a wealthy family who owns a coffee export business. I was expected to join the family business when I finished my schooling, but I did not want to live in Brazil, so I came to Belize."

I'm surprised at his candor. "You gave up your inheritance?" I blurt out.

"No, my younger brother bought my share, and I opened a banana export business."

"Your name sounds Spanish, and I detect a Spanish accent." I say, implying a level of competency.

He laughs. "I speak a little Spanish simply because there are so many Mexicans living here, but I grew up speaking Portuguese. That is the accent you incorrectly recognized."

"So, how's the banana business these days?" I change the subject to avoid discussing my blunder.

"Neither the soil nor the climate is as good as Brazil, but I do okay. I also have a few outside investments, so I live quite well. Do you have a wife?" he asks.

I feel he's established his elevated position, and is now sincerely interested in my life.

"Nope. No wife, and no kids," I tell hm.

"Are you divorced?" he asks. "So many Americans are."

I don't mention that I was married to a bitchy cousin of a friend for six months. "I'm afraid not. I had a lot of girlfriends, but I never got married." He doesn't need to know all my business.

"Ah, you are what the Americans call a *player*."

I laugh. "I'm a little too old to be a player." I raise the blind. Warm afternoon sun streams in. "Would you like me to leave the blind open?"

"No. I like it closed. Who knows what is lurking outside?"

That statement is truer than he knows. Down on the street, I see the fed's black Ford Lariat with the shiny chrome running board stopped next to a patrol car. I wonder what they are talking about. I wipe the window sill and close the blind.

"You cannot trust anyone these days. That is why I have a guard stationed at my door," Ramos says.

When I come back from carrying his empty food tray out to the cart in the hallway, he's sitting on the edge of the bed.

"Help me get up. I need to use the john."

"I'm not allowed to help you." I push the button for the nurse.

"Why did you push the button? I do not want the damn nurse," he snaps.

I see he's not always as polite as I thought.

"Javier! Get your butt in here!" Ramos shouts.

Javier charges into the room. "Yes, Mr. Ramos. What you need?"

"Help me to the john," Ernesto says.

As soon as he goes into the bathroom, I pack my stuff and leave. I've learned a lot today, but at the expense of mistaking his accent. I hope I haven't overstepped my boundaries by questioning him about where he's from. I want him to think of me as a friend, not a nosy American.

The next day, I come to work early. The head custodian has been inspecting the rooms and gives me a pat on the back.

"You did a good job," he says. "I'm going to ask Human Resource to put you on full time. The woman who does the first floor is slow. She could use a little help. After you finish the second floor, I want you to give her a hand."

Fat chance of that. "I'm sorry, boss. I have a previous engagement." As much as I would like to please him, I don't relish working a full eight-hour day. I only came here to infiltrate Ramos' organization. I don't need this friggin' job. The custodian is in for a big surprise. When Ramos leaves the hospital, I'm outta here.

"Let me think about it," I tell hm.

"No, I'm gonna ask today," he insists. "Maybe I can get you more money."

I don't argue with him. I'll be long gone before he can get me a raise.

After I put on the coveralls, I push the cart to the elevator and start my rounds. Actually, it's not a bad job, and I've met a lot of nice people. I hurry through the rooms and hallways and take a quick lunch so I can spend a little more time with Ramos.

Today, there is a new guard at the door. "What's your name" I ask.

"Gomez," he says. Then he asks me for identification. "How do you say your name?"

I don't think he can read English. "Rob-ert," I say.

"Si, Rob-ber. You have funny name."

"Yes." That's close enough.

He pats me down just like Javier, but he doesn't go into the room with me.

When I go into Ramos' room I nod my head to him and he nods back. I finish cleaning the bathroom and Ramos turns off the television and leans back against his pillow, but instead of stopping and talking, I stay busy mopping the floor. I move the chairs, and clean in the corners. I can see he is getting eager to have a conversation, but I want him to make the first move, so I keep my back to him and continue to clean. Several minutes go by before he says, "Could you please stop cleaning and say hello?"

"I didn't want to disturb you, Mr. Ramos. I saw you reading the *Belize news.*"

The headline read, "Alleged Drug-Queen, Lizzy Barrett, is wanted by U.S. Marshall's office."

I had read the article while I ate breakfast in the hospital cafeteria early this morning. The young lady from Virginia is accused of being a Queen Pin. She is charged with playing a pivotal role in trafficking drugs up and down America's east coast.

I hurry along, using the fresh antibacterial cloth on his table and nightstand.

He points to the article. "She is not from Belize. I do not know why our news reporters want to stir up the public by writing such articles."

"Who's not from Belize?" I act like I don't know what he is talking about.

"It is just a stupid story." He drops the newspaper into the trash can. "I like the *San Pedro Sun* better. Their articles are more accurate."

Noticing his obvious dislike for the newspaper article leads me to believe he might be more entrenched in the drug business than I first thought. When you compare the report the newspaper prints about the amount of drugs passing through Belize with the small amount Ramos claims to be in Belize, it's hard to tell which one is telling the truth.

The nurse comes in and says she's there to give him his shot. Her badge says Nurse Isabella, L.P.N. I've seen her several times, but she never speaks to me. Before she does anything, she checks all his vital signs. I've finished cleaning the room, so I pack up my supplies and start for the door.

"Are you coming back later today?" Ramos asks.

I guess he didn't expect me to come so early. "I'll be back tomorrow after lunch."

He looks at Nurse Isabella. "I want the waste basket emptied twice a day," he says. His eyes scan the room. "And I want this room thoroughly cleaned. I do not like this infection I've acquired. The next thing you'll be telling me is that I have a staph infection. Mr. Anderson does a good job, but germs spread quickly."

Ramos appears overly cautious about contamination. However, being allowed to see him twice a day is like being dealt a straight flush. The thrill of the game is exhilarating.

"I'll have to check to see if I'm permitted to clean the room twice a day," I say.

Isabella's head snaps in my direction. "See that Mr. Ramos' room is wiped down with an antibacterial cleaner twice each day. His doctor will place the order."

Holy crap! Anyone can see she's been advised to give Ramos whatever he wants. When I leave his room, I have a few anxious thoughts. If everyone jumps when he speaks, he must have a lot of authority in Belize, and most likely a number of tough guys to back him up. I didn't believe Cox, but if he's right, Ramos might be the major force behind the drugs that are moving through Belize and into the United States.

When I check Ramos' room in the afternoon, he's snoring. The room is clean. I straighten up the mess on his table, and wipe away a few crumbs left from lunch. I empty the waste basket and leave. He'll never know how long I was here.

It's too early for dinner, so before I leave the hospital, I stop at the cafeteria and get a package of cheese and crackers out of the vending machine. On my way home, I pick up a six pack of beer at a local bar. When I hear voices coming from the back room of the bar, I peek in the doorway and see Marco, one of the agents that snatched me out of the jungle, and a local cop shooting pool. This is the second time I've seen the local police and the US agents fraternizing. It seems odd, since Jeff says the feds are low profile and keep their distance from any other law enforcement in Belize.

A large number of empty bottles are on a table close by them, so I figure they've been here for a while. The few people in the bar are engrossed in conversation, and don't seem to be paying any attention to me. I slip out of the bar.

CHAPTER SEVEN

The following day, I return for the second time to Ramos' room. Since I skipped the bathroom this morning, I make it my starting point. This gives him time to formulate a few more questions. The sooner we talk about me, the quicker I can get information from him.

When I come out of the bathroom, sweat is pouring down my neck. "Do you mind if I sit for a minute?" My hand reaches for the comfortable chair that has been provided for his guests—not that I've ever seen any visitors in his room.

"Sit down, sit down," he repeats. "You are good company. It gets lonely in here."

"Does your wife come to see you?" It's a very personal question, but I need to find out about the dark-haired girl.

"I have no wife, but I have a pretty girlfriend." He makes the sexy shape of a girl with his hands. "She works for an airline and spends much of her time out of the country."

He answers truthfully and I take this as a good sign. Maybe he's beginning to trust me.

"You should get a woman," he says.

I wipe sweat from my face and laugh. "I'm better off by myself."

"A man needs to have a female around at least part of the time."

I nod, but I don't answer. I already have enough lies to remember.

"Why did you pick Belize to settle in?" he asks.

"It's a beautiful spot and I thought I could make some quick cash here."

"What can you do to make fast money?" he squints.

"I'm sort of a card dealer." The conversation is going better than I expected. Maybe I can reel him in by revealing a little of my past. "I pulled a lot of cash out of Miami dealing in the backroom of a nightclub, so if I make the right connection, I think I can do the same thing here."

"You do not want to try that in Belize." Ramos' voice drops to a whisper. "Not long ago the San Pedro police caught an owner of a restaurant running an illegal card game at his establishment. The Gaming Control Board came down hard on him. I heard he had to pay an exorbitant price to keep his business open. He did not go to prison, but two of his dealers served short jail terms."

"That doesn't surprise me. People often take the fall for their bosses," I say.

"Gambling laws are strictly enforced in Belize," he tells me.

"That's not what I heard. I was told the police don't even look for illegal card games."

"The police do not need to search. The gambling houses have moles combing the country for illegal betting. When they locate renegade wagering, the police are notified, and the government shuts them down. The law supports the establishments because their taxes pay the politicians huge salaries."

He turns over in bed and looks at me. "You even need to know someone to get a dealer's position in the casinos."

"I figured that, when they turned me down flat. That's why I started looking for an underground poker game." I tell him.

"The casino moles will find you," he says.

"If the government is so hard on illegal gambling, why do the politicians turn a blind eye to illegal drug trade?" I lean forward and speak softly. "Word on the street says drugs flow through Belize as smooth as fine whiskey."

"Drugs and gambling are two entirely different animals," he says. "Gambling, with all its curses, is usually found in high places. It is deemed a luxury sport. However, drugs are everywhere, and times are changing. The world is full of drug dealers. Even young children are peddling." He looks at the floor. "More often than not, words like homicide, suicide, and terrorism are connected to drugs."

I see an opening, and begin to tell Ramos the same story Cox told me about the Chicago murders.

"When I was in my twenties, I hung out with some bad company. I remember hearing about a family in Chicago. The young father apparently sold drugs in a part of the city that the mob controlled." I ramble on, embellishing the tale as I go. At the end I say, "He jumped out of a second story window."

"Did he die?" Ramos raises his eyebrows.

"I guess so, but he must have lived long enough to give the cops incriminating information because right after the incident, the law sent a lot of drug dealers to jail."

"That is what happens when you break the law." Ramos pushes the button to raise the head of his bed into an upright position. "Did it not bother you to be connected to a group of people whose life ambition is to deceive the public?"

Hmm, I wonder if he's really concerned about my morals, or if he's trying to ascertain whether or not I would be willing to do something illegal for him. "I didn't belong to any group. I was just dealing blackjack to a bunch of gamblers who knew what was going on. Sometimes they won, and sometimes they lost. That's the chance gamblers take."

"You must have worked for someone who provided you a place to deal cards and financial backing to make the amount of cash you talk about. Was it the Italian Mafia?"

I'm surprised at his frankness. "No. it was just one man who owned a dance hall. If he had connections to the Mafia, I didn't know about it."

"So, you are from New Jersey, you spent a year in Miami dealing cards, and then you suddenly move to Belize and end up a janitor. That is quite a journey." Ramos appears to be waiting for an explanation.

"That's not exactly what happened, but close enough." What little connection I had with the mob is over and done with. I lean back in the chair.

"And you think you can live on janitor wages?" He chuckles.

"No, I took the job to please your country's justice system. It appears that before you can become a citizen you must be gainfully employed."

66

"I see." He doesn't question me any further, but he continues to rock forward and gently crack his knuckles as he talks. "I am a father, I own a banana company, and I mind my own business."

"So you don't believe that your government is turning a blind eye to drugs being transported through Belize?"

"I pay my taxes and leave the running of the government to the politicians. Besides talk is cheap." He clears his throat and whether true or not, I know a story is coming.

"Recently, the *San Pedro Sun* reported a plane landed on a road in Belize with a large load of cocaine. When the culprits saw the police converging on the plane, the pilot and several passengers scattered into the jungle. The city of Belize confiscated the plane, and the police officers burned the drugs in a great bonfire on the beach." He raises his palms up in despair. "So who am I to believe?"

I stand. "This is all very interesting. I'm glad we had this talk. I think I need to look for a different country if I plan to continue my career."

"I enjoy speaking with you. I spent many years in your country. I graduated from the University of Miami."

"That's impressive. What was your major?"

"Mostly Cuban women, but I got a degree in engineering."

I laugh, and so does Ramos.

"I seldom meet a man of your profession who is educated well enough to have a good conversation. It makes me curious," he says.

"There's nothing to wonder about me. I'm just a guy out looking to make a buck." I glance at my watch. "It's almost time for me to go home, and I need to finish your room." I pick up my mop and go over the floor. By the time I finish cleaning, Ramos has fallen asleep. I load up the cleaning cart and head for the elevator.

My thoughts wander back to Ernesto. If he is the ruthless cocaine exporter, then he certainly is a good actor. His soft-spoken words and prudish morals are not typical of crooks I've met in the past.

Of course, it could all be an act.

CHAPTER EIGHT

After I get home from work, Jeff comes by the boarding house to see how I'm getting along.

"The best and cheapest place to rent a car in Belize City is Crystal Auto Rental, but before you do that, you need to get an international driver's license," he tells me.

"I don't think I need one."

"Maybe not, but you need it in some countries these days, so it's best to get it here. The place isn't busy, and the test is easier to pass in Belize. When you work for the DEA, you never know where they might send you."

"I'm not traveling anywhere. I'm staying right here. And I don't work for the DEA. I'm on a temporary assignment."

"Do me a favor. Get an international driver's license," Jeff repeats. "And don't get a flashy car. Rent one that no one will notice."

"Sometimes trying to look inconspicuous ends up being the most glaring mistake you can make," I say.

"Then get a Rolls Royce." He stomps out the door.

Against my wishes, Gerald Flowers gives me the following day off. No matter what I claim about the rooms needing additional work, he refuses to be persuaded otherwise. He tells me orders came from higher up. There is nothing I can do but stay home and loose another day of intelligence gathering on Ramos.

When Jeff finds out I'm not at work, he stops by the boarding house. He wants to see the car. This kid thinks just because he has a government badge, he's entitled to check up on me.

Sweat is dripping down his forehead and he is breathing heavily. "I parked at the restaurant down on the corner and walked here." He rolls his shoulders like he's just run a marathon.

What's he gonna do when he gets to be my age? I hand him a paper towel, and tell him about the conversation I had with Ramos.

"Don't you think it's a little early to be talking about drugs?" Jeff asks.

"I didn't intend for that to happen. We were discussing illegal gambling and drugs fell into the same category."

"It might have been a casual remark for you, but maybe it didn't seem so innocent to Ramos," Jeff says.

"We didn't say much. I talked a little about what I heard on the streets in Belize and what I learned about the mob when I was young. He told me a short story about a plane full of drugs landing on a road in Belize and the suspects disappearing into the jungle. That's when I said I had to leave, and the discussion was over." There was no need to tell Jeff the entire conversation. He'd only get upset.

"There was such a plane, but you'd do well to stay away from an exchange of ideas regarding drugs. What you need to do is tell him about your life in the Mafia."

"You make it sound like I'm a made man."

"Well, aren't you?"

"You don't understand how things work. I'm not even half a wiseguy. Besides, I don't think about it that way." Remembering Jeff's earlier remark, I add, "I only did what I had to do."

Jeff sighs, but he doesn't respond.

It's a hot day, so I turn on the air-conditioner. "I asked Marco why didn't they take me to the jungle in a helicopter and he said you don't have access to a helicopter. Is that true?"

"Yeah, it's true," Jeff says. "Occasionally there are circumstances that require the government to bring in a helicopter, but we couldn't have requisitioned one for you anyway."

"Why not?" I ask.

"They only do that for important people, like a real government agent, a politician, a famous entertainer, or someone with money." Jeff laughs.

"I don't see the humor in that," I say.

"We couldn't have dropped you off or picked you up in a helicopter because there's no public place in the jungle to land. You would've had to climb the rope ladder like the agents do."

"You're puttin' me on."

"No, I'm not. And even if you were able to climb the ladder, you might have been shot before you could make it all the way up."

"I get your point," I say.

"If this were a war zone, I guess they could have winched you up." He grins.

"Let's just drop the subject," I tell him.

Jeff stands. "I need to get going." He stops at the doorway. "Remember, before you make a left turn, you have to pull to the right side of the road and stop. In Belize, vehicles coming toward you and vehicles behind you have the right of way. Local law says you have to wait until both lanes are clear before you make a left turn."

"I've been noticing that."

"Listen to me," he says, like he's my boss. "If you get a ticket or cause an accident it might blow your cover. Besides, I don't want you to get yourself killed the first night out."

"I promise to obey the law." I salute.

"See you later." Jeff walks out the door.

He should know by now that a car accident isn't the only way to get killed in Belize.

That afternoon, I take the car and find a road that leads to Mexico. I'm not surprised to find it's heavily traveled by all kinds of vehicles. I'm driving along, minding my own business, when a patrol car pulls in behind me and lightly touches his siren.

I pull onto the berm. The officer sits in his car until a back-up patrol car parks behind him. Then he strolls up to my window.

70

"Step out of the car," he says.

I've danced to this music enough times to know better than to argue. I recognize him as the patrol officer that stopped the Ambassador's limo the same day I took a shot at Ramos.

"Let me see your credentials," he says.

I hand him my shiny, new international license.

Instead of being impressed, he asks. "Are you planning on traveling?"

"Not really, but there doesn't seem to be any decent paying jobs available in Belize, so I may have to move on."

"I was under the impression that you worked for Medical Associates," he says.

"I do, but only as a janitor."

"And you believe that's beneath you?"

I'm losing patience, but I smile. "Can you tell me why I'm being detained?"

"I'm not detaining you," he tells me.

I remain calm because I don't want to create a problem.

"It's just that your friend, Agent Cox, said you were taking steps to become a citizen of Belize, yet instead of buying a car you rented one. That doesn't sound like you plan to stick around."

"I'm not sure what I'll do. If I get a decent paying job, I'll buy a car and stay. If I don't, I guess I'll leave. I hate walking."

"Belize gets many travelers," the officer says. "Some are good, and some are nothing but trouble. We take pride in making sure unwanted visitors are deported."

The officer sounds more like a politician than a cop.

"Are you suggesting I'm a threat to Belize?" I ask.

"Of course not, but until you establish citizenship, we'll keep an eye on you."

"Then it's okay if I continue on my way?"

"Yes. I'm sure we will see each other again." He hands me my license.

I get in my car and leave. Things went okay out here on the crowded highway in broad daylight, but I'd hate to run into this hard-ass and his nosey buddies on a dark deserted road.

I branch off and proceed along an artery that leads to a gravel tour road running through the jungle. I breathe a sigh of relief when the patrol cars don't follow me.

The secondary trails are fenced off from the jungle, but it is still really something to see wild animals so close to the road. It's the same type of barrier that the feds had the key to the pad-locked gate to permit me access to the long, exposed walk I had to make to get to the spot directly across the river from Ramos' mansion. It's not like I had a GPS that would warn me of an approaching tiger.

I was hoping to use my phone to take a picture of one of the many wild animals that live in the Belize rainforest, but they run away and hide when my noisy car approaches.

It occurs to me that I haven't seen any gas stations, and I don't want to risk running into another patrol car. I think I've seen enough of Belize for one day. I want to send Angela a picture of the rainforest, so I settle for a snapshot of a slow moving armadillo, and turn back toward Belize City.

After I get gas, I follow signs that point to the beach. I park the car and walk toward the water. Large cruise ships anchor a good distance from port and shuttle boats travel back and forth between the ship and the shore. The passengers wave to the bathers who are already swimming along the coast.

A few people play in the surf, but most of the crowd is standing in long lines waiting their turn to take a tour bus into the city or around the countryside.

At the end of the port there is a large patio restaurant. They have a great menu, so I decide to eat. I order a beer and a platter of conch, shrimp, and lobster, which comes with fries and pickles.

A disc jockey is playing island music and here and there between the tables couples are dancing the salsa. The place is busy, the beer is cold and the service is slow, but when the food finally arrives, it's delicious. I wish Angela was here with me now. She would love the beach and all the shops.

While I'm enjoying the seafood, a guy dressed in jeans and a T-shirt comes into the restaurant. The advertisement on his T-shirt reads. "Beat the heat in Belize, Queen Street

Snorkeling." Standing beside a barstool, he places his camera on the bar and takes a mobile from his hip pocket. He holds the cell phone in the air, and appears to be taking a video of the interior. When he slowly scans the side of the bar I'm sitting on, I turn my head away. The patrons sitting next to me wave at the smart phone.

I want to snatch the phone from his hands and delete my picture, but decide I'm overreacting. He tucks the phone into his hip pocket, and orders a beer. I guess he's only a tourist. When I finish my dinner, I see him standing outside the entrance talking to a shabby looking guy in worn out jeans and a sleeveless T-shirt.

When I leave, I walk toward my car, then stop and pretend to look at a vendors table of necklaces. I glance over my shoulder and see the two guys are not far behind me. I wait until they pass. Neither one looks my way. In fact, both of their heads are facing the other direction.

I glance over to where they're looking and see a blank wall. They stop a little further down the sidewalk. The only vendor there is selling ladies apparel.

I make a beeline for my car and quickly leave the parking lot. When I turn the corner at the end of the street, I see the amateur photographer and his friend running toward the parking lot. After making a couple of turns I stop behind a building. If they're after me, I've apparently given them the slip because no one comes by. If the Belize police are suspicious of me, maybe some drug cartel or Ramos also feels skeptical. They all seem to be friends with each other. I feel like I can't trust anyone, not even the FBI.

By the time I find my way back to the boarding house, it's dark. I have to work tomorrow, so I crawl into bed and turn on the small screen television to help me fall asleep. The only thing that appeals to me is the old Turner Classic movie, *Key Largo*.

The next morning, I can't wait to hear what Ernesto has to say. I make his room my last stop. He's sitting in the guest chair. He puts the newspaper aside and smiles.

He seems to be in a good mood, so I drop my paraphernalia on the floor and walk over to his chair.

"I will be going home soon," he tells me.

I'm shocked, but I don't let it show. Jeff said he had spoken to a friend who works at the hospital. The information he received was that Ernesto would be hospitalized for at least another week.

"That's good news," I say. "I'm gonna miss our daily chats."

"Me too," he says.

"Are you strong enough to go home?" I inquire.

"They say I'm not, but I want to see my little four-year-old daughter."

"You have a four-year-old?" I blurt out.

"Her mother is my girlfriend. She is a bit younger than I am. My little girl tells me she can't sleep unless one of us is there with her."

"You said you were a father, but I didn't expect you to have such a young child."

"My daughter and I spend a lot of time together. She is an adorable youngster. She looks a lot like my pretty girlfriend, Daniela. She even has her mother's temperament." He shakes his index finger. "When Deedee wants something, she is just as determined as her mother to get what she wants. I love them both."

"Your daughter's name is Deedee?"

"No, her name is Delores, but I call her Deedee." He pulls a picture from his shirt pocket. "I carry her close to my heart."

I look at the picture. "She is very pretty. I remember you said your girlfriend works for an airline?"

"Yes. Daniela is not like most of the women I have met since my wife passed away."

"I'm sorry to have brought up the subject," I say.

"That's okay. It was a long time ago. She died in childbirth when we were very young and so did our baby. I never thought about remarrying until I met Daniela. She is a caring person,

74

and always wants to help people. She wants nice things, but she does not expect a man to give them to her. She wants to earn her own money and do something worthwhile with her life. She did not want to get married until Deedee came along. Now she thinks it is the right thing to do."

"That sounds like a good idea." I'm surprised that he is telling me so much about himself.

"I met her on a trip to Colombia. She was dancing with her girlfriends at a street fair. I had been shopping and I had a lot of coins in my pocket. I tossed them in the air, and they scattered all over the ground." He laughs.

I fail to see the humor, but I continue to listen intently.

"The girls ran to pick them up, but Daniela put her nose in the air. 'I can't be bought for a few coins,' she said and walked away swinging her hips."

He smiles, "I inquired about her name, and the next day I sent her a dozen roses to apologize."

Ramos shrugs. "Naturally I sent Daniela an invitation to dinner. Her father called me at the hotel and said she could come to dinner with me, but that her brother would be with her. That is how we met."

"That's a great story," I say. He's painting a pretty picture of Daniela, but I wonder how much of it is true. With all his money, I find it hard to believe that she wants to continue working.

"Yes," he says. "I immediately fell in love with her, and for fifteen years we wrote to each other."

"We should all have such wonderful memories." I tell him.

"I found out that her father owned a business and she and her brother worked for the company. Her mother had left her father for another man when Daniela was only four. Her mother left the country and Daniela no longer speaks about her.

"So you have known the family for a long time?" I ask.

"That is true, her father and I were good friends. Then unexpectedly, her father passed away, and I went to his funeral. The business had never done well, so after her father died, Daniela went to work for an airline. Later on, I loaned her brother money to get the business on its feet. When Daniela became pregnant, she came to live with me and we have been together ever since."

"And you think I have a strange life." I laugh.

"We do what we think is right." he says.

When I nod, he continues his story. He doesn't tell me whether he fathered the child or not, so I'm left with the possibility that the little girl might not be his.

"Since Daniela is away so much, I have hired a tutor for Deedee and already she is smarter than any other girl her age." He tucks the picture back into his shirt pocket.

I try to keep the dialogue going, however, I'm not good at talking about children and the communication wanes.

I'm hoping Jeff is right and that Ramos offers me some kind of position, but time is short and I don't think that's gonna happen. In desperation, I tell him that I have been back to the casinos to see if an opening may have come up for a dealer.

"I told you I did not think much of gambling, but for you I will put in a good word with the politicians. They will pass the information on to the casino managers."

As I presumed, he knew someone that could get me into the casino, but he probably didn't want to get involved in my problems. Besides, I don't want the job, I just want to keep in contact with him. I thank him and go to work cleaning his room. He smiles his approval as I carefully wipe each bedrail, but our discussion has ended.

I get off work early and drive into town. I park the car and stroll through the business section. I can tell by the different languages that many Europeans are shopping. Women wearing bathing suits cover themselves with flimsy tops and long, silky skirts. Most of the men wear shorts, and almost everyone has on a large straw hat to hide from the burning sun.

I feel out of place, so I unbutton my shirt and let it hang outside my pants. In one of the shops, I try on flip-flops, but they're uncomfortable, so I stuff my socks in my pocket and put my Bass penny-loafers back on.

Vacationing families giggle and laugh at the assortment of souvenirs as they walk along the sidewalk, while others chat about where they are from and where they are staying.

A young-man sits glassy-eyed in front of a sporting goods shop. He grins at everyone who passes, and occasionally tips his boater hat. When I walk past him, he draws a triangle in the air. I suppose he thinks he is putting a voodoo curse on me. I laugh, so he stands up and does a little dance. When I stomp my foot, he turns a couple of cart-wheels and runs away.

The onlookers boo me.

"Why did you chase him away?" a woman asks.

"He's just a boy having fun," a man with two young boys scolds.

"I didn't mean to run him off," I say.

"That's okay." An elderly gentleman puts his hand on my shoulder. "He comes into town every day. He'll be back tomorrow. We give him money for food."

"I don't wish him any harm. I was only joking with him, but I think the money you give him is more than likely being spent on drugs."

"Could be," he says, "but he brings joy to the children. Sometimes he does tricks on his bike. They call him Willy Wiggle."

The crowd drifts away, and I continue down the street. If you didn't know what was happening in the underground, you would see Belize as a fairytale country filled with laughter and love. I see Belize as a mixture of beauty and imperfection, wealth and poverty. Yet often the weak and the strong dwell in the same area.

Most of the country is touched by depression, but there is still much happiness. In a country riddled by corruption, a few ethical citizens seem determined to hold on by a hair. I'm beginning to have an attachment to this strange exotic place.

A short time later, Jeff calls. He always has his phone on speaker and everything he says echoes. He tells me Ernesto is getting out of the hospital in a couple of days. I tell him I already know and that Ramos said he would have the politicians put in a good word for me at the casinos.

"How's that going to further our situation?" he asks.

No wonder these guys can't get to Ramos. They don't know how to deal.

"You don't need a damn job," Jeff snaps.

I've had enough of his crap. "You think he's gonna spill his guts in two days? Maybe I should ask him to type up a confession and sign his name so we can convict him. I was only using the job idea to keep in touch with him."

He ignores my explanation. "While we're on the subject of Ramos, why didn't you call me as soon as you found out he was going home?"

"I just found out today and I did call, but you didn't answer your phone and your mailbox is full. Besides, I know your friend at the hospital tells you everything that's going on and every move I make, so I knew he'd let you know."

"Knock it off. He doesn't tell me what you're doing, and I've been here every day for you. I didn't know the box was full. I'll take care of it."

I couldn't seem to drop the subject. "If I was hangin' by my teeth somewhere, I'd hate to have you as my back up," I snap back.

"What's got into you today?" Jeff says. "You're upset over nothing. I'm sorry if I came on strong. We shouldn't be arguing."

"I'm not upset, but I was told I could do this my way without any interference from DEA or the FBI, but you continue to put me in impossible situations and expect miracles."

Jeff doesn't have a comeback. "I'll notify Cox." He ends the call.

I don't know what he expects me to do now. I shove my phone in my pocket.

CHAPTER NINE

The following day, I change into a clean pair of coveralls and check in with my boss.

"We're losin' a good patient." My boss looks at the floor.

I raise my eyebrows. "Who's that?" I ask, pretending I haven't heard that Ramos was going home.

"The Banana King, Mr. Ramos. The hospital's giving him a going home party. Everyone who works here is invited. A couple of the nurses think they can get a job taking care of him at his mansion. They say people who work for Ramos make a lot of money."

"After he gets better he won't need them, and by then they'll have lost their jobs at the hospital." I fill my cart with supplies.

"The nurses won't lose their jobs. The hospital wants them to help him get better. They want to please him. His company is the hospital's biggest contributor. I heard they're gonna hang his picture in the doctors' gallery."

I gape, as if his wealth was something I hadn't even thought about. "I presumed he was well off, but I didn't know he was that rich."

"Oh, yeah." The custodian beams. "He may look like a simple man, but he has power. Some folks say his money controls the politicians."

He's given me the perfect opportunity to talk about Ramos. "People love to spread gossip," I tell Gerald. "I talk to Ramos every day. He's always pleasant and caring. He doesn't strike me as a person who would exert his influence in order to control people. I doubt he has anything to do with politics. He even told me he has a little girl."

"That's true. He's got a daughter." Flower's taps his index finger on his desk. "She was born right here in this hospital."

I notice my statement has changed the atmosphere. "That must have been a big day."

"A big day for Doctor Palacio," Gerald says. "No one knew Ramos had a girlfriend, let alone that she was pregnant. They came in a limo, had a police escort, and in twenty-four hours the mother and the baby went home. Everything was secret. No birth notice appeared in the newspaper and no friends came to visit. It took a long time before the news got around that Ernesto Ramos was a father."

"Mr. Ramos didn't tell me about the day his daughter was born. He just said she was the love of his life."

"Some people still claim the little girl was spawned by a man in Colombia." Gerald whispers. "There was a lot of gossip back then, but like you say, people love to talk."

Good. I've squashed any questionable idea Flowers might have thought I had about Ramos. I don't want Gerald's daily gossip ruining any connection I make with Ramos. I push the cart toward the elevator while Gerald continues to put away supplies that were recently delivered.

However, the custodian's knowledge only adds to my problem. If Ramos was that secretive about a baby being born, I have no chance of getting invited to his home, much less his criminal organization if one exists. I start on the far side of the hospital, hoping to spend more time with Ramos in the afternoon. When I go in, Ernesto's sound asleep. I walk across the room and open the blind.

"What in the world?" I'm looking right into some guy's kisser. If the window was open I could've reached out and snatched his stocking cap. This is quite a surprise since I'm on the second floor.

The skinny man holds up a squeegee, releases the rope, and drops out of sight. He's apparently cleaning the outside of the windows, but he left this one a mess. Cleaning solution is still running down the glass. I wonder why he didn't finish cleaning the window, but then, most people don't do a good job these days.

The sun is bright, so I close the blind and leave the room. I'll come back a little later when Ramos is awake.

I think about the window washer as I walk along the hallway. It must be a hundred degrees outside, but the man was wearing a black knitted stocking cap. I only saw his face for a moment, but I remember it well. Long and thin. Large upper front teeth protruded from his mouth, and his nose was small and sharp.

I move on to the next room and start to clean. Nurse Isabella, who's in charge of the nurse's station on the second floor, comes into the room where I'm now working. She ignores me and checks on the patient, who is recovering from a broken leg. He looks to be in his late teens or early twenties. He has a head full of tight blond ringlets that curl around his ears.

She helps him get up. "You need to walk." She hands him crutches.

He doesn't appear to be able to put any weight on his broken leg. When he begins to lean toward Isabella, I see the fright on her face. I move quickly, pulling the kid into an upright position.

"I can't stand," he says.

"Sure you can. That's what that little bar underneath your foot is for. You just need to learn how to brace yourself before you stand up straight." I help him sit in the chair and pick up the crutches that have fallen to the floor.

Nurse Isabella snatches them from me and leans them against the bed. "Thank you for helping. I'll get an orderly. Go back to your job." She leaves the room in a huff.

"Thanks for catching me. My name's Donnie Logan." The young man reaches forward to shake my hand.

"Is that Donnie Logan as in U. S. Ambassador, Donald Logan?"

"You bet. He's my father. Do you know him?" he asks.

"I met him once." It's hard for me to believe that like Ramos, Ambassador Logan has a young son. I wonder if people would say the same thing about me if Angela and I had a child.

"How'd you break your leg?"

"Motorcycle."

"Did anyone else get hurt?"

"No, I was alone. Just took a corner a little sharp and laid it out."

"That's probably something you won't do again, or at least not anytime soon." I chuckle.

"I won't be doing that again, period." Donnie groans. "My father got rid of the bike and told me he will never buy me another one." He laughs. "You wanna show me how to use these sticks?"

"The hospital doesn't approve of janitors working with patients. You better wait for the orderly. He's a nice guy. You won't have any trouble."

"This place is a trip," Donnie says. "They wake you up to give you a sleeping pill, tell you to drink a lot of water and then they forget to give you a urinal and you have no way to get to the bathroom. My mom and I are going home to Miami as soon as I can get around."

"I understand completely," I tell him. "I'll come back when things quiet down in here."

"That's cool," he says.

I say goodbye to the young man and leave his room. Isabella and the orderly pass me in the hallway. He nods, but she looks straight ahead. I park my cart in front of the cleaning supply closet and go to the cafeteria for a much-needed cup of coffee.

While I relax with my lukewarm coffee, I think about the two head nurses. I can't help but wonder how Nurse Isabella and Nurse Marcie get along. They're both bossy and seem to be cut from the same cloth. I wonder if they ever butt heads.

In the afternoon, I go to Ernesto's room. I park my cart outside his door and go in to say hello. I suppose I should tell him about the window cleaner. However, I don't because he is so paranoid, I'm afraid it might upset him. Instead, we talk about him leaving the hospital. If the hospital thinks it's a good idea for nurses to help him get better, maybe I could suggest giving him a hand when he goes home to recuperate.

"Do you think you'll do okay at home, without any help?" I ask.

He laughs. "I have more than enough help. We have a maid to clean, one to take care of our clothes, another to cook, and a teacher for Deedee. They gather around me like mother hens. I do not want any more help."

It appears that a position at the mansion is out of the question. "All you need is someone to buy groceries and then you won't have to leave your bed."

"Most of the time I order the food and have it delivered. I do not like to go into the stores."

"If everything is done for you, what do you do to keep yourself occupied?"

"We have a little garden in the back. Between me and the gardener, we grow most of our fresh vegetables. It is peaceful there. It not only feeds my family, it gives me a reason to get up each day and go outside to see what God has nourished overnight. Of course, even though I hire competent employees, overseeing my banana business takes a lot of my time."

Again, I'm struck by this man's apparent sincerity. For the life of me, I can't see him as a ruthless killer. I'm happy he's alive. I would hate to have to think of how I would feel for the rest of my life if the bullet had hit its mark. I know now, I can't kill him. Even if he's a kingpin, he's entitled to his day in court.

Ramos strokes his mustache. "So, have you decided what you are going to do to make a lot of money?"

"I'm still looking for a dealer position at one of the casinos. I can't live on the wages I make here."

"Oh, yes. I had forgotten I promised to look into a position for you. As a matter of fact, I might have an opportunity that you may be interested in."

Did he say what I think he said? I feel like I'm falling off a cliff. I look at the floor and blink. A piece of paper has fallen to the floor. I take a deep breath to clear my head while I stoop to pick it up. "What do you have in mind?"

"I'm not sure what I plan to do, but it will require that I hire someone. I'll let you know tomorrow."

I thank him, but don't inquire any further. To question him now would be pushy.

Ramos has written two reminders on a scrap of paper. "Get present for Deedee and call to have helicopter pick up Daniela at airport."

"This must be your list." I hand the paper to him.

He lays the note on the table. "I have to write everything down. I think the medicine is causing me to forget."

"So, your girlfriend is coming home. That must make you happy."

"Yes, she is coming soon, but only for a day or two. She wants to make sure I get settled and that Deedee is being cared for."

"She sounds like a good mother," I say. "Do you know when the hospital is going to release you?"

"I am going to be sprung in two or three days."

His answer is an odd statement for a businessman to make. "You make it sound like you're in jail." I laugh.

"In a way I am. I do not like being confined." He rubs his hands together.

"Having body guards at home and a guard at my hospital door is mostly Daniela's notion. She says Belize is changing and that criminals now kill people for a few bucks. I believe she is over-protective. Besides, I do not keep anything of value at my home."

I grin. "You have to keep the little lady happy."

"I do not mind. She and Deedee have given me new life. I do not need anything else."

"That's a good enough reason," I say. "However, it's nice to be able to give the people you love a luxurious lifestyle."

Then he surprises me.

"I believe I mentioned I had a few investments. The truth is, when my father passed away he left my brother and me a large portfolio of securities. I placed mine in an off-shore account. I only use the dividends to help the poor people of Belize. It helps to offset my earnings and reduce my taxes."

This is interesting information since the FBI says he doesn't make any profit from Longview Banana Corporation, yet he still pays a lot of taxes to Belize. Maybe the FBI doesn't know about his additional wealth.

Nevertheless, time is slipping away, and I don't have any more information about Ramos being connected to drugs than I did the first day I arrived here.

"I understand they're planning a surprise 'leaving the hospital party' for me the night before I am discharged," he says. "I act like I don't know anything about it, but they contacted my people at the house to get an okay. I am having a couple of my friends over to help with the celebration. If you do not have other plans, I would like you to come to the party."

"I'll make it a point to be there," I tell him.

As I roll my cleaning cart out of his room, I see Ramos has already turned on his side and closed his eyes. Since I think I have finally earned his trust, I'm no longer sure I can betray him.

CHAPTER TEN

On the day of the party, I arrive at work early. I check all the rooms, and do only what is absolutely necessary. I want to be finished before lunch.

As I step into Ramos' room, I hear him leaving a message for Nurse Marcie. It takes a few minutes for Marcie to come to the second floor.

"What would you like, Mr. Ramos?" she asks.

"I want all this equipment that I am no longer using removed from my room. I do not want my friends to see it. They tend to make more out of my accident than is necessary."

"I'm really sorry." She clasps her hands together. "It takes two people and I only have one technician on duty today."

Now I understand why he called Marcie. She's a MSN and the head nurse of the whole hospital and this is probably a decision nurse Isabella couldn't make.

"Maybe I could help." I volunteer.

"I wish you could," Marcie says. "However, these are expensive electronics and only technicians are permitted to move them. I could get into trouble if any equipment were to be broken."

"Mr. Anderson is a retired engineer. I will personally be responsible if he does not properly store the equipment," Ramos tells Nurse Marcie.

Whadaya know? I've been miraculously promoted above the lowly technicians to engineer. I guess Ramos thinks if he's gonna lie, he might as well make it a big one. I also noticed he used his financial position to get what he wanted. Maybe Gerald was right.

"I didn't know that." She smiles at me. "Come with me." Nurse Marcie crooks her index finger as she walks toward the door. "I'll show you the storage area."

My volunteering did not mean I planned on moving the equipment alone. I assumed she would at least have the one qualified technician help me.

Ernesto grins. "Run along," he says. "We will talk when you get back."

I traipse along behind Marcie. We go down the stairs and along the hallway. When we pass the custodian's room, Gerald looks up.

"Robert!" he shouts. "I want you on the second floor. Don't be wandering around down here."

Marcie, as usual, doesn't miss a beat. "Ignore him."

Gerald rushes out of his office and catches up with me. He grabs my arm. "Did you hear me?" he shouts.

"Take your hands off me." I cuff him on the shoulder.

Marcie whips around. "Gerald, go back to your office."

He blinks and retreats in the other direction.

"That man will be the death of me. He doesn't know his place," she mumbles.

It makes me wonder exactly where I stand with her and reminds me to watch my P's and Q's.

At the end of the hallway is a chain-link, fenced-in area filled with equipment.

Marcie stops at the padlocked gate. "This is where the equipment is stored."

I look inside the fencing. Breathing machines, dialysis equipment, surgery lights—you name it. Everything is jammed together. There doesn't seem to be any order, and it doesn't look like anything else will fit into the space.

"Call me if you can't handle it." She hands me a key and walks away.

It almost sounds like she knows I'm not an engineer. I climb the stairs two at a time and go back to the second floor. I'll show her what a real man can do all by himself.

All the big devices are on wheels, but they're still heavy. I sweat like a pig while I maneuver the electronic equipment along the hallway and into the service elevator. Then I have to rearrange half the stuff in the storage area in order to make room for Ernesto's equipment.

When I finally finish, I rush back to Ernesto's room. He's asleep. Great, I've blown my only chance to talk with him and tonight's party will be the last time I see him. Dammit!

I go home to get cleaned up for the party.

When I return to the hospital, Ramos is already dressed and sitting in a wheelchair in the second floor waiting room. A long table has been set up and extra chairs have been brought up from the first floor. A few clerks from administration are milling around and talking to Ernesto.

The elevator door opens. A bushy-haired caterer and two waiters dressed in white uniforms step into the waiting room. Bushy Hair has on a tall white chef's hat and is pushing a hospital cart loaded with boxes and trays.

Before they can go near Ramos, Javier pats them down and checks out the contents of the boxes. They arrange the spiced tortilla's, grilled grouper, steak brochette, creamy chicken liver pate, eggplant and a host of other delicious dishes on the table. By the time they are ready to serve, more employees from the first floor have come up the stairs to join the party.

Ramos calls me over to his wheelchair. He looks up at me and says, "These are my friends, Eduardo Moralez and Jorge Diaz. They came to visit me and are staying for the party."

My brain clicks when I hear the name Diaz. This is the same last name Jeff used when he told me about Ramos' girlfriend, Daniela. I remember Ernesto saying she had a brother, but since they're not married yet, Ramos may only consider him a friend, or Jorge may not have any connection to the family at all, since Diaz is a common name in Belize.

Ramos points to me. "This is Robert Anderson." He introduces me to his friends.

I shake hands with the two men. "It's nice to meet you."

I'm uncomfortable when he tells the men that I'm the engineer who moved the equipment from his room. They both laugh, so I assume he has told them his made up story. Then, Marcie laughs and I laugh too. She knows I'm not a retired engineer. I can see it in her green eyes.

Some of the guests have placed small presents on the floor beside Ramos' wheelchair, and he looks embarrassed when a couple of elderly nurses kiss him gently on the cheek.

Laughter spreads as the guests fill their plates and chat with each other. Some of the staff tell Ramos how much they will miss him.

One of the other patients has come out of his room in a wheelchair and is rolling toward the waiting room. He seems to be having difficulty maneuvering the mobile chair.

Ramos touches my hand and points to the man. "Please help him," he says. "Bring him to the party."

Just as I move to help the guy, the elevator doors open. I turn around to see who's getting off and realize he's the window washer. He's pointing a black revolver at Ramos.

Two nurses scream, but everyone else seems to have lost their voices. I rush the shooter from the side, knock the gun from his hand, and go down on one knee. The pistol goes off when it slams against the marble floor. It spins along the hallway and slides under a couch.

The assailant crashes into the wall, but keeps his footing. He kicks at my head, but misses and hits my shoulder. A sharp pain goes up my neck. I grab his boot and he stumbles.

Someone shouts, "Get the gun!"

The intruder tries to get away, but I hang onto his boot and he drags me along. He comes to a stop and I begin to pull myself up off the floor. I look up just in time to see his fist headed for my chin. He scores a glancing blow, but he's a lightweight and I make it to my feet.

I haven't been in a fight for a long time. However, fisticuffs is ingrained in me, and I swing away, but I miss by a country mile. I chase him to the stairs. He's agile and fast. I, on the other hand, have been going out to dinner and eating rich foods. The extra pounds slow me down to what feels like a crawl.

I'm no match for the speedy window washer. He slides down the handrail, jumps over the last four steps, turns the corner and is gone.

Pandemonium ensues. People scream and knock over chairs in an effort to get out of the waiting room. I don't know where the hell they think they're going. Most of them are still on duty. I see a nurse pushing the patient in the wheelchair back to his room. He appears confused and she is trying to comfort him.

The waiting room is a tangle of overturned tables and chairs. Chow that was neatly arranged on the buffet is now scattered across the carpet. "Oh crap." I notice my pant leg is wet from when I bumped into the punch table.

I spot Ernesto's friends pushing him down the hallway toward his room. Javier is walking backwards behind them brandishing his gun.

Even after Ramos is secure in his room, Javier continues to stand outside the door with his gun drawn. Everyone has vacated the waiting room. I find the only comfortable chair still in an upright position and sit down. There isn't any blood on the carpet, so I assume no one was in the way of the one fired bullet. It most likely is lodged in the baseboard somewhere.

I realize that I'm going to be grilled by the police and they might discover my real identity. Even if I had left the building, they would've come after me. I make a quick call to Jeff and explain what happened.

There's a long pause. "Why didn't you let the idiot shoot Ramos? We would've had what we needed and you could've gone home."

I know he's a good agent. He never lets anything stand in the way of his agenda, but he hasn't had enough time on the street to learn how to change direction and do the obvious.

"Oh! That would've been great. I stand there while the gunman kills Ramos in front of thirty witnesses, and then let the culprit run away? Don't you realize he might have emptied his gun on a few more people?"

"It's possible, but not probable. More than likely he would've blasted Ramos and split. He's probably already halfway to Mexico or Honduras."

"You wish." I growl. "He has a job to finish. You're only thinking about what the FBI wants. The killer has his own agenda."

Sirens scream as the police approach the hospital.

"You're making too much of this," Jeff says.

"Me? I just called to give you the news and I gotta get off this phone before the police come in and want to know who I'm talking to."

"Stall them," Jeff says. "Pretend to be an upset janitor."

"I am an upset janitor."

"So it should be easy to pretend that you can hardly talk. Ask for water. Ask them to give you a few minutes. I'll be right there." He hangs up.

Bad enough I could've been killed, now he expects me to be an actor. This job sucks.

I delete the call and put the phone back in my pocket. If the police don't see anything on my phone, they might not think to check with the mobile company.

In spite of all the problems that will no doubt surface as a result of this fiasco, my thoughts turn to how hard it will be to get red punch stains out of the light blue carpet. I don't have long to obsess about it because a group of police officers arrive with guns drawn.

"Who are you?" A young cop asks me.

I stand. "I'm the janitor."

One police officer, dressed in a light tan suit, seems to be in charge. He and Nurse Marcie are engrossed in conversation. His bronze face glistens with sweat under the bright emergency spotlight at the top of the stairs that has somehow been turned on.

He turns and motions to the cop standing beside me and another officer who appears to be eyeballing a plate of tiny sandwiches that miraculously avoided being dumped on the floor.

"You two check on Mr. Ramos," the officer in charge says. He orders a third officer to go downstairs and talk to the guard. "See if he saw anyone leaving or noticed a strange car outside."

Then he and Marcie move closer to me. The bronze-faced man pushes his fedora back on his high forehead, revealing large dark eyes.

"This is Robert Anderson. He works in custodial service." Marcie says.

"I'm Detective Gonzalez," he tells me. "Were you on duty during the attempted murder of Ernesto Ramos?"

"No." Marcie interjects. "He was off duty, but Mr. Ramos invited him to the party."

"How long have you worked here?" he asks me.

"He's a new hire," she answers for me.

I guess I don't have to worry about answering questions.

"Do you know how the intruder got to the second floor?" the detective asks.

I wait to see if Marcie will answer.

"Mr. Anderson." Detective Gonzalez glares at me.

"Yes, sir," I answer.

"I'm talking to you." he says. "Do you know how the intruder got to the second floor?"

"He came up on the elevator." I wring my hands.

"What happened when the elevator door opened?"

"The man got off." I pause and squint like I'm thinking. "He had a large revolver and it was pointed at Mr. Ramos."

"Are you sure?" Gonzalez pulls a small notepad from his pocket.

I can't play this stupid acting game. "I'm positive!" My voice echoes across the room.

Unruffled, the detective asks. "Could you identify the intruder if you saw him again?"

"Yes, I also saw him two days ago."

"Where was that?" The detective continues to drill me.

"He was outside the window in Mr. Ramos' hospital room with a squeegee. I thought he was washing the windows, but now I think he may have had something else in mind."

"I'll check to see who we hired to wash windows," Marcie offers.

Detective Gonzalez scribbles something in his notepad. "What did you think when you saw he had a gun pointed at Ramos?"

"I didn't think. I reacted. I charged him from the side and grabbed at the gun."

"Did you tackle him?"

"No." There must be something wrong with the officer's hearing. "I was after the gun, but it fell to the floor. The gun fired when it hit the hard marble and slid under the couch." I point to the black leather couch next to the steps.

"Now we're getting somewhere," he says.

The Belize detective takes a plastic bag from his hip pocket and hands it to an officer in a blue uniform who has been tailing him.

"Get the gun," the detective tells him as he continues to interrogate me.

"Then what did you do?" He picks up his line of questioning.

I stop to think about what I said last. "The man went toward the steps, and I ran after him. He slid down the railing and jumped over the last few steps. Then he dropped out of sight. I turned around and came back to the waiting room." I'm not going to tell the cops about being dragged along hugging the guys boot or about the swing I took at him and missed, or how I gut cuffed by a skinny light-weight and make myself look like a bumbling idiot.

"Was that the last time you saw him?"

I nod. "Talking about this is upsetting my stomach." I tell the officer. Hell, I've probably said too much already.

"I need to check around, but I don't want you to leave the premises." He pulls Marcie aside, but his deep voice travels, so I can still hear him.

"What's with this janitor? Has he been here long?"

"No, he just recently started. He's an American, and new to Belize."

"Did he pass a background check?"

"I don't know. I'll have to check with human recourses."

"I want to know everything you have on him. I want to know how he got to know Ramos. I heard about him before. One of the patrolmen turned in a report with his name on it. He was riding in Ambassador Logon's limo. I don't think this is coincidental."

"I'll see what I can find out," Marcie says.

Before he leaves, he again reminds Marcie and I not to leave the premises. "I want to talk to you again." He glares at me.

"If you need me, I'll be at the main nurse's station on the first floor," Marcie tells Gonzalez, and then turns toward me. "Robert, I want you to clean up the waiting room."

Before I have a chance to remind her that I'm not on duty tonight, Gonzalez turns around.

"Don't touch anything!" the detective barks.

Blue Uniform returns with the gun. "Do you want me to tie off the room with tape?"

"No, just call Shorty. Tell him I want pictures of the waiting room. I understand the shooter got off the elevator and went straight down the steps. He never actually entered the room."

Gonzalez looks at the steps. "Yellow tape the steps, and call Forensics. The stairs have been used, but tell them we might be able to find a thread or something on the railing. Too many people have already used the elevator for us to get any good prints. Give the gun to Shorty. Tell him I want the results ASAP."

The second officer returns from Ramos' room. "Mr. Ramos wants to talk to the janitor."

"About what?" Gonzalez asks.

"He wouldn't say. He won't talk to us until he sees this Robert guy."

"You." Gonzalez points to me. "Stay right here until I come back."

CHAPTER ELEVEN

Donald Logan gets off the elevator and makes a bee-line to where I'm standing. "This is some mess." He looks around the waiting room.

"It just needs to be cleaned," I say. "The only bad place is where the punch got on the rug."

Logan rolls his eyes. "I'm not talking about the damn rug." He motions for me to walk with him to the far side of the room. He lowers his voice. "Who would've thought something like this would happen?"

"I already talked to Jeff," I tell Logan. "He should be here soon."

Ambassador Logan stops by the large plate glass window. "I put a stop to that. I don't want the FBI or the DEA to come anywhere near this place. They need to stay out of the loop."

This is no surprise to me. Logan appears to have his hands full. I didn't realize how hard it must be to make the U.S. agenda work and still stay on good terms with foreign governments.

Logan gazes out at the city. "This place is changing. Belize used to be a paradise. The country has always had its share of drugs, but now unrestrained gangs and hardcore criminals are taking over. I don't see how anything can ever be the same again."

He puts his hand on my shoulder. "It's important that we don't lie to the officials, but we need to say as little as possible. What have you told them so far?"

"All I said was that I saw the shooter a couple of days ago when he was cleaning the outside of Ramos' hospital window, and then I told the detective what happened when the shooter stepped out of the elevator tonight. It's no secret." I shrug. "Everyone in the room saw what happened. Detective Gonzalez has been too busy to talk to me about anything else."

"It won't be necessary to bring up your past. Give them the name the Federal Witness Protection Program originally issued to you. It already has a past built in. You shouldn't have a problem."

"I only glanced through the FBI's identification papers. I didn't have any reason to use the past life they set up for me and I don't recall what they said about it."

A vein stands out on Logan's temple. "I didn't know much about you, so when you first came to Belize I had to get special clearance to look at the FBI's Robert Anderson file."

I wonder what he found out.

"Here's what we're gonna do," he says. "We'll tell them you're upset and need a little time to settle down. We'll find a quiet spot and I'll tell you about Anderson's past. It's not much. Trust me, you'll be okay."

One of the local cops comes into the waiting room and says to me, "Mr. Ramos wants to talk to you."

"Ramos asked to see me a little while ago, and Detective Gonzalez said I was to stay right here," I tell the officer.

"Detective Gonzalez told me to take you to Mr. Ramos' new room," the officer says.

Logan's short nod tells me to go with the officer. I don't like being ordered around, but I've been in worse situations. The cop has on shorts and tennis shoes. The patch on his shirt says "Traffic Division"—Officer Leo Haylock.

The cop looks Logan up and down. "Who's your buddy?" he sneers.

He's in for it now. "Let me introduce you." I extend my hand toward Logan. "I'd like you to meet the United States Ambassador, Donald Logan. He's here to protect my rights."

Ambassador Logan shakes the officer's hand.

Stumbling over his words, Officer Haylock tips his cap to Logan. "I only saw your picture. I'm sorry I didn't recognize you. Would you like to come with us?" He puts his hand behind Logan's shoulder and urges him forward.

Logan brushes the officer's hand away. "That won't be necessary. Mr. Anderson is quite capable of answering any questions."

"I'm an American citizen." I glare at Haylock. "I'm new to this country. I'm sure you understand why I called the ambassador right after the incident."

"I'm sorry about the confusion. I did not mean to interfere. That was the right thing to do." He drips with apologies.

"I'm sure you meant well." I give him one of Cox's surface smiles and show him my newly whitened teeth that Angela insisted I get.

The officer turns to Logan. "I'll notify my commander that you're here."

"There's no need. I spoke with Commander Reyes on my way in."

"Yes, sir. Excuse us," he says.

"That's quite all right." Logan's reply is cordial, but his strong demeanor leaves no doubt as to who is in charge.

I follow the traffic cop. They must be short handed tonight.

Ramos has been moved to a different room. It's quite large and his bed is tucked in the corner, far away from the window and door. He's back in a hospital bed and holds his hand out to me. The cop leaves me with Ramos.

I glance around the room. Eduardo and two local police officers are standing by the window. Jorge is sitting by Ramos' bed.

"Jorge," Ramos whispers. "Due to the problems tonight, a nurse is unavailable. The cleaning man is going to bring me clean sheets and make my bed. Please take the men with you and step out of the room so I can change into my pajamas. We will talk more about the business when I get home from the hospital."

Reluctantly, Jorge, Eduardo, and the two officers leave.

I step close to his bed. "I'm happy to see you're okay."

"Yes, thanks to your quick response."

"Do you want me to close the door?" I ask Ramos.

"No, that will only make them suspicious."

The room is quiet except for a small beep from the machine that monitors his steady heartbeat, temperature, and blood pressure. The needle is back in his arm, providing a constant flow of glucose into his system.

"Come closer, Robert. I have something to tell you." He tunes his portable radio to soft music.

I pull a chair up to his bedside at an angle so I can keep my eye on the open doorway.

"Up until tonight, I must confess I liked you, but I did not trust you. I find it hard to trust anyone, especially an American who moves to another country without good reason." He sighs. "I do not believe either one of us has told each other the complete truth."

"You're probably right, but it's of little consequence. We're only ships passing in the night."

"I do not believe that is true. I think you were sent to me for a reason."

Oh, crap. He knows I'm the first guy who tried to kill him.

"Like you," Ramos says. "I have always been a loner, but now I find myself in an awkward position."

"If you think you owe me something for saving your life, you don't. The slate is clean. By the way, where was Javier when all the shooting was going on? I thought he was your bodyguard."

"Bad timing. He had just gone to the men's room."

"Do you think that might have been part of a plan?" I ask.

"No, he is a simple man. He has worked for me doing various jobs for many years. He only recently started to carry a gun. I am not sure he even knows how to use it."

"If he hasn't fired a gun before, you should have him trained."

"I wish all my problems were as uncomplicated as having Javier trained or thanking you for saving my life." He pauses. "It's important that you know I told everyone my rifle went off accidently and grazed my shoulder. The truth is, I was outside on my way to the helicopter pad when someone took a shot at me."

"Hmm, that's serious stuff. That's twice someone has tried to kill you. Do you know anyone who would want to take your life?"

"I think I do," he says.

Sweat forms on the back of my neck, but I play it cool and plaster a concerned look on my face.

"That is my reason for talking to you."

He couldn't know it was me unless he has an informer at the embassy. Maybe it's Marco or Butch. How ironic would that be?

"We often find ourselves in predicaments that are not of our making and we do whatever is necessary to survive," Ramos says.

"True." I say. He might just be baiting me.

"I am not a gossiping man, and I do not need to hear about your past. In fact, I want to talk to you about the assignment I mentioned." He leans forward.

"What kind of offer are you talking about?" I keep my voice steady, hoping he doesn't expect me to do something illegal.

"You see, Jorge is Daniela's brother," Ramos begins.

Oh, so there is a connection. I wait for him to continue.

"When her father fell ill, the already bungled business faltered. Their father willed the family house to Daniela and gave the business to Jorge. Upon his death, Daniela petitioned the court to get control of her father's business. She is a strong-willed girl and even though she was working for the airlines the court awarded her permission to run the business if she hired a qualified manager, which she did. She only did it because her brother tends to be incompetent. She wants to get the business on its feet before she turns it over to him."

"What kind of business did her father leave to Jorge?" I figure we might as well get whatever Ramos is mixed up in out in the open.

"Produce, mostly fruit," he says.

"Produce? Her father was in the fruit and vegetable business?"

"Yes. In the winter, Colombia ships a lot of produce to The United States."

"How is the business doing now?"

"She had to let the manager go. I don't remember the reason. Moralez took his place."

If this is true, the DEA's theory is completely blown out of the water. "And where do you come into this picture?" I ask

"Her father had been shipping their produce by boat to southern Mexico. Then, it was trucked into The United States. Daniela found out that when it got to Mexico, the transfer was often delayed and the produce spoiled. She changed the route and sent it by boat to Belize. From here it is being delivered by Longview's refrigerated trucks straight through Mexico and across the border into the United States." Leaning back into his pillow, he says. "I want to marry Daniela, so I am happy to help with this venture."

"Is that because you want your daughter to bear your surname?" I ask.

"My daughter's name is already legally Delores Ramos. I adopted Deedee when she was born and Daniela gave me full custody of the baby. Her job requires so much traveling she was afraid that if something happened to her, someone might try to take her away from me. He edges toward me and whispers. "I have not told anyone else, but my daughter is my sole beneficiary and naturally I named Daniela her guardian. My brother is the executor of the will and guardian of the property that Deedee will inherit."

"What about Daniela?" I ask.

"The best thing that has come from our partnership is that Daniela has accepted my proposal. After we're married I will change my will to include Daniela."

"I guess your brother will be happy. He probably doesn't want all that responsibility."

"He will still have many responsibilities," Ramos says. "In my tax bracket I couldn't expect Daniela to handle all my financial affairs. Besides, Daniela is a caring person. She is always busy helping someone. She has taken some of the poorest girls from Colombia and gotten them good-paying jobs in different countries. I am afraid that if something should happen to me, she could easily be taken in by unscrupulous people and lose everything we have." He frowns. "She works hard for the money she makes, and often gives it away to needy people. I love her very much and after I am gone, I want her and my daughter to be well taken care of."

"Then life is not so bad. You should be happy," I reply. "The rest is easy. All you have to do is tell the police to arrest the man who you think took a shot at you."

"You would think so, but it is not that easy. Jorge claims that Daniela offered to pay Moralez to get rid of me after we are married."

"Oh, my, gosh. Do you think she is capable of that?" I ask.

"Of course not. I do not buy into Jorge's lies. He is jealous of Daniela and would lie about anything to get his own way. When he is high on drugs or drunk on alcohol he tells lies and often threatens people. However, when it comes to actually doing something, he does not have the guts. No one in Columbia pays any attention to him. He says he is my friend, but I know better. I allow him to be close so I can keep an eye on him."

"What about Moralez? Is he trustworthy?"

"I believe he can be trusted, but I do not think he has any principles or feelings." Ramos rubs the stubble on his chin. "Moralez and Jorge were in my home the day of the shooting. So I know it was neither one of them. However, Moralez is good friends with Jon, Ambassador Logan's limo driver, and although I respect the ambassador, I do not trust his driver."

"So you don't worry about Moralez?"

"Nah, Moralez gets paid up front, and Daniela does not have that kind of money. Even if it were true, Moralez would come to me to up the ante. He works for the highest bidder." Ramos chuckles.

It's time to get to the meat of this conversation. I feel like bluntness is the only route Ramos understands. "Exactly what is the offer you want me to consider?"

"You told me you wanted to make a large sum of cash quickly." Ramos smiles. "I believe I have a proposition that will benefit us both."

I recall Jeff's first remark about Ramos. He expected the drug lord to make friends with someone from The United States that he could use to his advantage. Before I jump the gun, I need to let this play out. Ramos might have a lot of enemies, but I still don't see him as the ruthless man the government thinks he is.

An officer of the law in a tan uniform covered with braid and multiple gold and silver medals appears in the doorway of Ramos' room.

Ernesto waves to him. "Commander Reyes, come in."

I stand and Ramos whispers, "Reyes is the chief of police in Belize City and I need to speak to him alone."

I nod.

"Because of tonight's incident, the doctor wants me to spend another night or two in the hospital." Ramos pats my hand. "We can finish our conversation tomorrow."

As I leave, I pass by Reyes. He doesn't even look my way. When I get back to the waiting room, Ambassador Logan is sitting in a chair by the window.

"What did the kingpin have to say?" he asks.

"Not much. He claims he has a job for me, but Commander Reyes interrupted our conversation, so I don't know what he wants me to do."

"I've been told that the people who work for him are well paid," Logan says. "They no doubt earn every penny of it. God knows what he expects from them."

"I know he expects people to do their job, but I've haven't seen him ask for anything else."

Logan strokes his chin. "The police want you to sign a sworn statement that the man who was washing the windows is the same man who attempted to murder Ernesto Ramos."

"A lot of other people saw him. Why can't they identify him?"

"You're the only one who seems to know he was the window washer." Logan stands and motions for me to follow him to the elevator. "We need to go to the first floor."

"Who hired him to wash the windows? Why doesn't that person step forward?"

"They're checking into that, but right now they need a statement from you." Logan presses the button for the elevator.

"Officer Gonzalez has suggested that it might be best if you stay at the consulate until they can locate the would-be assassin. It shouldn't take long. Belize City isn't that big. They're combing the streets for him as we speak."

"So now I gotta worry about some crackpot window washer gunnin' me down."

"Staying at your rooming house would be dangerous. Commander Reyes is sending a couple of his officers with us. We'll pick up your belongings and one of the officers will drive your rental car to the embassy."

"Why can't I drive my own car?" I ask.

"That would not be safe."

We get off the elevator and walk along a hallway until we come to a makeshift police office that's been set up in an empty patient room. After I sign the statement, Logan's limo takes us to my boarding house. I don't have much in the way of clothes, so it doesn't take long to pack. Two armed officers guard the entrance and see that we return safely to the limo.

As usual, Jon opens and closes the door for Ambassador Logan. I'm amazed when he does the same for me. I look at him closely for some sign of hostility, but all he does is smile. When we're seated, I wait for Logan to tell me about my "Anderson" past, but he closes the partition and touches his finger to his lips. The only thing he talks about is the shooting at the hospital.

The police patrol car leading the way doesn't have its siren on, but the squad car's lights are flashing and vehicles pull off the road to let us pass. Another officer is driving shotgun in my car behind the limo. We don't stop at any intersection.

While the limo speeds along to the embassy, Logan turns on the light and hands me the Robert Anderson report. Information about my real past has been blacked out. Data about Robert Anderson states that he had a series of nothing jobs until he went to work for an insurance company. He's never been married and has no children.

I close the file and hand it to Logan. Ramos is spending another day in the hospital. I'm going into work tomorrow. I want to see Ramos about that job he mentioned."

The limo is sailing along at a good clip when Logan tells me. "Just as a precaution, I will arrange to have three armed men accompany you to the hospital tomorrow."

"FBI or DEA?" I ask.

"Neither. These young men work for the consulate. I trust them and the Belizean people like them."

"That's different."

"I'm sorry you're in this position." This is not the way I would have handled it." Logan gets out of the limo and goes into the embassy.

Jon drops me off at the hotel.

Jeff is waiting in the lobby. "Logan called me. He said you were on your way here. What happened—give me the details."

Jeff walks with me to my room. I drop my belongings on the bed and finish telling him about the bizarre evening.

"Damn. That was some night," Jeff says.

"And you were worried that I might get killed trying to make an illegal left turn."

Jeff stands with his hands in his pockets.

"Logan says he has three armed men who will accompany me tomorrow." I laugh.

"I hope he doesn't intend to send me." Jeff grins.

"He mentioned they're not DEA or FBI."

"The only other people here are the cook, the clerk and his secretary." Jeff bursts out laughing.

"Are you sure?" I ask.

"We'll there's a few guys back in administration, but they don't carry guns. Maybe Commander Reyes is sending someone over."

"I really don't want anyone to go with me. I can take care of myself, which reminds me, I need to get a good night's sleep. Tomorrow could get hairy."

"I was just leaving," Jeff says. "I'll see you in the morning."

After he leaves, I lock the door and look around the room. It's a small room, but it's clean and has a nice size shower. I check my nine-millimeter pistol and place it on the bed. One can't be too careful.

CHAPTER TWELVE

In the morning, I walk next door to the embassy. Ambassador Logan is in the small break room with three young men. The adolescents are drinking Coca Cola. Logan has a full cup of coffee, so he must have just arrived.

The ambassador motions for me to join them. I pour myself a cup of coffee and slide into a chair at their table. Logan introduces me to the trio he has chosen to accompany me on my way to work this morning.

"Let me see if I got this straight," I say. "Just in case the would-be assassin isn't exactly sure who I am, you're gonna send along a group to point me out."

"I was only thinking of your safety between here and the hospital," Logan tells me. "They weren't planning on spending the day with you, unless you want them to."

That's just what I need—three bellyaching kids to drag around. Although they're carrying weapons, they look more like Boy Scouts than armed protection against a gun totin' window washer. I'm even less impressed when I learn they're college graduates, speak five languages, and have spent two years in the Peace Corps. I don't think the window cleaner can be swayed by good deeds.

"Don't underestimate them," Logan says. "All three are trained sharp shooters. Just because they're young doesn't mean they don't have good heads on their shoulders."

"Commander Reyes called. He has tight security at the hospital, and you don't want to give me special attention. Ramos might suspect that I'm in Belize for a different reason," I tell him.

"You're probably right. Anyhow, I suspect the intruder is long gone."

I don't bother giving him my opinion of the gunman. Everyone seems to be taking the situation seriously, but if I run into trouble, I'm sure I'll be on my own.

"Reyes never keeps his word. I'm surprised you received a call from him," Logan says. "He said he would let me know as soon as they found out the name of the man the hospital hired to wash the windows, but I haven't heard from him."

"I'm going to work alone, like I usually do. Ernesto might get released from the hospital and this might be my last chance to put myself in a favorable position." I get up from the table. Regardless of how this turns out, Ramos and I have become friends. "I want to say good-bye to him. It might keep the door open."

Logan nods. "I understand. Be careful."

"If I'm not back at the consulate by four o'clock this afternoon, you can put out an all points bulletin for me."

"It's your call," Logan says.

"I'll be fine, Ambassador. Thank you for all you did last night."

"You're welcome," he tips his ball cap.

"Nice meeting you guys," I say to the Peace Corps trio.

"Likewise," one of them answers.

I swallow the last of the weak coffee and fill a to-go cup. A few minutes later, I'm on my way to the hospital in my rental car.

As soon as I arrive, I check in with the custodian. He's busy introducing the first-floor housekeeper to her new part-time helper. Good, I don't want to leave Gerald in a bind. He'll still be short-handed even if he puts the guy on full time, but at least he will have some help, until they can find a janitor to take my place. I don't tell him I plan to quit. He'll learn soon enough.

I can't wait to hear what Ramos has in mind. It can't be all that good or he would have picked someone else to do it.

I get my gear together and go to the second floor. Ramos is fully dressed and sitting on the edge of the bed waiting for the doctor to come in and release him.

"Hi," I say. "So, how are you feeling today?"

"Okay," he says. "Jorge and Eduardo are coming to pick me up. I do not trust either one of them, so both Javier and Gomez are coming with them."

"If you feel threatened, you shouldn't go with them," I tell Ramos.

"But then that would tip my hand." He waggles a finger at me. "I want them to think I believe the tall tales they are telling me about Daniela."

"What kind of trash are they peddling now?" I sit in the chair beside the bed.

"Just a bunch of lies about her drinking, drugging and running around on me. They even said she had a boyfriend in *Bombay*, and another one in Vancouver. She could not possibly do all they say and still do her job. They only say those things to torment me."

"You might be right, but you should be careful." I lean back in the chair and cross my legs. "So tell me the details about this great deal you have for me."

"I will explain the situation, and how we are going to handle this proposition this afternoon," he says. "It's important that you come to my house."

"What?" I can't believe I'm getting an invite to the house. It's exactly what I hoped for, but I don't want to appear too eager. "I'll agree to come to your house after you tell me what you want me to do. I want to think about what it entails before I make my decision."

"There is no time to think. I want you to come today. If you decide to take the offer, you will start right then. Bring enough clothes for a couple of weeks. If you do not take the job, my houseman, Pete, will drive you back to your hotel." He waits for my answer.

I doubt I have enough clothes with me to last two weeks. Nevertheless, I tell him that's not the way I work. "I'll agree to come to your house after you tell me about the job."

He's quiet for a moment. "I picked the right man for the job." Then he laughs." My house is built above a fallout shelter. The space is designed to protect occupants from radioactive debris or fallout from a nuclear explosion. No one has gone down there for a long time, but it has everything a family needs in case of an emergency. It also has a monitoring system that picks up audio and video that is installed in every room in the house, plus the patio and the veranda."

I'm beginning to think that I might be doing business with an unstable, over-reacting drug dealer. Who else in a small tourist country would go through all the trouble to build a fuckin' nuclear shelter?

"This is where I want you to stay hidden for a few days. Only Javier and I have a key to the door that leads from inside the house to the shelter. Daniela knows the shelter is there, but she does not have a key and she's claustrophobic, so there is no chance of her going down the steps."

"I was told your home is heavily guarded."

"Three of them have gone to the coast to pick up a piece of heavy equipment, the fourth man is stationed at the front gate. If you come on time, no one will see you. I need you to come to my home this afternoon at 4:00 p.m. I do not want anyone at my house to know you are there."

"I thought you said Jorge and Eduardo were going to be there with you?"

"Yes, they will be at my home, but I will arrange to have them in a different part of the house so they will not see you arrive." Ramos fidgets with the identity band on his wrist. "Javier will see to that."

"When are they leaving?"

"They will be gone the day after tomorrow. They want to see Daniela before they fly home to Colombia. She is bringing them gifts."

"How can you be sure they'll do what they tell you?" I begin to worry.

"My houseman will take them to the airport and stay with them until the plane takes off."

"What happens when Daniela comes home?" So far, his game plan sounds a little flimsy, and he still hasn't told me what the job is.

"She will be home tomorrow morning. She can only stay for a couple of days before her job takes her to *Bombay*. I want you to follow her to India. I want to know if what Jorge and Eduardo are saying is true or not. As soon as I get her schedule, I will let you know when my fiancée is supposed to leave and where she will be staying, Then, I will arrange for an airline ticket for you to fly to India on a different airline. If you miss her at the airport, you can pick up her trail at the hotel. I want to know exactly what she does on her layovers."

I can't believe my ears. All this time, I thought he wanted me to do something illegal, and it turns out he's only looking for a private investigator. "You said you didn't believe what Jorge and Eduardo told you about your girlfriend. Now you want her followed. When did you change your mind?"

"Only a foolish person would be so in love that they did not lend an ear to rumors. However, I have little faith in Jorge and Eduardo, so I think it is important to determine the truth before I make my decision to marry. I feel I owe this to my daughter. I think it will help to ensure her a happy and successful future."

I'm not sure this has anything to do with the child. I think it has more to do with his relationship with his girlfriend. "What if Javier decides to check the shelter out?"

"That is not likely, but I suppose I should let him know you are staying with us for a few days."

"How will I know if someone is coming down to the shelter?" My heart picks up speed.

"There is a long stairwell a person must descend. If someone tries to sneak down the steps, you will hear a warning beep and you can see them on the monitor. But do not worry. No one will be coming to the shelter."

"So you say, but what if?" I'm not convinced.

"The door is locked, so unless it is me or Javier, they will not be able to get in."

"What if they blow the lock off?"

"You have a wild imagination." He laughs. "Listen to me," he says.

"Okay, convince me."

"If someone gets in my house, which they will not, and they find a way to go down the stairs, which they will not, and they blow off the lock, you should try to close down the system and hide until you can get off a good shot." Ramos laughs.

"This is not funny. I'm a little concerned about being locked up underground."

He looks at his watch. I guess he doesn't want his friends to see me here with him.

"The house is completely protected by a sophisticated alarm system. No one can get past the primary system," he says. "On top of that, I have four men who guard the house with weapons twenty-four hours a day."

"Are you concerned that someone might try to break into your house?"

"Not right now. However, I do worry that Jorge and possibly Eduardo will come back. Neither one of them have good sense. They're always looking for easy money."

"Then why do you let them stay with you?" I ask.

"Like I said, I want to know what they are up to, but the main reason is because Daniela wants them here. She says they will protect me, but I have more faith in Javier and Gomez. Javier has been with me for twenty years. Gomez only recently came to Belize, but he is Javier's cousin."

"I understand." I nod.

"I am hoping that while you are here, you will be able to catch something on the monitors that I might have missed."

"That's all well and good, but this is a touchy job. I don't want to get myself killed for a few bucks," I remind him.

"The pay is much more than you can make dealing in a casino," he says. "You will not be disappointed."

"Exactly what is the amount you have in mind?" I ask.

"For the entire job?" Ramos asks.

"Yes."

He smiles. "Fifty grand plus expenses. We can discuss the details before you leave for India."

This guy has big bucks. I'm not gonna chase a woman all over the world for the next two weeks plus take the chance of losing Angela for fifty grand when I can go to another country and make a hundred grand in a week dealing cards. Besides, he's not pulling the wool over my eyes. This guy's in deep shit.

If he was as clean as he would like me to believe, he would hire a licensed private investigator for fifty bucks an hour plus expenses.

"Look," I say. "I had only planned on working for a casino until I found a connection to deal blackjack or poker. When I find a big game, I can easily make that much in a week. Sometimes, it only takes me two or three days."

"What! You steal?" he asks.

"No. That's my cut of the pot. If I skimmed I could make a hundred, but that's not my style."

"But you do not have a *Big Game* right now. You're mopping floors for minimum wages." He shrugs. "After you finish the job with me, I will introduce you to the pit boss at the Princess Casino." He smiles. "His brother is my transport manager."

"That's a different offer." I return his smile. "For three weeks work, I want a quarter-mil. I have an account at Alliance Bank. I want half before I leave and the balance when I give you the information." I stand to leave.

"First, you ask an unreasonable price."

"That's because I don't want the job."

He hesitates. "Second, that is a lot of money."

"Then get someone else."

"And third, you drive a hard bargain."

"The choice is yours." I rock back on my heels. All he thinks about is the money. He acts like there's no risk, but I know better.

Ernesto's lips tighten. "Give me your account number and I will deposit the amount today."

"I don't want anyone depositing money into my account. Have Javier meet me at the bank today at three o'clock. I want cash in US dollars. I'll handle my own transaction."

"You do not trust *me*? I pay this exorbitant amount and I cannot do it my way?"

"I'm not trying to be a hard ass." I pull a box of breath mints from my pocket. "Want one?" I pop one in my mouth.

"No." He refuses the mint. "I do not keep that kind of cash at the house. I'm a sick man, just getting out of a hospital. Do you realize what you are putting me through? I will have to get the money on my way home from the hospital."

"I'm sorry, but you're the one who waited until the last minute."

Ramos doesn't budge. "How do I know you will do the job? You might come back with a made-up story, or maybe you will not come back at all."

"I'd be pretty stupid not to come back for the other half of the cash. We all take chances. What happens if I find out information that you don't want to hear? Will you renege on the balance you owe me or, worse yet, knock me off?"

"Do I look like the sort of guy who would kill someone?" he asks.

"No, you look like the type of gentleman who would have someone do it for you."

"Ah, I see you still have a sense of humor." Ramos takes a new cigar from his pocket and bites the tip off. "Javier will bring your seven pounds of flesh. You have my word."

"I see you also have a sense of humor," I tell Ramos. "You got a deal. You'll get your information."

We shake hands.

"This is what I want you to do." Ramos takes a deep breath. "After you get your money, take a cab to the jungle resort. Do not check into the hotel. Look for a man named Roscoe. He wears a large sombrero with blue peacock feathers. He will be expecting you. He drives one of the jungle tour boats and also works for me. He will use the tour boat to bring you to my place. You can see the house from the river. There is a nice path for you to walk on. You will not get lost."

Oh, shit. I'm not crazy about being in the jungle again, miles from civilization with no outside contact or wheels to escape. I have some troubled thoughts and I guess they show.

"So what is bothering you now?" he asks.

"What about the wild animals?" I ask.

"My property is completely fenced. So far, no animal has breached the area."

I remember the tall cement fence. "What time did you say you wanted me at your house?"

"Arrive this afternoon at 4:00 p.m. I am planning a little party for Deedee. Jorge and Eduardo will be busy decorating the room. I will make an excuse to rest for a short time. Then, I will meet you about halfway down the path and take you to the shelter."

"It'll be daylight. Jorge and Eduardo might see me."

"Javier and Gomez will make sure they do not."

"You're not giving me much time to make arrangements."

"You do not strike me as a man who needs a lot of time. I know you flew in from Italy, not Miami, and went straight to the consulate, and within a week had a job at the hospital. You must have some worthwhile qualities for getting things done in a hurry."

I'm flabbergasted that he knew I flew in from Italy. I'm afraid to ask him just how much he really knows about me. I pull my thoughts together and attempt to establish my reason for coming to Belize.

"I'm still a U.S. citizen, so when I decided to become a citizen of Belize, I was told the first thing I should do was to check in with the embassy. That's supposed to be the proper way to take up citizenship. I guess I owe the Ambassador for all the help he has given me."

"Do not worry about your job, the consulate, the FBI, or the DEA. In Belize, they are not important."

My eyes open wide.

"I know you stay at the embassy sometimes. Do you think you need them to be safe in Belize?"

"To be honest with you, I had a little run in with the mob. I don't want to go into the details, but when the mob turned their back on me, I didn't have much of a choice. I told the cops what I knew, and they put me in the witness protection program and relocated me in Belize. I didn't like the program, so I went to Italy. The found me and brought me back to Belize. Naturally, the embassy was interested in what plans I had for employment. As a matter of fact, they helped to get me this piece of crap job at the hospital. I had to take the job or your justice system would return me to the United States."

He looks at me skeptically, so I add, "It was either stick it out here or go back to Miami and worry about the mob finding me." I hope that satisfies him. I've made up so much of this I hope I can remember what I said.

"So what did you do wrong that started all this trouble."

"I don't talk about it. I'm a free man and I plan to stay that way."

"For a guy who is looking for a job, and doesn't offer any references, you're pretty picky."

"The job is risky and worth what I asked for. I can make more money dealing cards. I found work before and I'll find it again. It's just a matter of time."

"I can give you more security and protection than the embassy and I have better contacts for higher paying jobs. All the U.S. operatives do is make noise. They are not significant."

This is a side of Ramos I haven't seen before. He is a strong pacesetter, and possibly a master of deception. This is the information the DEA needs and what I agreed to get, but now that the opportunity has presented itself, I'm wondering if I am up to the task.

"Tell me something. Why me?" I ask.

He looks straight into my eyes. "I thought you either wanted or needed money, you do not seem to have any real connections with anyone, and most of all—for whatever reason—you saved my life."

"Four o'clock. I'll be there." I reach into my pocket for my car keys.

"I have to leave now. I have a lot to do, and I'm not sure what I need to tell the hospital or the embassy to keep them from asking questions."

"Tell them you got a job as a dealer on one of the cruise ships. They will not check. Even if they do, half the time the cruise ship captain does not know what's going on. Many people have secretly left the country aboard a cruise ship. They are always looking to hire."

I don't tell him I already know what his house looks like and where it is. He thinks he knows all about me, but he doesn't know that I'm the one who took the first shot at him, or he wouldn't have swallowed that Italian story.

I return to the head custodian's office. Gerald's out to lunch. I go to the front desk, no one is there.

A woman volunteer at the front door whispers, "The clerk is in the ladies' room."

I ask the nice lady for an envelope and a piece of paper. I could just walk out, but that might raise questions.

The lady watches me scratch the note. I tell Marcie I'm leaving the job and give her my apologies. Then, I seal the envelope and hand it to the volunteer who smiles and says she'll see that Marcie gets my message. I suppose I should have given my notice to the Human Resource lady that hired me, but I know Marcie will handle it.

I drive straight to the embassy. All my gear is still packed from last night's episode. I take Jeff and Cox out of the man cave and hurry them into Ambassador Logan's office.

Logan is sitting at his desk. "Commander Reyes called me," he says. "They haven't located the window washer, but several reliable witnesses claimed they saw him boarding a good-size boat in the port town of Corozal."

"Oh, so they know who he is?" I say.

"No one seems to know his name, but they think he's been in town for almost a week. Reyes doesn't believe the guy lives in Belize because he asked the tour people a lot of questions about the city."

"I can't imagine anyone in Belize hiring someone to knock off Ramos," Jeff says. "Ernesto plays an important role for the drug smugglers and he's always there to help the poor people. Who would want to kill him?"

"A lot of people might want him gone—like maybe the FBI or the DEA." I look at Logan. "I guess you're not the only game in town. It could be a few honest people who don't share their government's views, or it might be a relative who stands to benefit financially from Ramos' demise."

Logan ignores my speculating and looks at the clock on the wall. "You're back early. Did your conversation with the kingpin not go well?"

"It went better than I expected. He invited me to his house at four o'clock today, and in a few days, I'll be on my way to India."

"India?" Logan's eyebrows rise.

"Yeah, his girlfriend's next flight is to Mumbai. I understand that's what they call Bombay now."

"What are you going to do there?" Jeff asks.

"Check on Ramos' girlfriend."

"Why are you leaving the country? You're supposed to be looking for drug smugglers here in Belize," Logan says.

Obviously, Logan is not pleased with how I'm handling the situation. Ramos might be right. Maybe Logan can't see any farther than his nose. "The U.S. Department of Justice wants me on the inside and this is the only position the banana king offered."

"It's better than nothing," Cox snorts.

"You're gonna be sorry you didn't get that international driver's license," Jeff says.

"I did. The same day I leased the car."

"That's great. I'm gonna go with you."

"How you gonna do that?" I ask.

"I'll hitch a ride on a government plane," Jeff says.

"If Ramos gets wind of you going with me, he'll back out of the deal and all I've accomplished will be for nothing."

"Give the FBI a break," Cox says. "We've got good connections in India. Besides, you can't take a weapon on the plane. You need Jeff to bring your Glock and extra clips."

"Why can't the FBI get me clearance for the weapon?"

"They probably could." Logan puts his hands together and steeples his fingers. "But then there might be a leak, and the wrong people would find out you're working for the US government. You need to go as a tourist, or some kind of trader."

"We can get you a license for a building contractor, a precious gem trader or something like that," Cox says.

"That's just freakin' wonderful. Get me a license for something I know nothing about." I give Cox an icy stare, but he's right. I don't know anything about India, and I'd feel a lot better knowing Jeff is there to back me up.

"Do you need anything else?" Jeff reaches for a pencil on Logan's desk.

"I don't know what I might need, but I'll tell you what I'd like to have."

"Shoot." Jeff picks up a scratch pad.

"I want an inside the pants holster with an under-hook clip in nylon. I like comfort."

"Anything else?" Jeff asks.

"Can you find me a .38 caliber 442 special, with a good ankle holster?"

"I know where I can get that," Jeff says.

"Make sure the ankle holster won't slide down." I grin.

"I'll see what I can do." Jeff shoves the list into his shirt pocket. "I'll bring everything with me when I fly to India. I should only be one day behind you."

Cox leaves the ambassador's office. I tell Logan I'll keep in touch and hurry to my room at the hotel. Jeff follows me. I hope I don't have to drag another lawman like my old pal, Joe Gaetano, all over India. Maybe it won't be so bad. Most of the time, Jeff does what I tell him. He's got that gotta-be-doin'-something perspective that I had when I was his age, but he channeled his energy in the right direction.

When we get to my room, Jeff walks in behind me.

"Hey, buddy," I say "I don't want to be rude, but I got a lot to do. I gotta get out of here quick."

"Not a problem. Give me all your dirty clothes. There's a place down the street I can have everything cleaned and pressed in an hour," Jeff tells me. "While your clothes are being cleaned, I'll get you something to eat."

"Like what?"

"I'll pick up a rockin' bowl of conch chowder, some real Bimini bread, and a cold beer. How's that for a rousing send-off?" Jeff asks.

"Sounds great," I say.

I go into the bathroom and take off the clothes I wore to the hospital this morning. A pair of walking shorts I wore to bed last night is hanging over the shower rod, so I put them on. I open my duffle bag. Almost everything is dirty, and it smells sweaty. I leave my cash in the duffle bag, and take one of the cleaning lady's plastic garbage bags from under the bathroom sink and throw in all my dirty clothes. I give the bag to Jeff. In a split second, he's out the door and gone.

So now I'm stuck in a pair of shorts with nothing else left in the room to wear. Not too smart. Jeff better not take long.

After a leisurely shower, I put my shorts back on, stretch out on the bed and call Angela.

"Are you at the condo?" I ask.

"No, I'm at Helen's."

"It's not Monday," I say.

She laughs. "I'm staying with Helen now. She works so I have the house all to myself."

"It's so good to hear your voice," I tell her.

"I'm so happy you called. I've been thinking about you. I miss you, darling."

"What made you decide to move in with Helen? Don't you want to spend time with your parents?"

"Well," she says dragging it out in her special way that lets me know this is gonna be something juicy.

"You just won't believe. Mom is working at the library."

"Your mother's working?"

"Yes, only she doesn't call it working. She calls it her 'intellectual time.' She just loves it. She also joined a reading club and is taking line dance classes at a senior center. When she's not doing those things, she goes to the beach and hangs out in a bikini."

"How do you feel about all this?" I ask.

"I miss shopping with her, but I think it's wonderful. I've never seen her so excited."

"How's your dad responding to all these changes?"

"I really don't know. He's rarely home. He golfs three times a week. And just last week, he met a guy who owns a fishing boat, so now when he has spare time he goes out on the water." Angela sighs.

"He told me he loved to golf, but he couldn't play in Chicago during the winter." I chuckle.

"Now I call before I go to the condo to see if anyone is home," Angela says.

There's a loud knock on my door. I crack the door and peek out. It's Jeff and he's loaded down with food. I open the door and motion for him to put it on the nightstand.

"Can you hold on a minute?" I ask Angela.

"Who's with you?" she asks.

"It's Jeff. He brought me food."

"Do you have someone attending to all your needs?" she asks.

"No," I say. "He's just giving me a hand today. I'm meeting some new people and I don't have much time to get to the conference."

Jeff is standing by the bed grinning.

"What do I owe you?" I ask Jeff.

"Nothing, I put it on my expense account. I'll be back soon. I have to pick up your clothes from the cleaners." He leaves, banging the door behind him.

"I'm back," I say to Angela.

"Sounds to me like you're getting a lot more than a little help." She giggles. "I'm jealous and getting homesick."

"Speaking of home, it looks like I'll be spending a little more time on this job," I say.

"I guess that's good. Not that I don't miss you, but this quilt has turned out to be a bigger task than I thought."

"How far along are you?" I ask.

"Actually, I haven't gotten very far. I was sewing like gangbusters before Helen looked at it and pointed out a lot of mistakes. She made me take most of it apart and do it over." Angela sounds like she's gonna cry.

"Don't be upset," I tell her. "Quilting probably has a long learning curve."

"Do you really think so?" she asks.

"Sure, honey. It'll be great this time. You'll see."

"I feel better now that you're going to be gone a little longer. I want to finish the blanket before you see it."

She'll probably have two quilts made before I get back from India. "I shouldn't be too long," I say. "Things are moving along nicely." There's no reason to ruin her day with my problems. "I'll call you as soon as I know when I'll be home. I love you."

"I love you too," she says. "Take care of yourself. Don't do anything foolish."

"Don't worry. I'm always careful."

We hang up. I wonder why she said that. She doesn't know I'm doing anything dangerous. Maybe she has paranormal powers and can perceive upcoming events. I wouldn't want her to know what's going on here in Belize.

I didn't have breakfast and now I'm starved. I devour my conch chowder and use the bread to soak up the last of the soup. It's delicious and I polish off the beer just as Jeff knocks on the door. He's carrying a bag of freshly washed laundry and a bunch of clothes on hangers from the cleaners.

"Think fast." Jeff tosses me a pair of jeans. "I bought you two pair of Wranglers. Try those on and see if they fit. They're comfortable. These will help, but you need sandals and shorts to blend into India."

I go into the bathroom to change.

"The cab will be here in fifteen minutes," Jeff hollers. "I'll be right back." The door slams.

Jeans aren't something I would buy, but since I'm only going to see Ramos, I wear them to please Jeff. He did a lot for me today. By the time I'm dressed and packed, he's pounding on the door again.

"I just wanted to let you know I was here. I'll wait for you outside."

We step outside the consulate entrance to wait for the taxi. Willy Wiggle is sitting on the sidewalk. A unicycle is propped up against a large tree trunk. Today, he's wearing a red tasseled hat, a blue polka dot shirt, and yellow shorts.

"Don't go any closer." I stop Jeff. "I scared him off the other day. I don't want to do it again."

When I wave my hand, he wiggles his big ears that stick out from underneath the tasseled hat.

"The kid is truly talented," I whisper. "It's a shame he's also into drugs. A guy in town said he didn't think Willy had a home. Maybe the consulate can do something to help him."

"I'll tell Logan to check it out." Jeff points to the unicycle. "Hey kid," he calls out. "Is that your bike?" Jeff walks a little closer.

Willy hunches his shoulders and sways back and forth, so Jeff takes another step toward him. The boy doesn't run.

Willy smiles and rolls his eyes so far back you can hardly see the pupils. "Tick, tack, toe. Guess what I know? Window washer laying low."

"What?" I rush over to him and grab the back of his shirt.

In an instant, his arms reach for the sky, and he drops out of the shirt. Like a shot, he jumps to the top of the tall bike and disappears down the road. I stand there holding a limp blue shirt. I hang it over the big embassy sign. He'll be back for the shirt.

"What do you think about that?" I ask Jeff.

"He's just making up rhymes. Probably something he heard on the street about the shooter, which reminds me. I've been meaning to tell you this, but everything happened so fast, I guess I forgot."

"Forgot to tell me what?'

Jeff hesitates.

"Spit it out, the cab just turned the corner."

Jeff looks at the approaching taxi. "The kid's right. The window washer is a convicted felon. The FBI got him an early-release. They brought him to Belize to knock off Ramos, but you disrupted the hit. They had it timed for the shooter to return to the states on a government plane, but when the job didn't pan out, he had to hide and the plane left without him. Now all the planes, boats and roads are being watched by the Belize military."

"So where is the so called 'window washer' now?" I ask.

"The FBI stashed him in your old room at the boarding house with a guard until they can come up with a way to get him back into the states."

I stare at him in disbelief. "Why didn't they put him on the next outbound government plane?"

"They're watching all planes including government and small privately owned." Jeff says. "Nothing leaves the ground until they check it out."

"It can't be much of a secret plan if a kid with half a brain knows the window washer is hiding out close to the police department."

Jeff shuffles his feet. "I want you to know that Logan and the DEA had nothing to do with it. We didn't know anything about it until it was over."

"If Belize checked the drug smugglers as close as you say they're watching transportation, the FBI wouldn't have needed me." I think back to the night the window washer tried to kill Ramos. I remember calling Jeff. He really didn't sound upset. In fact, he told me I should have let the assassin kill Ramos. I know if I open my mouth right now, I'll say something I'll regret.

The cab pulls up and I duck into the back seat. Ramos was right. I'll be a lot safer at his place.

CHAPTER THIRTEEN

Like a local sightseeing guide, the Chinese cab driver chugs through town pointing out places of interest.

"I don't need a tour," I tell him. "Just take me to Alliance Bank."

"Okey-dokey." The cabbie shuts up, but doesn't drive any faster.

"Look, Charlie, I'm in a bit of a hurry. I'll only be in the bank a few minutes. After that, I need to get to the jungle resort as quick as possible. I'm meeting a lady and she likes me to be on time."

"My name not Charlie, I Wong, fastest cabbie in Belize."

"If you're the fastest, I'd hate to see the slowest. You get me there on time and I'll pay you double what you're worth."

"I drive lickety-split," he says. "You pay thirty dollar."

"Only if I arrive on time."

Wong's cab lurches into the fast lane, swerves to miss a truck and runs a stop sign. I slide back and forth on the black leather seat.

This gig is not worth losing my life. "I don't want you to wreck the cab. I just don't want to creep along."

"I no creep—I good man—I have family." He turns and glares at me.

I struggle to keep from laughing. When I get out of the cab I walk toward the bank entrance. I spot Javier in a Ford SUV. He gets out and hurries toward me.

"Mr. Ramos send you this." He hands me a briefcase.

I thank him and he turns to leave. "Wait a minute." I hold up my hand for him to stop. "I'm going into the bank. Wait a few minutes, I'll bring Ramos' case back to you. I don't need to be dragging it around.

He nods and goes back to his vehicle. I step into the bank. It's a friendly place and people are eager to help.

"I need someone in safekeeping," I tell a savings counselor.

"I'll be glad to help you." She checks my identification, goes behind a counter and pulls a card from a file drawer. While I'm signing my name, she says, "We can help you set up an off-shore account."

I'm thinking she might have x-ray vision, but I know I'm blowing this out of proportion. "Not today, I'm in a hurry."

"It only takes a few minutes." She smiles.

"*Not today,*" I hand her my key and she unlocks the box.

She leads me to a private room, where I pack one hundred and twenty-five thousand American dollars into my safe deposit box and leave the bank. When I return the briefcase to Javier, he snatches it from me.

"I don't get paid to sit around and wait on you," he snarls. And pulls out of the parking lot.

I go back to my taxi.

Wong is waiting for me. "I charge to wait," he says.

"That's okay," I tell him.

"Time is money." He looks at me in his rearview mirror.

"That's true," I agree.

"Now cab ride thirty-five dollar."

"I understand."

Wong flashes a large set of white teeth as he smiles and turns into a road beside a billboard advertising "Belize Jungle Resort." It's a two-lane highway with no passing signs posted every half mile. Of course we pass everything in sight.

"Don't get a ticket," I tell him.

"I no worry—you in hurry—you pay ticket."

I figure if I tell him I'm not going to pay the ticket, he'll slow down to a crawl again, so I hold on and hope for the best.

The place is farther out in the jungle than I thought and time is passing quickly. I'm happy when the resort comes into view. The taxi screeches to a halt in front of the hotel. I pay my fare and top it off with a ten-dollar tip.

Wong bows his head three times. "Thank you—thank you—thank you."

I grab my bag and I jump out. As soon as the cab pulls away, I hear the deep guttural sound of someone clearing their throat. I turn around. Standing right behind me is a husky man sporting a full six-inch beard, and he's wearing a sombrero decorated with blue peacock feathers. He jerks his head toward the tour boats tied up at the dock.

No doubt about it. This is Roscoe. I follow him to a boat with dancing monkeys painted all over the hull. He snatches my bag, jumps from the dock into the stern of the boat and motions for me to come aboard.

There are no other passengers waiting. I begin to worry. What if he's not Roscoe? Maybe all the boat drivers wear sombreros with blue peacock feathers.

"Me?" I inquire. "You want me to come on board?"

"No, your brother," he says.

I grasp the railing and swing onto the boat.

"The monkey boat was runnin' rough this morning," he says to a young man fueling the boat next to us. "I added a quart of oil. I'm gonna check her out. I'll be right back."

The young man peels the rope from around the post on the dock and tosses it into our boat. Roscoe starts the motor. It sputters once before he revs up the engine. Then, it runs smoothly. He backs the boat out slowly, but when we're clear of the other vessels, he takes off fast and speeds down the river. I grab the railing to keep from falling.

"Are you Roscoe?" I inquire just to make sure.

"The one and only," he tells me.

"How did you know I was the man you were looking for?"

"Is your name Anderson?" he asks.

"Yes." I move away from the railing to miss a spray of water that's coming my way.

"Then I guessed right." He swerves the boat like a water skier.

The front of the boat bounces against the water. "What if you had picked the wrong man?"

"I never pick the wrong man," he says.

I give him a hard look.

"Who pissed you off today?" he asks.

When I don't answer, he straightens out the boat and runs at full speed. It's not long before he throttles the motor back and we slow way down. He maneuvers the tour boat toward the edge of the river.

"There's a big rock here." He points to a boulder wedged in the river bank and almost covered in water. "Climb over the railing. I'll get you close enough to jump onto the rock. Take one more leap and you'll be on dry land. Then, I'll toss your bag to you."

Roscoe points to his left. "The compound is right round the bend. It's a clear shot from the river to the big house.

This could be a setup. I have no idea where I am. Ramos' men could be waiting to feed me to the crocs. I reach behind my back to feel for the loaded Glock I keep stuck down inside the waistband. Damn. It's not there. I gave it to Jeff to take to India.

This isn't going well, but he's telling the truth about the wide path. Still, it's hard to trust people you don't know.

"Come on, fellow. Get off my boat," Roscoe says. "I did my job. I gotta go back to work."

I look at the big cement wall. "Where's the entrance?" I ask. How do I get on the other side of this barrier wall?"

He didn't tell you?" Roscoe grins.

"No."

He points a short distance down the barrier. A rope ladder is hanging over the wall. "He only told me to tell you when you get to the top, you're to flip the rope ladder to the inside wall."

"Is that how I get down the other side?"

"I don't know. I've never been there," Roscoe says.

"I think you better turn this boat around and take me back to the resort." I sit on one of the padded seats.

Roscoe uses his fist to knock on the cabin. "I can't do that," he says. "Boss's orders. It's time to get off my boat,"

Another man comes up from the cabin. He's sporting a shoulder holster. He doesn't pull the gun, but I feel certain he will if I don't get off the boat.

I climb over the railing and hesitate at the distance between me and the rock.

"You can make it," he says. "Jump!"

I lunge for the rock, wobble for a second on one foot, and leap onto dry land. My Gucci Horsebit loafers sink into the muck.

"Atta-boy." Rossco throws my bag onto the shore and takes off.

Why did I agree to do this? I gaze at the surroundings, pick up my bag and walk along the river bank. I have one eye on where I'm walking and the other watching for crocodiles.

When I come to the rope ladder, I give it a good pull to see how strong it is. There is no use standing here, I tell myself. There is no other way out.

I swing the strap of my bag over my shoulder, and stick my shoe onto the first rung. The ladder shifts under my weight and promptly sags leaving no room for my other foot. All the way up the ladder, it twists back and forth. I bang my knees on the cement and scrape my knuckles knowing all the while, it will be the same going down the other side.

My bag has slipped to my elbow, making it even more difficult to climb. When I reach the top, I find the wall is about a foot thick, so I sit down to rest. I don't know exactly what I expected, but what I find is cement block steps. I'm so thankful for the steps that I pull the rope ladder up over the wall like Ramos requested.

I head in the direction Roscoe pointed. When I come around the bend, the first thing I see is the helicopter pad. Charged with new optimism, I walk faster. The path is wide open and covered with course jungle grass. When I'm about halfway to the mansion, I hear Ramos shouting to me.

"Robert!" he waves. "Over here!"

He's a good way off under a stand of trees. I hurry to where he's waiting.

"Why didn't you tell me about the rope ladder?" I growl.

"Because you would not have come." he says.

"You got that right. I don't want anymore surprises. You got that?"

"I understand. However, life is full of unexpected happenings, but I will honor your wishes to the best of my ability."

"See that you do." I think about the money he is paying me and don't say anymore.

"We can take this old trail. No one uses it anymore. Be careful not to fall." He looks at his watch. "So you didn't have any trouble finding Roscoe?"

"No, he found me," I tell Ramos. "He's a peculiar sort."

"That is true, but I can always depend on him and you can, too."

"I'd rather not," I say.

"You should not be hasty," Ramos says. "You might need him one day."

I won't be in Belize long enough to need anyone.

When we reach his house, Ramos electronically opens a panel, which reveals a hidden door. The place looks like something you'd see in a "Star-Trek" episode. It's filled with monitors, computers, electronic doors, vaults, push buttons, and weird lighting on different levels. There are also microphones, headsets, and accessories I don't even recognize. A Ruger lays next to the key board.

"This is unbelievable," I say. "Are you expecting World War III?"

"I like to feel safe." He claims he's the only one who has the combination to the outside door, and when we reach the surveillance device he quickly shows me how to turn the equipment on and off. "Spread the screen with your fingers to make it larger, click on this to turn the audio up, click on that if you want a different camera angle, click on—"

"Stop! I can't remember all that shit."

Ramos laughs. "Watch the screens. Nothing is going to happen. I have to go now. I will come back later tonight. If you get hungry, the kitchen has been freshly stocked." Ramos leaves the system up and running.

One of the screens shows a woman gathering dirty dishes from a table that's recently been used to serve a meal for at least ten or twelve people.

I open the refrigerator, find a beer and plop down on a comfortable chair in front of the monitors. The woman is the only one in the room and she hums a little tune while she works.

Deedee's party seems to be in a family room. Presents are stacked everywhere. She has just opened a baby buggy, which includes a doll dressed in gold material. The toy has long, black hair. It's wearing a crown, and has a red spot in the middle of its forehead. It looks as if it may have come from India.

Jorge sits on the floor pretending to play with one of her birthday games. Eduardo is staring out the window and appears to be bored. They sing "Happy Birthday" to Ramos' daughter, and she blows out her four candles. Ramos gives her a bite of cake and she kisses him.

Party dresses and beaded jeans are scattered on the floor, and a pile of jeweled bracelets rest on top of the table next to the cake. Several women help Deedee open the boxes and try on her pretty new dresses.

On another monitor, four men dressed in black T-shirts and cargo pants watch a soccer game on television. I'm not sure what part of the house it's in, but I see a glass enclosed gun cabinet filled with weapons. I use my fingers like Ramos did to enlarge the picture. I don't know much about rifles, but I can tell they're all automatics.

There is a bank of monitors on one side of the room, but I can't make out what is on them, because they are sitting at an angle.

The rest of the room looks like a police station. There are boxes of hand guns and ammunition. Bullet proof vests hang on a rack. These guys must be the patrol Ramos uses to protect the compound. "Whew!" I'm glad they didn't come after me.

Watching the screen is boring. A couple of times I nod off, but each time I raise my head not much has changed. I check out the Ruger. It's loaded and the safety is on. At least this is a gun I can recognize and know how to shoot.

The system has about fifty buttons with labels like fast forward, auto record, search and effects. I'm not sure what they all do, but I believe that the system could be left running all the time. Ramos could come down at his leisure and see everything that has taken place in his house over a period of time. He doesn't need me.

I lean back in the chair. Why would he even want me to know about this place? Maybe he found it just as boring as I do. Watching the screen is sleep inducing.

About a half hour later, Deedee's party comes to an end. She's saying goodnight to Ramos. One of the women takes her hand and they leave the room together. Ramos reaches into a desk drawer and pulls out a cigar. He excuses himself and walks through a door that looks like it leads outside. Then, I see him on a different screen. He's on the patio. He clips the end off the cigar before lighting up.

Soon Jorge and Eduardo are the only people left in the family room.

Jorge tunes the television to the same soccer game Ramos' guards are watching, and then pours two drinks from a decanter for him and Eduardo.

Eduardo watches the patio while Jorge snorts what appears to be a line of cocaine.

I turn up the volume on the monitoring system so I can hear what Edwardo and Jorge are saying.

"This is exactly why I don't trust you. You can't deal and use," Eduardo says.

"It's just a little something to help me relax," Jorge says.

"It hasn't been that long since you took those Mollies." Eduardo walks to the window and looks outside. "Just so you know, I don't intend to go down with you."

"It was only a couple of pills. Don't worry. I can handle myself. I know where to draw the line."

"You don't even know where the line is unless it's coke. You're gonna kill yourself mixing all that crap together."

Jorge waves his hand. "You worry too much." He settles his skinny body into a comfortable corner of the couch to watch the soccer game.

I thought Ramos might return to the shelter, but apparently he's chosen to stay on the patio. I think about the trip to India.

Eduardo leaves the window and sits on the couch.

"She'll be here tomorrow," Jorge whispers. "We could make it look like an accident."

"I'm not doin' nothin' until I see some scratch," Eduardo tells Jorge.

"When she's gone, the produce company and everything else she has will be mine."

"What if she has a will that gives everything she has to the kid?" Eduardo asks.

Jorge leans close to Eduardo and lowers his voice. "Everything's in the corporation's name and my name is on the corporation books. She keeps it that way because she doesn't want to pay taxes. Her accountant makes it look like the business never makes a profit."

Eduardo shoves Jorge away. "If she turns up dead, the courts will freeze everything. It could take years before I see any bread."

"That's why we need Ramos." Jorge takes a slug of the booze. "He'll help us straighten out the court system. He's got an older brother who's an attorney and owns a coffee business in Brazil. He's in tight with all the political establishments."

Holy shit! It sounds like everyone is out to get rid of someone. I glance at the patio monitor. Ramos is still puffing on his cigar.

"Ernesto's in love." Eduardo sips his drink. "He don't see nothin' bad about Daniela. Wait 'til he finds out she's just another *puta.*"

"Don't call my sister a whore," Jorge snaps.

"You care about what people call her, but it's okay if she gets knocked off so you can take over the business. Besides, there's no tellin' what her death would do to Ramos. He might go wacko. Then where would we be?"

"If I leave things up to you, we'll be in the same place we are now," Jorge says.

Eduardo cocks his head. "Shut up. He's comin' this way."

Ramos walks into the family room and looks at the soccer game. "Who is winning?" he asks.

Edwardo and Jorge look at each other.

"Brazil," Eduardo says. "Don't they always?"

"That's because Brazil is the best." Ramos takes a puff of the cigar.

"When did that happen?" Jorge asks Ramos.

"When I was just a boy, and in my heart, win or lose, they will always be the best."

Jorge shakes his head and laughs.

"We have a big day tomorrow. I am going to bed. Your rooms are ready. Get some sleep." Ramos leaves the room.

Soon, most of the lights go out, and the monitors go dark. The only place still going strong is the room with the men dressed in black. The game is still on, but now the men are playing cards and drinking heavily.

Ramos showed me a bed where I could sleep, but I feel better watching the screens. I take off my shoes, stick the alarm plug in my ear and stretch out on the couch.

An hour later, I hear a warning beep in my ear. Someone is coming down the stairs. I keep my gaze fixed on the monitor and pickup the Ruger. It might be a test, or Ramos might be coming down to talk. My hand reaches for the shut down switch. Ramos appears on the monitor. He's alone. I lay down the gun and meet him at the door.

"Ah," he says. "You are still dressed. I thought you might have gone to bed."

"I'm afraid I won't get much sleep tonight."

"Sure you will. Everyone has turned in. No one will be doing anything tonight. I have had a long day, and I am tired. I only came down tonight because I told you I would. We will have plenty of time to talk tomorrow." Ramos reaches for the off switch.

"Why are you turning it off?" I ask. "Your guards are still playing cards."

"There is no need to leave it on. They are not going to do any harm, and everyone else is asleep."

"I don't agree. This is the most logical time for an attack."

"What do you think is going to happen?" he laughs.

"I don't know, but I heard Jorge talking to Eduardo. It sounds like they may be planning on taking Daniela out of the picture permanently. You might be included."

"You do not understand. Jorge loves his sister. It is the drugs and the liquor. He likes to hear himself talk."

"How can you be sure?" I ask.

"Jorge and Daniela have been my friends for a long time. They get a lot of this craziness from their father. The man lived in fantasyland. He wanted to be a millionaire, but he did not have much business sense. He passed those bad traits along to his children. Daniela is trying to build the business before she turns it over to Jorge. I told you before, Jorge is not a killer. He panics at the sight of blood."

"What about Eduardo? You said he works for a price."

"That is what he brags about, but I have seen him back down more than once. He is all talk."

"It sounded serious to me. Maybe this time he means it." I thought Ramos was smart, but I don't think he's handling this situation very well. "I overheard Jorge trying to get Eduardo to get rid of Daniela when she comes home and make it look like an accident."

"Please, do not let their drunken talk get in the way of what I want you to concentrate on, but if it makes you happy I will leave the system running."

"This is not a good situation," I say.

"Let me worry about Jorge and Eduardo," Ramos says. "You need to relax. Would you like something to drink?"

"No thanks, I want to have a clear head tonight.

"I see you drink beer. I have some excellent wine." Ramos stands.

"I'm determined to get some answers. Exactly what do you expect from me?"

I'm surprised when he sits back down. "I want to know what Daniela does with her free time when she has a layover in another country. I am not concerned with her having a companion at dinner or wherever she goes. A person gets lonely when their work takes them away from home. She usually tells me everything that she does, but I want to know if she is really contemplating our marriage."

"So, you're basically looking for a private investigator. I've always thought snooping into people's personal lives to be unsportsmanlike. Not the kind of work I'm used to doing." I want him to know that I want a job that pays a lot of money, but I don't want him to think I'm interested in his private affairs, or that I'm the type who would do anything for a buck.

"We will discuss the details later."

Before I can press for more information, a light comes on in Jorge's room.

"Look." I point to the monitor. The light is only on for a few minutes before it goes out. "Maybe he left his room." I continue to look at the dark screen.

"He does not like to go to sleep early," Ramos says. "However, the infrared comes on every time an entrance is opened between eleven in the evening and eight in the morning. If the connection is broken, you will get a warning signal and be able to see the interior of the room. "

I continue to watch the blank screen, but nothing happens. I wonder if Ramos is telling me the truth. I'm also puzzled about why it would help to see in the room, if Jorge has gone out the door. Ramos appears agitated, so I don't ask any more questions about Jorge.

"I notice the system is set to record everything that happens in the house, so you don't need me to watch the monitors. You can come down and check them anytime you want." I want him to know he's not talking to a dummy.

"That is true, but I want you to be familiar with my surroundings and the people who visit. One must be educated on how to deal with the people you have transactions with. Preparation is everything."

I focus on each thing he says and still I'm not sure what he is trying to tell me.

Ramos starts for the door. "We will continue our talk tomorrow."

Before he leaves, he tells me, "I will put Javier on notice. He will bring your meals and get you anything you need or want."

"I don't think Javier cares much for me," I say.

"He will do his job and be friendly. Goodnight." Ramos leaves the shelter.

CHAPTER FOURTEEN

In the morning, Javier brings my breakfast. It's quite a feast; scrambled eggs, a thick piece of freshly sliced ham, fried potatoes, bagels, orange juice and coffee. If no one knows I'm here, does the cook think Javier is eating a second breakfast?

Everyone in the mansion is up and ready for a new day. All screens are lit. The busiest place is the big dining room. The same four men dressed in black are eating at the end of what looks like a boardroom table. I wonder which guard is on duty now. There's another man, well-built and well-dressed, who looks to be about forty-five or fifty. He has dark slicked down hair and is sitting next to Deedee.

"Good morning, Mister Pete."

"Good morning, birthday girl," Mister Pete says.

"That was yesterday." She giggles.

On the other side of Deedee is a mature woman with brown hair pulled back in a French twist. "Are you ready for your studies today?" she asks Deedee.

"Not today, Miss Wright," Deedee says. "Mommy's coming home. She said no school work today or tomorrow."

That has to be the tutor Ramos mentioned. Deedee appears to be well-schooled, well-mannered and exceptionally mature. Ramos has gone to great lengths to see that his daughter has an educational beginning and a meaningful future.

"Good morning, Uncle Jorge." Deedee blows him a kiss.

Eduardo and Jorge sit on the far side of the table.

Jorge puts his thumbs in his ears and wiggles his fingers. Deedee laughs.

"Mommy's coming home today," Deedee tells her uncle. "We're going to have another party."

"We are?" Jorge laughs. "Your daddy didn't tell me that. I need to buy you another present!"

"The party is just for me, Daddy, and Mommy. No one else can come."

Everyone laughs, except Jorge. Eduardo doesn't say anything to anyone, but he looks over at Deedee and smiles. She sticks her tongue out. I guess she's not so well mannered after all.

On another monitor, I see two women who are not eating breakfast in the dining room with the others. They're already at work changing bedding, cleaning bedrooms and bathrooms.

"Rosie and Sylvia are late," Mr. Pete says.

"Hey, Frenchie," Jorge says to the cook. "Did they eat earlier?"

"Don't call me that." The cook raises her big wooden spoon.

Jorge laughs. "They must have gone shopping to buy satin sheets for the mistress. Am I right, Nanette?"

"No, you are not right. They had breakfast and are busy cleaning the house. You need to watch your mouth." Nanette heads for the kitchen when Ramos arrives.

The room grows quiet, and Jorge digs into his plate.

"Good morning," Ramos says. "I am sorry to be late. I had a lot to do this morning. I want everything to be nice when Daniela gets here. Make sure your work is done early. I want the house to be quiet during the day. She works hard, and when she is home, it is the only time she has any real peace. I want her to rest before the party tonight."

Everyone gets serious about finishing their breakfast, and soon they all leave the table. Nanette quickly picks up the dirty dishes and carries them into the kitchen.

I spend the next few hours watching the monitors and memorizing the players. Then I sit down with a sandwich I put together from stuff in the fridge. I see that sandwiches are also being served on paper plates on the patio. Later, the patio is decorated with crepe paper and strings of small white lights for an evening party. It looks like it might be fun.

I didn't see Gomez and Javier yesterday, and they weren't on the monitors last night, but today they had breakfast with the others. Now I can see they're getting instructions from Miss Wright on how to decorate the patio.

At two o'clock, the helicopter pilot and Daniela arrive. It's the same pilot and pretty girl I saw the day I shot Ramos. Daniela brought gifts for everyone, and the men in black bring all the packages into the house.

Daniela hugs Deedee and Ramos and then plays with Deedee.

"I'm sorry I couldn't come to your birthday party yesterday, but we'll have our own party this afternoon while everyone is busy preparing for tonight's festivities," Daniela tells her daughter. "Nanette has made us a picnic basket to take to the gazebo. While we celebrate you and daddy can play cards, and I'll braid your hair."

They're such a happy family, I can't help but feel guilty about working for the FBI. I cheer myself up as I think how I can prove to the DEA that even though Ramos is a rather strong-willed man and possibly politically involved, he isn't the evil person trafficking drugs through Belize. If anyone is dealing drugs it's Jorge and Edwardo.

Apparently there is no camera at the gazebo, because a couple of hours pass before I begin to see Daniela, Ramos, and Deedee again.

I watch the monitors throughout the afternoon, but nothing interesting happens.

When the evening meal is served, I notice two new guests have arrived. One is Commander Reyes and the other is Logan's chauffeur, Jon. Now that's a Quinella I would have never thought about, but if you wheel them with Ramos— hmm—I can see some possible collusion. Maybe I've stumbled onto something the FBI missed.

Commander Reyes and Ramos talk about plans for a new administration building, but the banana company and drugs are not mentioned.

Rosie is the only employee at the party. She and Jon are sitting rather close on the couch and I wonder if something is going on between them. She is telling him about going to one of the clubs and dancing the Salsa. He smiles and nods.

After dinner there is much drinking, conversation, and laughter. Drugs are not mentioned, but Jorge goes to his room several times to snort coke. Marco and a young woman arrive late. They're not dressed for the party, but they each get a drink and make themselves at home. I wonder if Marco is the leaker, or if Ramos just invited them to be polite. They certainly look comfortable. Marco talks with the Commander and Jon, but only casually speaks to Ramos. I wonder which side Marco is on. Jeff needs to look into this. At least now I know why Ramos didn't want anyone to know I was here.

When things start to get a little rowdy, Daniela tells Rosie to put the child to bed, while she goes into another room that appears to belong basically to her. Luggage is scattered everywhere. She grabs a few items from the closet and goes into the bathroom. When she comes out she has on a frilly, see-through blouse and a tight skirt with a slit up the side.

She sits on the floor, reaches under the bed and pulls out a small box. She swallows a number of different colored pills and polishes off the drink she brought with her. Then, she smears on another layer of bright red lipstick. She and her brother are birds of a feather. I shake my head. Jorge and Daniela both seem to do their share of drinking and drugging.

I notice Ramos and Commander Reyes standing by the window talking.

"The *Americana's* have not been able to make much headway. They have not been able to determine who is transporting the large amounts of drugs from our country into the United States," Commander Reyes says. "Our country has always been a small contingent of the drug world, but our police force is well trained and keeps our country safe and free from the big cartels. I believe the U.S. government will soon leave our country in peace." Reyes sips his drink.

This is a surprise. Ramos knows I can hear their conversations. Maybe it's all being said for my benefit.

Jon joins their conversation. "I do not believe the gentleman from Italy has ever been a threat to us."

Oh, so they did wonder about me.

"What makes you say that?" Ramos asks. "He was in the jungle the day I was shot."

"Holy shit. Jon and Marco are in on it.

"That's true, but I saw him fifteen minutes after you were shot. There are no drivable roads from where the sniper had been located. He could not have taken a shot at you and made it to where I saw him in the amount of time he had. The sniper had to be someone else."

"I'm not so sure." Ramos relights his cigar.

It sounds like he suspects me.

"I spoke with the ambassador," Jon says. "He told me that Mr. Anderson is in the U.S. Federal Witness Protection Program, and that a contract killer was sent to Belize to kill him. They gave Mr. Anderson food and supplies to stay in the jungle for a few days. They captured the hired assassin and sent him back to America to stand trial for attempted murder. I thought you knew," he tells Reyes.

"You mentioned that before, but it's hard for me to believe."

"I drove Agent Cox to pick up Mr. Anderson when the FBI brought him back from the jungle. He did not have a long-range rifle. He only had a small backpack."

"That doesn't mean anything. He could have ditched it. Just because the police never found a rifle doesn't mean it's not out there someplace." Ramos is adamant.

I believe he thinks I tried to kill him, and he's got me locked up in his basement. This could get a little hairy.

"They thought I could not hear them speaking, but with that new bug we installed behind the back seat I could hear every word." Jon smirks. "I was told the ambassador had permission from the Belize police to hide Mr. Anderson in the jungle until they caught the contract killer."

"That's true." Commander Reyes says. "We gave our permission for him to hide in the northern part of the jungle."

"That's exactly where I picked him up." Jon says. "They only gave him a pistol. He was also supposed to bring back a mountain lion for Logan, but he turned out to be a lousy shot."

"These Americans are nothing but trouble. We should not be accepting these immigrants," Commander Reyes says.

"Trouble or no trouble, it would have been impossible for him to arrive in less than fifteen minutes at the northern part of the jungle."

"The FBI truck is a four-wheel-drive," Ramos says.

Jon laughs, "The truck could not have driven through the jungle brush, besides your men would have seen tire tracks."

"Maybe he used a helicopter," Ramos suggests.

"There was no helicopter. The only helicopter in the sky on the day you were shot was Longview Banana and it took you to the hospital," Commander Reyes says. "I checked that out myself."

"From what I have gathered, Robert Anderson does not seem to get along well with the FBI or the DEA. He seems to be at odds with the establishment at every turn," Jon says.

How'd he come to that conclusion? I wonder if everybody here is crazy.

I can see right now that I have a major problem. I can't trust Ramos. Still, I did try to kill him, and if it were me, I'd be suspicious, too. I need to think about this.

Daniela returns to the party. She weaves across the room to where Ramos is standing and gives him a kiss. He pulls her close and whispers, "Where did you change clothes?"

"I changed in the bathroom, my darling. I know that pervert, Javier, who you think so much of, sneaks down to the basement to get an eyeful whenever I come home. You need to put one of those off buttons in my room."

"I'll take care of it." He kisses her on the tip of her nose.

When Jon comes out of the bathroom, Daniela swoops away from Ramos, hooks her arm around Jon and struts across the room to where everyone else has gathered. "So what's the latest gossip in Belize City?" She looks into Jon's eyes and bats her lashes.

Ramos takes a deep breath, but says nothing. As the stories are told, Daniela becomes more talkative. In fact, she is quite funny and soon everyone except Ramos is laughing at her antics. She doesn't do anything ludicrous, but she does wobble.

When the party ends, Jon and Commander Reyes say their good-byes and leave, and so does Marco and his friend. Rosie, Jorge, and Eduardo sit down to finish their drinks and Daniela and Ramos say goodnight. Ramos holds onto her arm as they walk to his room. After they go into the bedroom, his screen suddenly goes black. At first, I think something is wrong. Then I realize he has blocked his room from the system. Not that I want to see what they're doing in the bedroom, but it could be dangerous not to have it monitored considering Jorge and Eduardo's conversation.

Very early the next morning, I wake to the sound of voices coming from one of the monitors. I sit up on the couch and look at the screens. Jorge and Daniela are sitting alone at a small table in the kitchen drinking coffee. I can't see the whole kitchen, and I don't know how to move the camera for a different view, but I don't think anyone else is there.

"How long do you intend to keep the produce company?" Jorge stirs his coffee.

"How long before you're gonna grow up, quit using drugs and do your job?" Daniela crosses her legs.

"I'm perfectly capable of running the business. If you hadn't stroked the judge's rooster, our father's company would have been mine from the start."

"Nothing happened between me and Judge Henry. He made me guardian of the property because it was in your best interest. He knew you couldn't handle it." Daniela leaves the table and comes back with a basket containing a few leftover petite sweet rolls.

"Are you kiddin'? I do all the work and you take all the credit. When things go right, Julio gets a pat on the back. When things go wrong, I get the blame."

"I hired Julio to manage the business because you weren't doing anything." She gets up again to get more coffee, and brings back a chunk of cheese and fancy crackers.

"You're gonna get fat. All you eat is junk." Jorge cuts off a thick slice of cheese.

"Plenty of men think I have a great body," she snaps.

"Don't change the subject," Jorge says.

"I didn't, you did."

"Julio doesn't run the business. I do," Jorge reiterates. "All he does is make sure that the truck is packed correctly. The rest of the time, he's in town getting laid."

"Keep your voice down." Daniela digs into the basket for another blueberry pastry.

While Daniela pours Jorge's coffee, I sip my own hot coffee that Javier dropped off. It sounds like Julio has found himself a tit job.

"Julio doesn't go into town to get laid," Daniela tells Jorge. "He's helping me find girls who need a job so they can send money home to take care of their families. Sometimes he has to get close to them, to give them the courage to leave home and travel to a foreign country. When that happens, he might get laid. It's all part of the process."

"Is that what Julio told you?" Jorge cracks up laughing.

"What does it matter? I needed a manager. There's nothing between us."

"Did you say nothing? Is that what you call a four-year-old daughter?" Jorge lights a cigarillo.

"Whoa! Did I hear right? Deedee is Julio's child. I wonder if Ramos knows this."

"I didn't mean that." Daniela sighs.

"I suppose you expect me to believe you don't meet him in Medellin every time you have a layover in Colombia?"

"We meet, but only to talk about how to improve the business."

"And I guess part of his job is seeing that no one stands in your way?" Jorge blows smoke in her direction.

"No, that's Eduardo's job." She laughs. "I really don't need anyone. I'm capable of handling everything myself."

"Really." Jorge says between clenched teeth.

"By the way," she says. "I shipped a case of baby diapers. They're cheaper and smell stronger than what we've been using. Let me know if they work better and I'll order more."

"Holy shit." I heard something about this once before, but I didn't pay any attention. I make a note to tell Ramos.

"Anything will be better than what we're using," Jorge says.

So the drug smugglers wrap the drugs in baby diapers so the dogs can't sniff out the smell of the drugs. Ramos doesn't know what he's in for. Daniela's the drug smuggler, and he's so crazy about her, he can't see the forest for the trees.

"I almost forgot." Jorge gulps his coffee. "Julio wants more of those anabolic steroids you sent last month."

"More?" she asks. "I sent him a three-month supply. What's he doing, selling them?"

"I don't know. He asked me to tell you to send more." Jorge raises his palms. "Don't shoot the messenger. I don't have anything to do with steroids. They'll kill you quicker than drugs."

She grins. "They are drugs. I don't want him to use them. That's why I only sent a small amount. I don't like to buy that kind of medicine from another country. I only did it as a favor to him. They came from China. I don't know if I can get any more right now."

"Julio's not gonna be happy when I tell him that."

"I don't care if he's happy or not. I have my own problems." Daniela pours cream in her coffee.

"Julio said you bought a house in Paris. He said he'd soon be living in it."

"You know how Julio lies. I saw a house I liked, and I may have mentioned it, but I didn't buy it. Don't believe every word he says. Tell him I'll try to get the steroids from India, if not he can use mollies like you do."

"He don't want to feel good, he wants to get big and strong."

"All right—I'll check out India. If I find anything I'll send it." She smears a glob of cream cheese on the small blueberry pastry.

"Speaking of India," Jorge says. "What does Kadam think about you and Samir?"

"Of course, Kadam gave me a bad time when I broke up with him, but it doesn't matter what he thinks. Samir is rich and he supports my handling the medical nutriments."

"Kadam told me he dumped you." Jorge leans forward and waits for her reply.

She waves her fork back and forth in the air as she talks. "You know how he used to put me down. He didn't think I could make it on my own. As a matter of fact, no one else thought I could make it either, but I'm doing great and now they're all trying to muscle in. He wanted out and I said good riddance. Who cares about who dumped who."

"Why do you insist on calling the drugs you ship to Belize nutriments when you know damn well I know they're drugs?"

"It's a habit I got into so that I never make a mistake and use the wrong word."

"How long do you think India's Mafia is going to let a woman cut into their business?"

"I don't know." She shrugs. "Samir has already told me he might not be able to hold the Punjabi Mafia out."

"Doesn't that bother you? Don't you know they'll get rid of you?" Jorge says.

"It's Samir who doesn't know what's going on. I'm working on a plan with the Punjabi's top dog. Mr. Fat Ass may soon be on the outside looking in. They're all idiots."

I lean back in the chair. Maybe the party was put on for my benefit, but I feel certain that Ramos didn't expect this conversation to take place, at least not in front of a monitor. My problem now is how Ramos is going to take this new information. Maybe he'll call off the whole deal.

"You better be careful, girl. Those guys are hardened criminals. Most of them have spent time in the pen. When it comes to drugs and money, they're smart."

"You would think so, but I find them stupid. Most of them can't even control the men who work for them."

"What does Kadam think about you knocking him out of his position with Samir?"

"I don't know." Daniela casually pushes her hair back from her face. "I haven't talked to him in months. I heard he's been living with that woman Julio sent from Colombia. You know the one I mean. She's the one that resembles me."

"What's her name?" Jorge asks.

"Sophia. Kadam told Samir she wasn't feeling good and wants to stop flying."

"Is she gonna keep making deliveries?" Jorge asks.

"You're damn right she is. I have a lot of rupees invested in her."

"You think Samir will side with Kadam or you?"

"What do you think?" She smirks. "Samir asked me to quit my job with the airline and move in with him. Like that's ever gonna happen. My job is my cover. Besides, I can hardly stand to be around him for the little time I spend in India." Daniela tops off their coffee.

"Were you happier with Kadam?" Jorge asks.

"Not really. I don't miss him, and I think he's happier with Sophia. He is the most misogynistic man I have ever met. He thinks women were made to clean house and please men. He once told me I was too bossy."

"Is that what that word means, or did you make it up?"

"I didn't make it up." She glares at him. "You never heard it before, because you hang around with people who have no class."

"I don't know why he would think you're bossy." Jorge's upper lip curls into a sneer. "It's probably because he doesn't really know you." Jorge turns his head and rolls his eyes toward the monitor.

I laugh. This sounds like daytime television.

"That's exactly what Samir said. I told Samir I wasn't imperious, I just couldn't stand Kadam's stupidity."

"What the hell is imperious?" Jorge asks.

"It just means I know what I'm talking about."

"Yeah, yeah," Jorge says. "We all suffer from that." He clears his throat. "Before we get off the subject of business, I want to give you fair warning. I'm only waiting until next month for you to step down and put the business in my name like Daddy's will says, or I'm gonna take you to court. We'll see what happens when the newspaper gets hold of the story."

146

My jaw drops. I know they're smuggling drugs, but up to now I figured it was just an argument between addicts. I think he's really going to do it. He's dumb enough.

"Right, like you're gonna put our business in the newspaper. How stupid can you be? The reporters would love that, and we would both be out of business, and maybe in jail. You better think long and hard before you cut your nose off."

"If I can't have the business, I don't want you to have it either."

"You can have Daddy's business, but you stay away from my medical connections."

It's all falling together. They're using Ramos' refrigerated trucks to deliver Colombian produce. They just forgot to tell him that her so-called medical supplies are really drugs and are part of the shipment. Looks like I already got the answers for Ramos and the DEA. We should be able to wrap this up in a hurry. All I have to do is have Ramos come down and listen to this conversation. Wait until he hears that Deedee is not his child.

Jorge shakes his head. "Without the produce business your medical supplies won't make it into the United States. After all, they're not exactly FDA approved."

"So now you not only want the produce business, you want a piece of the nutriment action. What makes you think you're entitled to that?" She sighs.

"All I want is a small cut," Jorge snaps. "You're the one who doesn't play fair. If I had been running the business, it would be in better shape than it is now, and unlike you, I would've given you a fair share of the profits."

"Bullshit." Daniela points her index finger at Jorge.

"You say 'bullshit,' but I've always done right by my family while you only thought about yourself. Even though you took what our father wanted me to have, I still supported my wife and children."

"Yeah, on the money I pay you to run a business, which you don't bother to do." She picks up her cup of hot coffee and glares at him.

My eyes are glued to the monitor. I think she's gonna throw the coffee in his face. I sit on the edge of the couch waiting.

"You don't run the business either," Jorge says. "You hired me and Julio."

"For your information, dear brother, the produce isn't making a profit."

"If you had let me run it right, it would." Jorge chucks a roll into his mouth.

"I paid you out of the cash I made on what you call my 'FDA unapproved medical supplies and nutriments,'" Daniela says.

"Well it's pretty clear how you get what you want in the quote-unquote business world."

"How would you know?" she asks.

"I've seen you perform since you were sixteen. You've had more action in the field than Colombia's National Liberation Army."

Daniela rolls her eyes. "Why do you always stoop to vulgar accusations in order to win an argument? I admit I had to do a few things when I was young to get a start in life, but it's not that way anymore. I call the shots. When I talk, men jump."

"Jump what? Your bones?" he laughs.

"Vete a carajo!"

"Don't tell me to fuck off," Jorge says.

"You know, Jorge, you're pathetic. If you insist on talking about me, why don't you tell Eduardo I said to quit paying someone to kill Ramos? I intend to marry him. Then maybe I'll be in a better position to help you." Daniela dunks the last of her roll in her coffee.

"I told you Eduardo didn't pay anyone to kill Ramos. We don't know who did that." Jorge glares at Daniela. "You say you got control over everything being shipped through Ramos' Banana Company. Well maybe you should ask your own people who's trying to knock Ramos off." Jorge adds more sugar to his coffee.

"Mentir, mentir, mentir. You'd lie to God."

"You're thick-headed. I'm telling you the truth." He shoves his chair back.

"I'd rather be brainless than on drugs like you. You'll always be a junkie!" She shakes her head.

"Like you don't use?" He spits back at her.

"Not like you," Daniela sneers.

"Get outta here. Maybe the rest of the party didn't know, but I'm sure you used a little happy powder or you wouldn't have pulled off that performance last night."

"I didn't do anything wrong. I was just having a little fun." She giggles.

"I'll tell you right now—if I could tell, Ramos could tell, and he did not look pleased."

"He loves me and nothing or nobody is going to change his mind. I make him happy. If there was anything he wasn't pleased with last night, it was you and your stupid remarks."

"It's always the same with you. You're always right and I'm always wrong." Jorge says. "I gave you fair warning. I'm taking what's mine."

Suddenly, Daniela seems to have had enough conversation. She stands up and slams her coffee cup on the table. "Stay outta my way, you fuckin' idiot. You ruin it for me and you won't see a dime." She stomps out of the room.

All at once I see a shadow moving across the wall of the kitchen monitor screen, but I can't make out who it is.

Jorge sits at the table alone, puffing his cigar. "What the hell was she so pissed about?" he mumbles. "I'm the one who's getting screwed."

Then Jorge also notices the shadow. "Who's there?" he asks.

The person moves into the range of the monitor and I see it's the French cook.

"Who were you talking to?" she asks.

"I wasn't talking to anyone. I was thinking out loud."

"It didn't sound like that to me." Nanette picks up a dish towel.

Jorge gets up and leaves the kitchen. "Bitch," he says over his shoulder before the door closes behind him.

That afternoon, before Mister Pete takes Jorge and Eduardo to the airport for their flight back to Colombia, I watch as they say good-bye. If I hadn't heard their earlier conversation, I would think they were a normal loving family. How could their altitudes change so quickly?

When it's time for Jorge to leave, Ramos shakes his hand.

"I wish you both a pleasant and safe trip," Ramos says.

Daniela hugs her brother and kisses him. "I love you." Real tears seep from her eyes. "I'll miss you. Tell everyone back home I said hello."

"I will, sweetie. Don't work so many hours. It's not good for you." He kisses his sister again and picks up Deedee. "Take care of Mommy."

"Okay." Deedee hugs her uncle's neck.

He kisses her and puts her down. Daniela takes her daughter's hand.

Jorge and Daniela remind me of the old Italian men at the local social bar back in Jersey. They would fight, argue and scream at each other all day long, then, at dinner time, they would hug each other and go home. The next day they would do it all over again.

Jorge and Eduardo leave in Ramos' Lincoln Town Car, and the family goes back into the house. I don't see much of Ramos and Daniela, but when I do, they're lovey-dovey and walk hand-in-hand. Sometimes Deedee is with them, but most of the time it's just the 'happy couple.' Daniela is always kissing Ramos and telling him how much she loves him.

What a two-timing bitch. I realize how lucky I am to have a nice girlfriend.

Late that evening, when Ramos comes to see me, I feel obligated to tell him about Jorge using drugs at the party, and about the argument between him and Daniela. Ramos passes the quarrel off as a family squabble between two spoiled siblings that meant nothing.

I ask him to look at the video but he refuses. "I have been through this before. Javier has dragged me down here with the same idea. You cannot believe anything Jorge says. He does a lot of drugs. I know Daniela does a little, too, but that is

150

because she works so many hours. She will be fine after we are married and she no longer works. You can see how happy she is when she is home."

"You might be right about Daniela, but I don't think you should trust Jorge."

"You do not understand them the way I do," Ramos says. "Jorge lives in Colombia. Drugs are an accepted way of life. The two siblings say things to hurt each other. They always do that." Ramos waves his hand. "Forget it."

"I don't know how you can be so calm. They were talking about doing business in other countries and bringing unapproved products into Belize. Doesn't that sound suspicious to you? Don't you think it's more than medical supplies?"

"Let me explain something to you," Ramos says. "Daniela is a lot like her father. She's started a little business. It's mostly cures from India and China. They are not approved by the FDA, but they're not harmful, and she only sells them to her friends. She's never going to get rich. It just makes her feel good to be a businesswoman."

"You hired me to find out what she does when you are not with her, and now you refuse to listen to the truth."

"I hired you to see what she does in India. Jorge will not be there. After you do that, I'm sure you will see her in a different light." He pats my shoulder.

I don't blame Ramos for not trusting my judgment. I wouldn't have believed it either if I hadn't seen and heard it myself. This time Ramos is wrong. I think this is more than just a small nutrient business. I'm gonna have Jeff check it out.

The following day, everyone at the mansion is helping Daniela get ready to go to the airport. Ramos comes into the shelter. "Your plane leaves before Daniela's but she has to get to the airport early."

I nod and wait for him to continue.

"She will be leaving in the helicopter and everyone will be going out back and down the path to the helicopter pad to see her off. It is something we always do."

"It's a good idea to stick to your usual activities." I say.

"Be ready to leave before noon."

"I will be prompt," I assure him.

"I will call you when it's good to go. Wait five minutes and then go out the hidden door. It will automatically lock behind you. Get into my Lincoln Town Car. It will be parked close. My houseman, Pete, will take you to the airport. He has a package with your airline ticket, a cell phone and cash. I will contact you on the cell phone after you get to India."

"Got it." Now I have a DEA mobile, Ramos's cell and my own smart phone. Even if I could take a gun on the plane, I wouldn't have room in my pockets.

I think this is a good time to bring up the conversation I heard during the party on his security system. I need to get things out in the open. "I heard you discussing my possible connection to your shooting incident. If you think I was responsible, then why did you hire me?"

"During the conversation, I thought you might not be the person for the job. However, I also do not believe the FBI's story about a hit man looking for you. This is a troubled world we live in. You can't always believe the obvious. Sometimes you must trust your own feelings." He turns and walks away.

It's extremely difficult to figure out how this man ticks. I don't know if Ramos is so in love with Daniela that he's in denial and refuses to believe she is capable of being involved in drug smuggling, or if he's the real drug trafficker and is purposely leading me astray. Either way, I have made a deal to do the job in India for a hefty price and at the same time, I might be able to dig up details the DEA needs to put a halt on drug smuggling through Belize and into The United States. And if nothing else, I get to see a new country.

CHAPTER FIFTEEN
Mumbai. (Bombay) India

I arrive at *Chhatrapati Shivaji* International Airport and rent a car. I stop in a no parking zone, roll down the window and rest my arm on the door. "Hey buddy," I say to one of the airport security men.

The guard turns around and looks at me.

"Can you do me a favor?" I ask. "I'm here to pick up a lady. She should be out in a few minutes. Her plane has already landed."

He leans down close to the window and squints at the Andrew Jackson in my hand. "You got no rupee?"

I shake my head.

He points to a spot just ahead. "Over there—ten minutes."

"Thank you," I say while tucking the bill into his breast pocket.

He nods. I can tell this isn't his first parking rodeo.

I have picked this spot because it is close to the baggage exit. This is the quickest way out of the airport and I'm hoping Daniela agrees. If not, I've wasted my time and money. Even worse, I'll have to go to her hotel early in the morning and wait in the lobby.

Five minutes later, Daniela waltzes through the automatic doorway. She crosses to the center island and heads straight to the front of the taxi line. She is wearing her flight attendant uniform and pulling a medium-size suitcase.

I follow her taxi, but instead of going to the Marriott, where Ramos told me she would be staying, we're traveling on a busy thoroughfare. Cars try to cut me off at every intersection. Horns blast when traffic slows, and it's difficult to keep up with an experienced cabby. It's late but brightly lit shops are still open and doing a brisk business.

At the end of a thriving trade district, the road narrows, traffic becomes lighter and street lights disappear. Not wanting to be noticed, I lag a little farther behind. Up ahead, the cab makes a right turn. I cut my headlights before turning onto the same deserted gravel road. I creep along until I see the glare of brake lights. When the taxi comes to a standstill, I'm scarcely moving, so I'm able to coast to a stop.

A shadowy figure gets out of the cab, is briefly lit by the headlights and disappears around the corner of a building. I assume it's Daniela since she's the only passenger.

When the taxi continues down the dark road, I turn on my parking lights and ease the rented Chevy forward. Several cars are parked in front of the building, but Daniela is nowhere in sight. On the side of the structure is a single green door. "Lunickbox Pharmaceuticals" is printed in faded, almost illegible, gold lettering, under a dingy, overhead light. Daniela must have gone inside.

I turn the car around, staying as far away as I can while still keeping the green door in sight. I park on the side of the road, kill the engine and sit in the darkness. Dim lights glow nearby, so I know there are other buildings in the area, even if I can't see what they look like.

A few minutes later, Daniela walks out of the green door pulling her suitcase. However, now she's also carrying an extra-large shopping bag. A seedy looking guy with a heavy beard is with her. They fade into the night and I lose track of them. I look around. There's no taxi in sight. I wonder what they're up to. I'm about to get out of the car when I see bright headlights coming from one of the vehicles parked in front of the building. It pulls onto the deserted road and moves slowly toward the thoroughfare. Either someone was waiting for them or one of them is driving.

The bearded man comes out from the shadows and goes back into the building. That eliminates him.

The vehicle has already turned left and is almost out of sight when I reach the highway. I turn on my headlights to follow. By the time I catch up, we're in a lighted area. I'm relieved to see the burgundy Ford Expedition is being driven by Daniela. She stays in the slow lane—never going over the speed limit—so it's easy to drop back and still keep her in sight.

She heads back toward the airport stops at the Marriott Hotel and leaves the SUV with the valet. It's late and business must be good, because I have to search for a parking place.

When I get to the entrance, I step into the atrium and stop abruptly. Daniela is leaving the desk and walking toward the elevators. She's still dragging her suitcase and carrying the shopping bag. She pushes the button for the elevator and waits. Impatient, she tries the service elevator and its door opens immediately. She's the only person getting on.

The elevator lights indicate it has stopped on the second floor. The lobby is empty, and the clerk lowers the lights and walks through a doorway behind the desk. I move swiftly across the room and press the up button. The lift returns and no one gets off. I leave the lobby and walk down the hallway until I come to a hotel phone. I call room service and request a bucket of ice for Daniela Diaz, and hang up before they can ask any questions.

I hurry up the stairs to the second floor and hang out at the end of the corridor. Room service knocks at door 209. Just as I expected, they want to please their guest. The door opens and the employee hands over a bucket of ice to Daniela.

"No charge," he says.

I'm proud of myself for successfully shadowing Daniela without being noticed. It's late, but I decide to stop in the hotel bar for a quick nip to celebrate my triumph. Now that I've had time to assess the scope of the job, I'm glad Jeff is flying in tomorrow.

Looking through the glass door, I see only one guy at the bar. His hand is wrapped around a tall glass and his head is slung low. He appears to be three sheets to the wind. I open the door and step inside.

"We're closed," the bartender tells me.

"The sign says you're closed, but I see you still have a guest with a drink in his hand." I lean against the bar.

"I wait for the desk clerk to send someone to take Mr. Jackson to his suite." The bartender drops a few things in a topless box.

"It takes a mighty nice guy to go the extra mile." I smile. "While you're waiting, would you mind pouring me a nightcap?"

He continues to wipe down the back bar. "Bar is closed." He points to the open drawer of the cash register.

"Can you take a credit card?" I ask.

He drapes his cleaning rag over the water faucet and turns around to face me. He frowns. "Nothing fancy." He sets an empty glass on the bar.

"Scotch and water will do." I lay the card beside the glass.

He scoops a few watery ice cubes from a container, pours the drink and runs the card. "When Mr. Jackson leaves, lights go out, and so do you."

"I can live with that," I say. "I had a long day and I'm a little dry."

Ten minutes go by and the bartender is still waiting.

"Looks like you're here for the night." I nod my head toward Jackson.

"If you walk Jackson to his room, I cancel credit card charge," he tells me.

"Is there any reason why you can't do the same thing?" I ask.

He holds up five fingers. "When I lock door, I have only five minutes to get to kitchen before alarm go off."

I must have rocks in my head, but he looks tired and seems like a nice guy, so I agree.

The bartender sticks out his hand. "My name Cano. Stop in again. I set you up."

"Thanks," I say. "You don't have to do that."

"Hey, Jackson," Cano calls out. "Gimme door key."

"I'm not ready," Jackson mumbles.

"Yes you are," Cano says.

The bartender takes Jackson's key and hands it to me.

"About the credit card?" I smile.

He runs the card through the machine again. "I cancelled charge," he says.

I sign the slip and he gives the card back to me.

"What's Jackson's room number?" I ask.

"Suite 210." Cano picks up the box that holds his money bag and the rest of the paraphernalia he's taking to the kitchen.

"You have suites on the second floor?" I ask.

"We have a few for special guests."

Cano helps me get the drunk through the door, and while I pull him toward the elevator, Cano takes the steps to the basement kitchen.

Everything is working out great. I have access to a place directly across from Daniela and Jackson is too drunk to remember how much time I spent with him. I know it's late, but when Jorge and Daniela were arguing, Jorge mentioned that she had a thing for some guy named Kadam. I'll wait a while and see if anyone shows.

When I let go of Jackson to unlock the door, he sags to his knees. I put my foot in the doorway to keep it from closing, and hear the click of door 209 opening.

"Come on, Jackson, get up." I hold the key card between my teeth, put my arm under his shoulder and lift him into a standing position. Still, his feet don't budge.

I get a gander at the back of a woman in flowered pajamas, who I assume is Daniela. I turn my face away.

As I start to drag Jackson through the doorway, I sneak one more peek.

Unfortunately, the woman is now staring directly at me. I quickly pivot my head, but maybe too late. She might have seen my face. I'm struggling to pull Jackson's long legs inside the doorway when her voice rings out.

"Do you need a little help?" Flowered Pajamas asks.

I'd know that sweet sugary voice anywhere. "No," I growl around the card, while keeping my head lowered and my shoulders hunched.

Just as the drunk's feet clear the door, she turns into the alcove next to her room that is filled with snacks and refrigerated drinks.

Jackson's door slams shut. I drop him on the floor and search for a light switch. I stumble into a small room just off the sitting room that only has a pedestal sink and toilet.

I've slobbered on the door key, so I drop the card into the sink to rinse it off. I wash my hands and use a clean cloth to wipe my sweaty face. I'm using my fingers to smooth back my damp hair, when I hear a light tapping on the door. It's her. I know it's her. I'm not gonna open the door.

Fifteen minutes later, the door is tapped on again. This time a man calls out. "Room service!"

This is almost the same trick I pulled on her thirty minutes ago. Daniela might think she's smart, but she's can't beat me at this game.

I call the front desk. "This is Mr. Jackson in suite 210. I didn't order anything from your kitchen and someone from room service is banging on my door. Get them the hell outta here. I hang up and grab a clean glass from the bathroom.

I rip off the paper wrapper and press the bottom of a glass against the door. Then I put my ear close to the open end of the glass. I hear someone talking.

"What's the name of the man who's in this room?" a woman asks.

I was right. It's Daniela.

A male voice answers. "I don't know."

"Yes, you do. You just won't tell me. Do you want currency? I've got many rupees," she whines. "My husband sent someone to check on me before, and he's doing it again. The man pretended he was drunk. When I looked at him, he turned his head."

I listen to hear if the man tells her Jackson's name, but then I hear shouting and people are being questioned.

"I got the wrong room," Daniela says.

Then I hear a door slam. The hallway is quiet.

Jackson opens his eyes. "What's goin' on?" he slurs.

He gets to his feet, staggers toward the bedroom and falls across the bed face down. Jackson must have already been here for a couple of days because clothes are draped over all the chairs. A pile of dirty towels is on the floor of the gigantic bathroom just off the bedroom. I look in his fridge and find a cold beer. I sit on the sofa and let the cold liquid cool my throat. I've been awake a long time, but my mind is still going sixty miles an hour.

After almost thirty minutes, I peer outside the door. No one is there. I hurry down the hallway, take the stairs and slip into the darkness. I don't breathe until I'm locked in my car and driving out of the parking lot.

I guess Jeff knew what he was talking about when he said, "Don't stay at the Marriott. You might accidently run into Daniela."

I look for a hotel close by and register at *The Lalit Mumbai.* When I walk into my room I'm happy to see a large screen television. I need something to calm my nerves.

I page through the menu until I find a local station. *Barfi,* a movie made locally in Bollywood, is playing tonight on channel five. I fluff the pillows and lie down to watch the flick, but I can't stop my mind from wandering back to Daniela.

I gotta find out what's in that shopping bag. Anything that can't wait until tomorrow after flying almost ten thousand miles has got to be mighty important. As soon as Jeff gets to India, I'll have him check on Lunickbox Pharmaceutical. Even if Daniela is smuggling drugs, a commercial drug company wouldn't deal with an airline attendant. She's gotta be working for someone else.

CHAPTER SIXTEEN

It's Tuesday morning, and my seven a.m. wake up call is ringing on the hotel phone.

I turn off the television that's been blaring all night, jump in the shower, shave and dress—all in fifteen minutes. I've got to get to the Marriott before Daniela leaves her room.

On my way, I put in a quick call to Ramos, but I'm only on the line long enough for him to give me several worthless instructions. "Like what?" I ask Ramos. "I'm getting close to Daniela's hotel and need to hang up."

I've barely started the job and already Ramos is concerned with how I'm spending my time and his money.

"Hell, yeah, I'm on the job. I never let her out of my sight. I'll call you as soon as I get any information whatsoever," I say before cutting him off.

The ride only takes a few minutes. When I get there, I search the Marriott's parking lot, including valet. The big-ass Expedition is nowhere to be found. In the lobby, I use the hotel phone to dial Daniela's room number.

When no one answers, I leave knowing I've missed my chance to follow her. Upset for not coming earlier, I go to Café Frangipani in nearby Nariman Point Shopping Mall, which—who would have guessed—serves Belgian waffles. The coffee is made with real Arabica beans, strong enough to curl your hair, but so delicious I can't resist asking for a second cup. After breakfast, I walk around the mall. Zenith and Fujitsu are apparently the big electronic names in Mumbai. I notice a Deutsche Bank sandwiched between two clothing stores, but what amazes me most is Ruby Tuesday's has made it to this far-away land.

By noon, the temperature outside is scorching, so I return to the hotel to see if Daniela has come back. The SUV is still not there. I stop for a cool drink in the Marriott bar. It isn't long before I meet a road engineer from Michigan named Sinclair Jaworski.

"I'm Robert." I don't give him my last name.

He tells me he's here to help rebuild the road system. He says when it was first built, a large portion of the funds found their way into corrupt politician's pockets, and most of the substandard roads have now crumbled.

"The same thing happens in a lot of countries," I say.

"I'm here to see that it don't happen again," he says.

"That's quite an undertaking." I twirl the wooden swizzle in my drink.

Jaworski hands me one of his business cards. "It's hard to focus on road problems when it seems like everyone is trying to get their hand in your pocket. Most of the cement and construction companies I deal with are owned or controlled by the Punjabi Mafia."

Finally, something he says catches my interest. "What kind of Mafia is that?"

"It's India's version of organized crime, but it also operates in other countries. Some folks say it's affiliated with terrorist groups." Jaworski takes a gulp of scotch.

"I've never heard of organized crime sharing profits with subversives—or any other organization—for that matter."

Jaworski mumbles something about mobsters and the high crime rate in India before he blurts out, "What do you think about India's drug problems?"

I'd like to hear what he has to say, but I don't want people in the bar to think I agree with his raving rationality. It's time for me to bail out of this conversation. "All I know about drugs is that India is the largest legal grower of opium."

The bar begins to fill up and the noise level rises. My acquaintance raises his voice to be heard over the clamor. Patrons look our way and I notice two men staring at us.

"A large portion of the opium is converted into illegal heroin and it's consumed as concentrated liquid. People overdose and drop dead," he informs me.

"I assume that's true with any drug," I tell him. Then I ask the bartender for my tab.

"If that's not bad enough, India's pharmaceutical manufacturers are responsible for the legal drug production finding its way to India's addicts without a prescription."

I don't want to talk about drugs to anyone publicly, especially in a bar filled with people who may have a vested interest in the drug industry. When I don't reply, he says, "I'm sorry. I have a habit of running on about things. What brings you to India?"

The bartender says, "I was born here."

"I was talking to Robert," Jaworski says.

The road engineer knows we want him to shut up, but the dumbass has no manners.

"I came to buy silver." When I say silver, it arouses the bartender's interest. He's a different barkeep than the one who was here last night.

"Where do you buy your silver?" the bartender asks.

"I'm gonna try the *Zaveri Bazaar,*" I tell him. "I hear it's a good place to find bargains on precious metals and gems."

The bartender hands me a card. "If you don't find what you're looking for, I have some connections you might be interested in."

I pay my tab and finish my drink.

"You're not leaving, are you?" Jaworski asks.

"Yeah, I have an appointment with a jeweler." I leave a tip, shove the change into my pocket and extend my hand to the windbag.

He pumps my hand. "Nice to meet you," he says.

"You bet." I think he enjoyed hearing himself talk.

When I leave the cool sanctuary, I check the parking lots again, but there's no sign of the Ford. I don't like hanging around a bar with a fanatic, so I drive back toward the pharmaceutical manufacturing plant that Daniela visited last night. I wanna get a look inside. It might give me a clue to what was in Daniela's shopping bag.

A half hour later, I arrive at the pharmaceutical company. Security is posted at both the front entrance that I hadn't noticed last night and the side door. Foolishly, I explain to them that I'm an American businessman interested in investing in manufacturing and would like a tour of their processing plant.

Apparently, the pharmaceutical company's security has heard this line before, maybe from an undercover cop. The guard hands me a business card with the address of the corporate office. "No admittance without company approval." He shoos me away.

Standing on the dirt road in the hot sun, I tuck the freakin' card into my pocket with the others. In daylight, the area takes on a completely different appearance. This section of town must have been rezoned into an industrial area. Many factories are built right to their property lines, literally within inches of the dilapidated shacks where families are still living. It looks like an unsuccessful attempt to squeeze out the occupants, who continue to live with smoke, dirt, and factory wastewater discharge rather than move. They probably have no where to go.

According to the business card, Lunickbox corporate office appears to be in a place called Dharavi. I get into my car and check the map I picked up at the hotel. The highway I'm looking for is only a short distance from the plant.

It's a nice day for a drive. However, I was told there are millions of people in Mumbai, and it seems as if most of them are using this road. It's not far to Dharavi, but in stop and go traffic, it takes a while. My stomach growls and I look at my watch. It's already noon.

The hotel clerk had mentioned that one of the most popular places to eat is the Taj Mahal Grill, so when I see the large billboard advertisement, I stop there for lunch. I see three older men and three gorgeous young women dressed to the nines seated at a round table. One girl in particular stands out. She is wearing a blue and green saree. I suppose it could be just business, but I watch the body language while I drink my coffee. Nah, it's obvious—they're sugar daddies.

The waiter brings my order. I love spicy Indian food and these are dishes you don't often find in the United States or even in other European countries. When the waiter comes by to check on my table, I ask him about Bollywood.

"The girl in the blue and green is one of India's movie stars," he tells me in a stage whisper. "She recently had a small part in an American movie. For a few rupees I can get her autograph for you."

"No thank you," I say.

The road engineer had mentioned that India's movie stars hang out with some pretty nasty criminals. He told me that mobsters use threats to get young stars speaking parts in various movies in exchange for sex. I seem to recall several New Jersey gangsters whose pictures hit the front pages of the weekly tabloids with movie actresses on their arms.

I finish my lunch, and while I'm waiting for the check, I pile my dishes. It's a habit I picked up from Angela, which was probably because she was once a waitress.

When the waiter brings a second cup of coffee, he looks suspiciously at the pile of dirty dishes. "Are you looking for work," he asks.

"No," I say softly. "The food and service were quite good." I smile. I pay my tab, leave the restaurant and continue on the road to Dharavi. As I get closer to my destination, I see graffiti scratched crudely on fences and walls along with some remarkably good drawings. The area appears to be one of the major slums of Mumbai. It's old and worn out. Quite a few buildings are collapsing and those still standing have boarded windows.

Barefoot children play on top of piles of garbage that litter the streets. Hundreds of people fill the trains that run through the thickly populated area, while others cling to the railings or ride on top. I can't imagine an office for a huge pharmaceutical company being in this part of town.

The address is a lot further away than I expected, and the buildings here are fairly new. The front door and all the windows of the corporate building are protected by black metal bars. Several other places have bars on their windows, but most of the buildings do not. Why would only a few buildings have bars on their windows? I ask myself.

I suppose a corporate office could mean either there's unaccountable cash or incriminating information about their business stored inside. Everything else would be covered by insurance. If they have something to hide, it might also be the reason why the office would be located this close to a slum area.

I decide to wait until I talk to Jeff before I investigate further. I'll let him run the information through the UN Office on Drugs and Crime and India's Ministry of Social Justice. I'm sure they have figured this out. I leave Dharavi and go back to the Marriott.

The big Expedition is again valet parked. I go into the lobby and find an out-of-the-way chair overlooking a flower garden. I hope to get a lead soon.

Ramos did tell me that Daniela usually has a long layover when she flies to India. This time she isn't coming directly back to the states. Her next flight takes her to Vancouver.

When Jeff gets here, he'll check her flight schedule. I still have a little time to see what she does in India. I'd like to see what secrets are in suite 209.

I sit in the lobby for more than an hour before Daniela gets off the elevator alone and walks toward the dining room. I partially cover half of my face with a sports magazine, but she never looks my way. The maitre d', dressed in a colorful satin robe and white turban, hurries to the doorway to greet her. He gives her a big hug like they're old friends. He hooks his arm around Daniela's and leads her toward the bar.

When she disappears from my sight, I venture toward the dining room. The hostess meets me at the door.

"How many?" she asks.

"I'm not sure." I tell her. "I'm looking for a man I met this afternoon."

"You're welcome to come in and look around," she says.

I glance around the room. The maitre d' is now attending to another table and Daniela is sitting at the bar with a heavy-set gentleman. She's taken off the silk wrap she was wearing, exposing a shimmering bronze tan in her off-the-shoulder dress. She takes a cigarette from a silver case, places it in a long slim holder while flaunting a huge diamond ring. I wonder if Ramos knows about the ring, or it might be just a fake she bought.

Her dinner partner reaches out to light her cigarette. She blows him a kiss. He smiles as he attempts to settle his obese body back onto the high back stool.

I don't think this is the Kadam, she and Jorge were talking about, since she said he dropped her. If it is one of them it must be the one she called "fat ass" or someone from the Punjabi mob.

Even though he appears to be fascinated by the soon-to-be Mrs. Ramos, I don't think he's the boyfriend. He might be a local acquaintance she uses for dinner dates, or maybe he has something to do with the airline, although he doesn't look the part. If he's connected to drugs, my guess is he could be close to the top echelon.

The bartender sets a bottle of champagne on the bar. He places two crystal glasses in front of them. This guy has no class. I can't even imagine taking a lady out for champagne and having it served at the bar. However, it doesn't seem to bother Daniela.

The hostess observes me watching them. "Do you see your friend?"

"No, I'm afraid not. He must have gone somewhere else for dinner. I was just admiring the fabulous bar."

"You mean the pretty lady." The hostess winks at me.

Caught red-handed, I grin. "Yes her, too."

I leave the restaurant and go to the second floor. I want to see if Jackson's in his room. Since I was the one who helped him to his room last night, he might go to dinner with me and that way I could keep an eye on Daniela, where I may even be able to overhear some of her conversation. It's not much of a plan, but right now I'm batting zero.

When I reach the second floor, I see the door to suite 209 is held open by a pile of dirty towels. They appear to have an overabundance of what looks like lipstick and makeup smeared on them. I move closer, until I'm standing right in front of the door when the cleaning lady walks out.

She frowns at me, picks up the dirty towels and raises her eyebrows. "You can go in now. I brought the clean towels your lady requested,"

I stop the door before it swings shut. "Hum." The maid thinks I belong in this room. Talk about an opportunity. But what if I get caught? Hell, she won't be back until at least after they finish dinner. I slip inside. An abundance of clean towels hangs neatly in both bathrooms. The rest of the place is in total disarray.

There is a sitting room, just like Jackson's. Paperwork from the airline is strewn across a small table. Two extravagant dresses and Daniela's black airline uniform hang in the bedroom closet. The main bathroom has makeup, hair products, and perfume scattered across the vanity. Wet panties hang over the shower rod. Everything else is still in her suitcase, which is on the floor in the middle of the bedroom next to a pair of three-inch heels.

I check the closet, the unlocked safe, dresser drawers and all the corners of the room. The shopping bag isn't here. No pharmaceutical or other products are lying around. I haven't found any new worthwhile information. Then, as I turn to leave the bedroom, I hear the door click. Not knowing which way to turn, I freeze. All kinds of thoughts race through my mind. I have no gun—I'll be put in jail—the story will hit the newspapers. The mob will send a hit man to kill me.

Then my worst thoughts prevail. I might never see Angela again. They might even go after her and I won't be there to protect her.

CHAPTER SEVENTEEN

I'm on the far side of Daniela's hotel bedroom. Double hung heavy drapes, made to keep the heat out and the air conditioning in, are pulled open and bunched up on each side of the huge plate glass window. I hear mumbling, and then the door slams shut.

"I see they left the clean towels I had to call for," Daniela says.

I ease myself behind the scrunched-up drapes. I'm sure they're sticking out further than normal, but with all the crap spread around the room, maybe Daniela won't notice the bulging material. My mind is racing to come up with a plan to get out of here.

"Give me a few seconds to freshen up," she sing-songs. The patter of her soft shoes fades.

"Take your time, darling," a masculine voice utters.

Stuck behind the drapes, I can only assume it's the obese gentleman I thought she was going to have dinner with. Only now do I realize that I should have waited for a time when I was sure she had left the building, but I just couldn't resist the open invitation. I press my body against the wall.

Footsteps make their way to the bedroom. I pray the clutter will distract the intruder from noticing my hiding place. The breathing of the unwelcome guest comes in short bursts. My confidence builds. I know I can handle the fat man, so I poise ready to pounce and wait for the drapes to be pulled away.

He meanders over to the window. I can see his nose and chin as he leans forward and peers at the busy street below. I don't know what he is looking at, but he watches intently. I'm afraid to breathe. About three minutes pass in silence, but it feels like an eternity.

"I'm ready, Samir!" Her voice is muffled.

She must still be in the bathroom.

Then, only a short distance from where I am standing, she asks. "Did you find what you were looking for?"

"No, my dear. I was not searching your bedroom. I just looked out the window to check the traffic."

"You know, it's not polite to scrutinize a lady's *boudoir*," she complains in her sultry voice. "I'm sorry the place is such a mess."

I could imagine her innocent eyes and sexy smile tormenting him, but to my amazement his answer is far from what I expect.

"This is not a *boudoir*, and you're not a lady, but I love you anyway," he grunts.

"Remarks like that will get you nothing," she jeers.

"That is true, but if one has enough rupees, even the greatest of problems can be resolved."

There is a slight rustle, but I can't determine where the sound is coming from.

"Is all that for me?" she asks.

"Yes, and there's more where that came from," he says.

There are a few muffled oohh's and aahh's.

I hope they are not planning on closing the deal right now.

"Come Samir. It's getting late."

"Give me one little kiss," Samir begs.

There is a quick smack of lips, like she's kissing the air.

"I'm sure you can do better than that, my precious. I love the feel of your body close to mine."

It seems like a long time before Daniela quips, "Let's hit the road, I'm hungry."

He apparently doesn't mind her aloof approach. "I'm glad you thought of going to dinner at the Taj Hotel," he says. "Their delicious Kaffir lime martini is known around the world."

"My mouth is watering already." She sighs.

"Save your taste buds for Tamari scallops and me," he coos.

"Samir, you say the sweetest things."

"Only for you, my precious." He gushes.

"Let's go," she says again.

I hear high heels clunking toward the sitting room. She must have changed her shoes. I picture her the first day I saw her getting out of the helicopter. She looked so innocent, so in love with Ernesto. What's she doing with this horny pig?

"Oh," she says. "I forgot my purse."

"Leave it," he says. "You don't need it. I'll take care of you."

"But—"

"Come along. The hotel's dining room closes early," he says.

That's odd. He didn't seem to be concerned about the time when he was trying to get her to smooch.

The door slams shut, but I stay behind the drape without moving. Daniela might come back for her purse or on some other whim.

When it seems safe to step from behind the drapes, I peek into the room. All the lights are on, but no one's there. I take one last look around and gaze at the tiny pink purse. I feel like someone is watching me.

I undo the flap and look inside. There's a pair of sunglasses, lipstick, comb, and a bottle of Temazepam 30mg. It reads *"Take at bedtime."* I turn the bottle around. It doesn't have a doctor or pharmacy name on it. I see only a few rupees at the bottom of her purse.

Sewn in the purse is a little pocket. Inside the pocket is a piece of a napkin. Several phone numbers are written on one side. On the back of the napkin are two names—Kadam and Mehta.

Hum. I heard about Kadam before, but who's this Mehta?

I copy the names and numbers on the hotel's breakfast menu. I tuck it into my pocket and slip out the door. The hall is deserted. I take the stairs to the lobby.

The hotel lobby is fairly empty, so I head to my comfy chair and call Jeff. He doesn't answer. I leave him a message about the names and telephone numbers I found in Daniela's purse, and ask him to check them out and get back to me.

A few minutes later he calls me back. "I'm on it," Jeff says. "I also got your message about staying at *The Latit Mumbai,* on Sahar Airport Road. I'm at the same hotel in room 603. You can stop by for your gun on your way in tonight."

"I may be late. Daniela has gone out to dinner and I don't know when she'll get back. I'd like to hang around the Marriott for a while."

"That's okay. I'll be up late. You picked a great place. My room is really big. It has a desk with computer connections, a king-size bed and a recliner. I intend to do most of my work from this room."

"I'm glad we're in the same hotel. The traffic here is horrible," I tell Jeff.

"By the way," he says. "I contacted the NCB."

"What's the NCB?"

"It's the Narcotics Control Bureau," Jeff says. "It's like our DEA. They wired Daniela Diaz's room yesterday morning while she was out. It will pick up and record conversations in the room and on the hotel phone."

I don't warn Jeff about Samir's foreplay. I'll let it be a surprise. "She probably won't use the hotel phone," I tell Jeff. "What about her mobile?"

"They're working on her smart phone, but that's not likely to happen."

Another guest of the hotel walks over and sits across from me. When I get up and move, my cell phone starts to cut in and out. Jeff is rattling on about the NCB.

"Say that again." I say.

"NCB. . .quartered in Delhi. . .office in Mum. . .assign a Narc. . .work with. . .his name. . . arrange. . .meet."

I only hear half of what he's saying, but it doesn't matter. Jeff always tells me everything at least twice. I guess the Narc is another team player.

"Can you hear me now?" Jeff asks.

"Yes, that's much better."

"Trust me. The narcotics detective will make this job a lot easier for both of us," he says.

"So you say." I laugh. "Just how much do you plan on telling this guy about me?"

"Only that you're a private investigator working for us. We won't bring Ramos into the picture unless it becomes necessary. Are you okay with that?"

"Yeah. I guess so." What I really mean is, there's not much I can do about it.

It's still early in the evening, so I look into the Marriott's bar to make sure Jaworski isn't there. Only a couple of men are sitting at the other end of the bar. I've learned a lot about India, but all I know about Daniela is that she has given one man a quick smooch and now she's gone out for dinner. So far, I haven't been able to verify any of the information I've dug up.

I guess I should feel guilty for getting so much money with nothing to show for it, but I didn't want either job. However, they insisted, so it's up to them to pay. Since I'm doing this job, I'll be able to take Angela on that trip to Australia that she's been talking about.

Again, I think about the shopping bag Daniela picked up at the pharmacy plant. It was too big to be carrying the anabolic steroids Julio uses. I close my eyes and picture Daniela coming out of the pharmacy plant. I don't think this place makes the baby diapers she uses to wrap her so called vitamins and nutriments. I remember her swinging the bag, so it couldn't have been very heavy. Yet it had to be something important.

For all I know it might just be a fancy dress she borrowed from a friend to go out in. It appears I'm even less of a detective than a sharpshooter.

I've only taken a couple of sips from my Amrut martini when Jaworski, the mouthy Pollock comes in and plops himself on a bar stool next to me.

"Hey, Robert." Jaworski says. I thought you might stop by here after your appointment. How'd everything go?" he asks.

It's been a long day and I don't want to get into another discourse on road construction. "The jeweler didn't have anything I was interested in."

"Sorry about that. I was hoping you'd find some good deals and stick around for a few days."

Jodi Ceraldi

"There are plenty of brokers in India. I'll make another connection."

"You deal on the black market?" He pulls a red workingman's handkerchief from his hip pocket and wipes the sweat from his brow. "Maybe you could make a connection for me?"

"Why? Have you taken a sudden interest in silver?" I ask

"Not silver, but a connection's a connection." Jaworski grins.

"I don't know what you're talkin' about, but it's getting late and I'm gonna turn in." I pull my wallet from my pocket and motion to the bartender.

"You've hardly touched your drink," Jaworski says.

I stand, pick up the martini, and drain the glass. "All gone."

I can't wait for my tab while this blowhard fans his mouth about the black market.

"Would you like another drink?" the bartender asks.

"No thank you." I hand the barkeep enough rupees to more than cover my drink. "Keep the change," I say.

The bartender nods. "Come back again. You have a drink comin' your way."

"I hope I didn't run you off," Jaworski says.

"Not at all," I say. When I walk away, I hear Jaworski talking to a guy who has just sat down beside him.

"He's a good friend of mine," Jaworski tells the man. "He had a hard day—lost his black-market connection with a silver broker."

I look back at Jaworski and glare, but he's already involved in a new conversation and doesn't pay any attention to me. This is the last time I stop here.

My thoughts return to Daniela. Instead of going to my hotel, I decide to try and find her. I walk outside where several cabs wait. Not having any idea of where this place is, I slide into the backseat of a taxi. "Taj Hotel," I tell the cabbie.

"Which one?" he asks.

"Damn," I mumble. "The closest one." Looks like I might strike out again.

When the driver stops in front of the hotel, I lean forward and pay the high-priced minimum for the two-block ride.

A guy opens my door. "I'll be happy to see to your luggage."

"I don't have a suitcase," I tell him. "I'm only stopping in for dinner."

"The dining room is about to close. They will not prepare any more tables," the prim and proper gentleman says. "You might like to try the hotel's hors d'oeuvres at the bar."

"Thank you. I'll give it a go."

I proceed briskly to the hotel dining room, where I'm encouraged to go to the bar. Only a few people are left from the dinner crowd. Bingo! Daniela and her friend Samir are sitting at a table right in the middle of the lavish room.

Before entering the bar, I wander around pretending to look for a restroom while I check out the exits. The only way out of the dining room is the hallway next to the bar. I pick a barstool close to the doorway and order a Kaffir lime martini. Samir is right. The drink is fantastic.

Soon after I arrive, another man dressed in an expensive looking American style suit enters the dining room. I get up as if to stretch my legs and meander over to the doorway. The man who just came in is now sitting with Daniela and Samir. He appears to me to be a native of India. I can't hear them, but their hands and arms move excitedly. Their voices must be raised somewhat, because customers at other tables turn to look at them.

Daniela holds up her palms and they all stop talking. A waiter goes over to their table, and I return to my barstool. I wonder what that was all about. I need to ask Jeff if he can get me some kind of listening device so I can hear what people are saying on the other side of the room.

The waiter comes into the bar. "Kadam wants his special drink," he says to the bartender.

My ears perk up.

The bartender mixes shots from six different bottles with ice, shakes it up, and pours it through a strainer into a fancy glass. The waiter takes the concoction into the dining room. After a little while I slide off the stool and peek inside the dining room door. The tall fancy glass is sitting in front of the man at the table with Daniela and Samir. Hum, so that's Kadam.

When I return to the bar, the bartender looks at me suspiciously. "Are you looking for someone?" he asks

"No, I wanted to have dinner, and was told the dining room was closed. I thought the new customer was being served, but I see he's only having a drink."

"We have a variety of hors d'oeuvres," the bartender says. "I can place your order."

"I think I'll finish my drink and find a place where I can get a meal."

"Try the Kebab Shop. It's just one block north," he says. "Tell them Edgar sent you. They serve complete meals and stay open all night."

It's not long before I hear voices. Daniela, Samir, and Kadam pass by the bar as they leave the restaurant.

"I'll see you later," I say. "I'll try the diner you mentioned."

As I reach the lobby, Daniela and Samir are saying good-bye to Kadam. Samir pulls a room key from his pocket and wiggles the card in front of Daniela's nose. She bats her eyelashes, and they get on the elevator.

Now that's something I can tell Ramos that he won't believe. The geezer is older than Ramos, fat as a hog and bald. He must have something she wants.

I follow Kadam outside. While he waits for the next cab to pull up, he glances back at me and does a double take. He shouts an address through the passenger side window to the cab driver and gets into the taxi.

I walk to the next cab and repeat the address.

After two blocks, Kadam's cab turns right and my cab goes left. "I think you went the wrong way," I tell the driver, but he pays no attention to me.

A few seconds later, we're driving through another slum area. Streets zigzag between small huts. Garbage is piled higher than the houses, and the smell of human waste permeates the evening air.

I wonder why Kadam turned to take a second look at me—then I remembered where I had seen his face. He was one of the two men at the Marriot hotel bar who was staring at me the day Jaworski was runnin' his mouth.

"Turn around. Let's get the hell out of here," I tell the driver.

"You fell for the oldest trick in the book," the guy says.

"What?" I glare. "You heard the address the man ahead of me requested?"

"Yeah, I heard Kadam and so did some of the other drivers. If you wanted to go where your friend was going, you should have told me."

"He's not my friend. I just wanted to talk to him."

"You lookin' for drugs? I can help you with that, too."

"No, I'm not into drugs, and you don't sound like you're from India."

"Me? My name's Gus. I'm from Manhattan, been here for twelve years."

"If I had asked, would you have followed the cab Kadam was in?"

He tilts his head from side to side. "That depends on how much you had been willing to pay."

"Take me to the Marriott Hotel on Sabar Airport Road," I say.

"You got it." He gets us back on the highway. "Don't you just love the traffic?" He chuckles. "It reminds me of home."

We ride along quietly for a while. I fear I have already become too friendly with this man, and I don't want to get in any deeper, but then he asks me a question.

"What brings you to Mumbai?" he asks.

He's never gonna buy *I'm just a tourist*. "I deal in silver. I came to see what the *Zaveri Bazaar* has to offer."

"Ah, now I know what you were doing at the Taj Hotel. You shouldn't trust Kadam, and you better watch out for Maharaja Samir Mehta. He'll steal you blind. You can do better at the bazaar."

"Maharaja Mehta?" I sputter.

"For him it's only a nickname. I suppose he thinks it makes him important, but Maharajas haven't had any power since way back in the late forties. Nevertheless, some of the old guys cling to the title." He laughs.

I watch the road signs. Many of the streets run at an angle and the name of the street changes despite the fact that the road continues straight ahead.

Then he says, "A lotta Americans spend a ton of money in Dharavi dealing with men like Samir. However, if you're an educated precious metal dealer, you can find a handsome piece of jewelry at a bargain price at the bazaar."

I lucked out on this trip. Taxi drivers always know about the best deals, but this one gave me more information than he realizes. Maybe I should listen to what he has to say about India. I lean back against the plush seat. "Do you find it difficult living here?"

"Nah, I love it. I make good money. I have a beautiful wife who keeps our little place clean as a whistle, cooks the best Indian dishes and makes me happy."

"Do you have children?" I ask

"Not yet, but very soon. That's why I work late. I want a bigger place to live. I want my baby to have the best. After he graduates from college, he's going to be a sports star."

"You know your baby is going to be a boy?"

"Yes, we checked as soon as the doctor could tell. I have a picture if you'd like to see."

"No, that's okay. I believe you," I say quickly. "What kind of a sports star?"

"He can pick any sport—cricket, soccer, whatever he wants. I'll see that he has the best training."

None of this matters to me, so I change the subject. "You drive an extra nice cab. How did you happen to come to India and get a job like this?" I wait for his version of how he ended up in a foreign country.

"Twelve years ago, I got into some heavy shit." He looks in his rearview mirror.

"Drugs?" I ask.

"No, well, yeah, there were drugs involved, but I wasn't into that." He slows down at an intersection. "People over here don't know how to drive."

"It's the dense traffic," I say.

"I hung out with some college kids who thought they could save the world. We caused problems at civic centers and interrupted political speeches. In general we were just a pain in the ass to the city. I got arrested a couple of times for petty shit and my dad bailed me out." He turns around and looks at me. "That's what money can do."

"When I was growing up, my old man rarely gave me the time of day." I lurch forward when the cab comes to a quick stop at a red light.

"You okay?" he asks.

"I'm fine." I wave off his concern. "Finish your story."

"Then, things changed. The group got out of control. Some of them got into drugs and a few began to carry guns. I didn't think anything would happen, but one night two cops got shot. I didn't pull the trigger, I didn't even have a gun, but just being in the wrong place is enough to get you in a whole pile of trouble."

"Damn, how'd you get out of that?"

"I don't know how my dad managed to get me out of jail, but I got shipped to India and my uncle bought me this big ass Buick."

"That was nice of him," I say.

"I don't work for a company. I'm what you call an independent." He turns into the hotel courtyard and pulls in front of the main entrance.

I pay my tab and get out. "Thanks."

"No need to thank me. You paid the fare and didn't give me any trouble." He hands me his card.

I shove it into my pocket with the rest of the business cards. At least I don't have to remember where I've been tonight. "If I ever come back, I'll give you a call."

"You do that," he says. "I know Mumbai like the back of my hand. I can tell you where to go and where not to go."

As I walk toward the main door, the big taxi lumbers out of the lot. When his cab turns onto the highway, I turn around and walk back to my car. I drive the short distance to *The Latit Mumbai* and go directly to room 603 and tap on the door.

"Who's there?" Jeff calls from inside the room.

"Nick."

He cracks the door, and I push it open. I don't see Jeff until I step inside. He's standing with his back against the wall with his gun drawn.

"What's with the gun?" I ask.

"I don't take chances."

I walk to his bed and bank the pillows against the headboard. I take off my shoes, drop my tired body on the bed and lean back. I want to stretch my legs. "Ah, man this feels good. Whatcha got for me?"

"Get your feet off my bed," Jeff says.

I ignore him. "You got a beer?"

He motions toward the small fridge beside his desk.

A few minutes later, he tosses a package to me. "Here's your nine-millimeter Glock and the pants holster you wanted. Try it on and see how it fits."

I stand up, put on the holster and tuck the gun inside. I puff up my cheeks. "I feel like Vito Corleone. You did a good job."

"I'm glad you agreed to let me tag along. I was getting bored in Belize."

"Fuhguddaboudit." I laugh and so does Jeff.

Jeff works hard and most of the time the DEA doesn't give him much credit. I guess sometimes I don't either.

Jeff stands up when he hands over the 442 snub-nosed .38 special.

"Look at this. It's fuckin' beautiful and just what I wanted—small and powerful," I say.

"Try this on for size." He tosses me an ankle holster.

"You gotta be kiddin'." I strap on the ankle holster and it fits perfectly.

"When you're not carrying the guns, lock them in the safe in your room," Jeff tells me.

"You wanna come with me and make sure I get to my room?"

"Damn you, Nick. I busted my ass to get you all this stuff."

I snap my heels together and almost fall. "I'm just kiddin'." I walk over and make myself comfortable on his bed again.

Jeff takes a deep breath and puts extra ammo on the desk. "Take this back to your room."

"And don't forget to put it in the safe." I mimic Jeff.

He frowns. "Sometimes you can be such an asshole."

"Don't worry so much," I tell him. "We're gonna do okay."

I share everything with Jeff that I have learned so far, which isn't much. I fill him in on my silver dealer M.O., and he tells me that according to the NCB, Kadam is a known drug supplier.

"They have him on their radar, but haven't arrested him yet," Jeff says. "Although he's not aware of it, he's leading them to other drug operations."

"That's a cool idea. Get the bad guys to work for you without promising them anything in return."

Jeff picks up a document he's been looking at. "The first telephone number you gave me is registered to Kadam's son."

"That wasn't very clever." I roll my eyes. "I tried to follow Kadam tonight, but I lost him."

"Stay away from him. The NCB has him covered. Most of the drug dealers think they're above the law, but the NCB is gaining ground. India's making progress," Jeff says.

"If you would've been with me in Dharavi tonight, you might not feel that way. It makes the Bronx look like a Miami resort."

"I was talking about the drug problem." Jeff says. "You must have gotten lost in the slums. Dharavi has some nice areas."

When I get off his bed to get myself another beer, he hands me Daniela's airline schedule.

I glance at the information.

"You need to call Ramos and see what he wants you to do. Let him call the shots." Jeff pauses. "We don't want him to get suspicious."

"I'll call him before I go to bed."

Jeff nods and sifts through his papers. "This is what we know about Samir Mehta. He's suspected of belonging to the Punjabi Mafia. Some cops think he's the top dog, but the NCB says he reports to someone higher.

"The second telephone number belongs to a library, and the third isn't a working number." He hands me a new neatly typed list with the addresses and telephone numbers of Kadam, Samir and the library.

I drop the paper on the bed.

"I need the name of the hotel where Daniela and Samir are at tonight," Jeff adds. "We'll put the room under surveillance to see where they go when they leave the hotel. The NCB will send in forensics before the room is cleaned. We should be able to get fingerprints. If we get lucky we might find something else that can give us a lead."

"It's the Taj Hotel. It's not far from here. And speaking of leads, I saw an ad on television that they have a listening device that you can put in your ear and it enables you to hear a conversation that's taking place on the other side of the street. Have you heard about that?" I ask.

"Yeah, I got two of them." Jeff says. "It was buy one get one free. I don't know how they could get you a lead, but you're welcome to have one."

"Do they really work?"

"Sometimes," Jeff shrugs. "It depends on the noise level, how far away you are, and how loud the people are talking."

"I could've used it tonight. Daniela and Samir were having dinner at the Taj Hotel. They did a lot of talking, but I was too far away to hear what they said."

Jeff reaches into a box sitting next to the desk. He tosses me a small package. "Give it a try," he says. "You need to put a triple A battery in it."

When I shove his typed list into my pocket, I feel the business cards I put there earlier. "These are for you." I hand them to Jeff one at a time. "I picked this one up at the Taj Hotel where Daniela is tonight. This other card is from the taxi driver who brought me home. He's a young guy from Manhattan sent here by his father to keep him out of trouble."

Jeff reads the taxi driver's card. "Gus? His name is Gus? He doesn't have a last name?"

"He didn't tell me his name. He just handed me the card when I got out of the cab. I didn't look at it."

"How'd you get involved with this guy?" Jeff asks.

"It's a long story. I'll tell you later."

"Tell me now," he says.

I lean against the desk and rattle off the details of how I lost Kadam and made friends with the taxi driver.

"And you let him bring you right to the hotel you're staying at? You know you could have had him drop you off at one of the fifty hotels around here and walked to the *Latit.*"

"No, I didn't have him bring me here. He took me back to the Marriott. After he left, I got in my rental car and drove here."

Sinclair Jaworski's business card is the next one I pull out. "You can deep-six this. He's the loudmouth road construction engineer who can't wait to talk my ear off every day."

"I'll hang on to it for a while," Jeff says. "You don't know how things will play out. We might need him."

"Why? You have a road you want repaired?"

He drops the card into the pile with the rest of the business cards. "I'll take care of it."

"The two bartenders I told you about from the Marriott are pretty savvy. Cano is the one I did the favor for and damn near got caught. The other bartender gave me his card, but his name isn't on it. It just has a company name. He claims he can set me up with a good jeweler."

"What's this little mark here in the corner?" Jeff asks.

I hold the card under the light. "Too small to see, but it looks like some kind of logo."

"Odd business card—looks homemade," Jeff says. "I'll see what I can find out."

"This last one is the corporate office of the pharmacy plant that Daniela visited the first night she got here. Jaworski might be some help with that one. He thinks some of the pharmacy plants are saturating India with drugs without prescriptions."

"These big companies wouldn't take a chance like that," Jeff says. "They have too much riding on the drugs they ship to other countries. They wouldn't want to get closed down for a criminal action that couldn't come close to making them what they earn on exports."

I don't mention the bottle of sleeping pills I saw in Daniela's purse. "If you have everything you need, I'm going to bed." I open the door.

"Follow that cab." Jeff busts out laughing.

Back in my room, I call Ramos. "Ernesto, I hope I didn't wake you." The line cuts in and out. I think he said he was having breakfast.

"Yes, everything is cool. She had dinner at the Taj Hotel with an elderly gentleman. Later, she went to her room. She's no doubt sleeping by now," I report.

He says she doesn't get enough sleep and I'm beginning to think he's right. She's out late and always up early.

"I have a couple of questions for you," I tell Ramos. "You said Daniela was going to Canada when she leaves here. Do you know her flight number and departure time?" Again, I only hear every other word. "Did you say her flight leaves at eight-thirty?" I turn up the volume on my phone, but it doesn't help.

"Okay," I say. "If I don't answer, leave me a message. I may be able to hear the information better on my voice mail." After that, I can't hear what he's saying, only that it's something about how much he worries about Daniela. Dumb ass, should be more concerned about his own life.

"I'll wait for your call tomorrow. Hopefully, we'll have a better connection and I'll have some solid information for you."

But what I really mean is if I can prove that Daniela is smuggling drugs from India into Belize and using the banana company to transport them into the United States, the DEA will have all the evidence they need to prosecute Ramos and Daniela. I guess it's best to keep this news to myself.

CHAPTER EIGHTEEN

The next morning, the phone rings. I rub my eyes and look at the small hotel clock. I've overslept again.

Jeff gets right to the point. "The Narcotics Control Board is loaning us a detective to work with us. We're going to meet him this morning at the Café Frangipani."

"Meeting a Narc in a public place isn't a smart move," I tell him. "If the Punjabi Mafia operates anything like organized crime in the States, they know what's going on at the headquarters of law enforcement before word filters down to the police force."

"India's a crowded country. What are the chances that someone would even notice three men drinking coffee in a café?" Jeff chuckles.

My mind flashes back to Jersey. "Listen, there are thousands of meaningless individuals waiting to spot something that could make them a few bucks or move them up the ladder in organized crime. There are more mob soldiers on the street than there are servicemen defending our country."

"You're making too much out of this," Jeff says. "I already told him we'd meet him at the café. He'll be there in an hour."

"Call him back. Tell him the meeting is in your room and to make sure he's not followed. After he arrives, call me. I'll bring coffee."

For a moment, Jeff is quiet. Then he says, "He'll probably get a little huffy if I tell him to make sure he's not followed. How would you like it if I told you how to do your job?"

"You already have, many times."

"I don't do that to you," Jeff barks.

Now he sounds like my old nemesis, Gaetano. "Get over it, Jeff. Remind the guy. It's important."

I take my time getting dressed, go to the lobby and pick up a newspaper. I find a seat close to the entrance. People are checking out. Businessmen with briefcases are rushing to various appointments. An old man pushes a dry mop over the marble floor while the sun streams through the atrium and reflects off the glossy surface.

Then I spot him—head held high, sharply dressed, European style, all piss and vinegar. No question about it. The guy's a street cop recently promoted to the Narcotics Control Bureau. One thing he didn't change are his sturdy, polished, black shoes.

I glance around the room. It doesn't appear that anyone has followed him. As he's getting on the elevator, his cell phone rings. When he answers it, he smiles. Some people can't go anywhere without their phone. I go outside. Almost everyone has left the hotel. Only a few cars remain parked in the hot, humid air rising from the asphalt.

There it is—a plain, black, Ford Escape with no markings, toting a big, bright, government plate. Oh, yeah, don't forget the car's number. It's 222.

A few minutes later, I'm standing at the counter of a little shop down the street from the hotel ordering coffee and rolls when my phone rings.

"Bring the coffee," Jeff says.

I laugh.

"What's so funny?" he asks.

"Nothing, see you in a few."

Five minutes later, I arrive at Jeff's room with three coffees and a bag of sweet rolls. I sit them on the desk.

"Yo." I wipe the sweat from my forehead. "It's really hot out there."

Jeff introduces me to Rajat Singh. "He's our contact with the NCB."

Singh and I shake hands. He has a firm grip, and the muscles in his upper arms ripple.

I observe the ever-so-slightly raised imprint of a shoulder holster against his soft silk shirt. I turn and look in the mirror on the closet door to see if I can detect an imprint of my own. Son-of-a-gun, it's barely noticeable, but it's definitely there. The Glock is well-fitted, but the bulge at my waist doesn't look normal. What I need is a bigger shirt that hangs loose over my trousers.

Over breakfast, I find out that Rajat has a girlfriend who takes up a lot of his time. He appears to be quite fond of her, and says he has given up smoking at her request. I also discover that Singh is knowledgeable about the Punjabi and Indo-Canadian Mafia. He gives us a little background on the rise of the Hindu drug dealers, not only in Canada and India, but in the United States.

He's really well informed for a flatfoot just promoted to the NCB.

"The Punjabi and the Indo-Canadian Mafia have a working relationship," he says. "However, they're rivals and always attempt to undermine each other's territory."

Singh reminds me of my third-grade teacher who always kept her eyes on me to make sure I was listening.

"Mob bosses act first, and settle their differences later." Singh continues, "Most of the time, innocent people who are in the wrong place at the right time end up dead."

Then Singh singles me out. "You might want to keep that in mind if you have any thoughts of investigating on your own without proper backup. In today's Vancouver, that would be a big mistake."

"I'll make a note of that," I say with a trace of sarcasm.

"If you need me, I have received permission to travel with you to Canada," Singh says.

He sounds a little too eager to help. I think maybe I should do a little investigating on our new buddy, Singh, but I say, "I don't think we'll need any help in Canada. If we do, Jeff will let you know."

Rajat's phone rings again and he walks over to the window while he whispers into the device.

Jeff looks up from his paperwork. "Think about this, Nick. We should decide now. We're leaving tomorrow, and Singh has experience with the Indo-Canadian drug cartels. He could be a significant help."

"If the NCB is all that good, why doesn't the DEA deal directly with them? Why'd they bring me here?"

"You know we're here to deal with one specific area of drug smuggling. Singh can fill us in on the overall picture to help us get that information."

I'm sure Rajat can hear us talking about him. He comes back to where we are standing.

"I will not be in your way," Singh says. "If you have questions, I will answer. That is my task. I'm not here to do your job. NCB does not want anyone to know I am working with you. I am just another tourist, observing the country. I will wear plain clothes."

"Sound good to you, Nick?" Jeff asks.

"That's fine, but the first time you interfere, you're on the next plane back to India. And lose the black cop shoes. Don't even bring them with you."

Rajat looks down at his shoes and flushes, but says nothing.

Arrangements are made to keep in touch while we get packed and wait for approval for the government flight. Jeff and Singh are still working out details for our Canadian trip when I leave the room.

My plan for arriving early at the Marriott Hotel has fallen by the wayside. I look at my watch. I've probably already missed Daniela, so I stop off at my room.

I'm standing by the window, which overlooks the visitors' parking lot, when Ramos calls back with the information on Daniela's flight to Canada and her hotel accommodations. The connection is much better this time. Still, he hasn't been able to book a Canadian flight for me.

"I can handle it," I tell him. "Yes, I have enough money for now. Maybe you can send funds through Western Union to Mumbai since we'll be returning to India in a few days."

He asks where to send the money.

"There are a number of currency agents close to the airport," I tell him. "The Andhra Bank and Reliance Money Express both handle Western Union."

Looking out the window I see Singh leaving the hotel. He's headed toward his car. "Hold on a minute," I tell Ramos.

I was right. Singh goes directly to the black Ford Escape. He stands outside the car to light a cigarette and make a call. I guess he didn't really give up smoking, but he only takes a couple of puffs before throwing it away. He gets into the government car and leaves his parking space. A lone dark blue Chevrolet sedan appears to be following him. Singh drives to the far end of the lot and stops. The dark blue car stops behind him. A female in the second car gets out and walks to the driver's side of Singh's Ford.

"Are you still there?" Ramos yells through the phone.

"Yes, give me another minute," I call out to Ramos. I can't see what's going on, but the driver of the second car quickly walks back to her car and leaves the area. Then Singh's Ford also pulls on to the highway.

"Sorry about the interruption," I tell Ramos. "The toilet was running over and I had to turn the water off to stop it." I laugh and add, "I'll call you when I get to Canada."

"Have a safe trip," he tells me.

"I certainly hope so." I end the call.

I call Jeff. "Guess what I just saw?" I put my phone on speaker while I finish dressing.

"What?" he asks.

I explain about the woman following Singh.

Jeff is not concerned. "He probably had someone with him to make sure no one else followed." Jeff pauses. "Could have been his partner; or it might have been his girlfriend."

"If it was his girlfriend, she caught him smoking." I laugh. "Let's keep this little secret just between us until we find out how much we can trust Singh." I slip into my loafers and pick up my car keys while I'm talking. "By the way, Ramos didn't get me a plane ticket. I told him I could handle it."

"I'll take care of it," Jeff says.

"Thanks," I say. "I knew I could count on you."

"I'll get all three of us passes on a government plane. We'll get there ahead of Daniela and this time we'll be more prepared," Jeff says.

"Have you heard anything back from forensics about what they found out from the Taj Hotel?"

"For now, they just have fingerprints on file. We'll get more information later."

"Great, I'll call you when I get back today," I say.

As soon as I hang up, I'm out the door and headed for the elevator. It's almost ten-thirty. If Daniela was out really out late last night, she might still be in her room.

I pull into the parking lot at the Marriott. There aren't many cars. I choose a space in the middle of the lot beside a panel truck. I listen to the last few bars of *Leaving on a Jet Plane* by John Denver before stepping out into the hot sun. The music makes me think about Angela and how long it's been since we've been together. The lyrics don't match our situation, but it reminds me that I'm flying away. I'm gonna call her tonight no matter what happens today.

A Cadillac parks a few rows away from me. A man gets out and walks toward the entrance. I slip on a pair of sunglasses and get out of my car. He turns around and I hear the beep as he uses his electronic key to lock his car. He hesitates when he sees me, but by the time I realize that I'm looking straight at Kadam he turns and continues toward the entrance.

Maybe he didn't recognize me. That's a stupid thought. He saw me at the Marriott, and he got a good look at me the night I tried to follow him from the Taj Hotel. He's not gonna think this is a coincidence. I step behind the panel truck and sneak a peek, but he doesn't look back. He's concentrating on the burgundy Ford Expedition whipping along the edge of the parking lot.

I wait to see what happens.

Just as the valet driver stops the SUV in front of the hotel, Daniela walks out the door with the bellhop. He's pulling a luggage cart loaded with small boxes. The valet gets out of the vehicle and helps load everything into the back of the Ford.

Daniela is dressed in a beautiful multi-colored, floor length saree with a large scarf covering her shoulders. Her hair is pulled back in a plain bun the way Angela used to wear her hair at work, and Daniela isn't wearing any of her gaudy jewelry. She looks positively elegant.

189

Kadam steps in front of Daniela, puts his hand on her arm, and appears to be saying something to her. I reach into my pocket for my new listening device. Their voices are as clear as if I was standing right beside them.

"Get your hands off me." She brushes his hand from her arm.

He leans over and touches one of the boxes. "This is quite a load. Does Samir know about this?"

"Not yet, I'm telling him tonight. They're thank-you gifts for Samir's clients."

"You're sending thank you gifts? I've never heard of doing that for our customers."

"I ship a lot of packages for Samir. I think this gives his business a personal touch."

"Personal touch, my ass," he says. "You think he's stupid. When he catches on, he'll squash you like a bug."

"He won't catch on, unless you tell him."

"Don't worry about me, I keep my nose clean, just remember I gave you fair warning."

"Samir doesn't want to lose the best thing he ever had," she tells her past lover.

Kadam runs his tongue along his upper lip. "You could be right, but is it worth taking the chance?"

She shrugs.

"By the way, I wanted you to know I'm not seeing Sophia anymore. Maybe we could get together again. We used to have some great times. Samir doesn't need to know."

"You think you can just walk in and out of my life anytime you choose?"

"I'm admitting it was a mistake. It won't happen again. I miss you. Think about it. I'll give you call." He smiles.

She looks down at the ground. I think she's gonna cave.

"I'm not going through that again," she says.

Wow! That's a surprise. I'm shocked.

"Take your time," he says. "Think it over. I won't mention anything to Samir about the thank-you-gifts. He's not like me. I don't think he would appreciate your thoughtfulness."

It sounds like he's giving her an ultimatum.

The bellhop closes the back of the SUV and Daniella settles into the driver's seat. Kadam follows her to the driver's side open window.

I walk back to my car so I'll be ready to follow her. I think Kadam has caught her shipping drugs without Samir's knowledge and making a hefty profit on the side, and Kadam is using it to get back into her good graces.

She blows him a kiss. "I'll think about it."

Kadam turns away and goes into the Marriot. He seems to spend a lot of time at this hotel. Maybe the bar is part of a money laundering association.

We don't go far before Daniela pulls up to a FedEx store and goes inside. I park a short distance away on the other side of a tourist van. A few minutes later, she returns with a young man pushing a dolly. He unloads all her boxes and moves them inside the building. She's in the store for a long time while I wait outside in the sweltering heat.

When Daniela finally comes out, she goes next door to a coffee shop. I wait until she's inside before I cross the parking lot and go into FedEx.

"Excuse me." I say to the clerk. I point to the SUV sitting out front. "I work for Miss Diaz. She asked me to find out how soon her packages will arrive at their destinations."

"I already told her seven days to the U.S. That's what she paid for," the clerk says.

"Thank you," I tell him. "I guess she forgot. I'll give her the information."

A few of Daniela's boxes are still sitting beside the counter. I can see three of the addresses. They're being delivered to small town independent pharmacies in the U.S.

I hurry back to my car to write down the name and address of the one pharmacy I can remember. I look up and see Daniela in a window seat. She appears to be eating a sandwich and drinking something. I pull out of the parking lot and head for the exit. I hope she doesn't notice my car.

I stop before I reach the highway and wait until the Expedition leaves the parking lot. Then I follow. Two cars turn off the road and for a short distance I'm directly behind her.

Her hand is resting on her side mirror with a cigarette between her fingers. This time I write down the license plate number for Jeff. If Daniela always drives the same car, the NCB should already have the Ford's plate number.

Today, we are taking the highway, so I back off and give her more space. Places begin to look familiar. We have arrived in Dharavi, but we have traveled here on a different road.

It appears we are going to the pharmaceutical company's corporate office. Then she passes right by the building without even slowing down. Now I'm a long way behind her and the street is filled with traffic. I wonder if Daniela passed the building because she thinks she's being followed.

To be on the safe side, I wait until she stops for a red light and then I cut through an alley to the next street. Traffic is heavy and I pull in between a couple of fast-moving vehicles and the second car blasts his horn. I give him a thank you wave and he gives me the finger. He rides my bumper for the next two blocks until I turn again to go back to the street Daniela is driving on. I need to catch up quick, or I might lose her.

Thankfully, she's still traveling on the same street. Even though she drives slowly, she stays in the fast lane, and cars are continually beeping their horns and passing her on the right. I stay mostly in the slower lane several cars behind. When the road narrows, she and several other cars turn off the main road into a densely populated area. It's different from the one I was in last night, and not quite as bad. There are larger buildings and trash isn't piled as high. The Mumbai train system runs right through the middle of it.

"Damn." She crosses the tracks and I get stopped by the train. The speedy train is short and doesn't slow down for the crossing. After the train passes, the cars quickly cross the tracks. I continue along the same road.

I look down each street for her car. Soon, the streets become wider. I see a burgundy Expedition parked all by itself in a no parking zone, right in front of a hospital. The sign reads "Lonely Beginnings Orphanage Hospital." I check the license plate. Yep, it's Daniela's. I turn into the parking lot and park behind several other cars and wait.

Soon, Daniela is followed outside by two men. They walk to the back of her car. She pushes the button that opens the rear door. The men take out six medium-sized boxes. I reach for my pocket telescope. On the side of the boxes in large letters is printed "Medical Supplies."

I put the hearing device in my ear. I can hear them talking, but they're speaking in another language. I have no idea what they are saying.

One of the men takes a bundle of bills from inside his jacket. Daniela quickly shoves it into her blue tote bag.

They look around, I guess to see if anyone is watching them. However, there are no other people in the parking lot. I'm slouched down in the seat, and I don't think they can see me behind the other cars.

I can't believe my eyes. Why is she delivering medical supplies to a hospital? If she were making a regular delivery, doctors or technicians or whoever those people are, would not have come outside. This is very fishy. And all that cash. Did I just witness a drug deal?

The men bow, and one of them hugs her. When she drives away, the men go back inside. I believe Daniela is done with her business and will head back to the highway. Still, it takes me almost ten minutes to catch up with her. I can't figure out what this woman is up to. First, she's a loving girlfriend to Ramos. Then, she turns into a shrew, and now this. I don't understand, but I do remember Ramos saying she was a caring person. At the time, I thought he was talking about her helping people, but maybe she is just helping herself.

When I see a few lines starting to form in front of the restaurants, I realize it's already time for dinner. Daylight is slipping away. The amount of vehicles on this road is unbelievable. Daniela and I sit only a few cars apart waiting for an overturned truck to be towed off the highway.

While waiting, I think about the day I missed getting to the hotel early and she was gone. What transpired that day? My mind wanders to the Taj Hotel. Maybe the room she and

Samir shared was used for something besides sex or sleep. I hope Mumbai's forensic team comes up with more than just fingerprints.

Back in town, close to the airport, there is a string of shops. Daniela parks right on the sidewalk and disappears into one of the ladies' apparel stores. Now, I'm sure we'll be detained for some time. I've gone shopping with women before.

I park and window-shop on the other side of the street. Some of the store owners try to coax me inside. I figure as long as I'm here, I'll buy that oversized shirt I need. After I try one on, I decide to wear it.

The day is going by fast and all I had for breakfast was coffee and a roll. I mosey along the sidewalk to a street vendor and get a sandwich and a cold drink.

Ten minutes later, Daniela comes out of the shop. Carrying a small tote bag, she scrambles toward her car, but a cop has been watching it. He meets her on the driver's side and holds up a ticket. She stands on tiptoe and kisses him on the check. He smiles and holds out his hand. She reaches into her purse and hands him several bills. He tears up the ticket.

She gets into the Expedition and pulls out, squealing her tires. It's a wonder she didn't get another ticket. I don't know what she thought would happen, but one could hardly expect a peck on the cheek to cover the price of a parking ticket. I thought she was lucky to get away by paying him off.

This has been quite a day. I'm hoping she will go back to the hotel, but we aren't headed that way. We soon arrive in Mumbai's Meri Jaan district. It is the life of the city with bars, restaurants, and shops.

Daniela wedges her car into a parking space across the street from a string of shops. She crosses the road, strolls toward a shabby door with *Restaurant* printed on it and goes inside. There are no other signs, no windows, nothing—just a door jammed between two shops. I wait a while, but she doesn't come out. I don't know if she's in there eating or even if it's a place of business, but I have to find out. I guess I'll play dumb.

I approach the door and try the handle. It's locked. I knock lightly.

A huge young man opens the door. "Welcome to Baywatch Dance Bar,"

He's built like a bouncer.

Another well-dressed gentleman leads me through a corridor. All I can hear is the soft thump of Hindi film music. When the last door opens, my ears are jarred as the sound ramps up.

"Good evening, sir." A young woman gives me a warm handshake. "Thank you for patronizing our dance bar"

I find myself in a dark room. The noise is deafening. When my eyes adjust to the barely lit area, I can see that I'm at the end of a room with reclining sofas and plush chairs.

The patrons are close to a hundred percent male, but it doesn't appear to be a gay bar. But then one can never be sure. I wonder what kind of business deal Daniela has with this bar, or if it has something to do with drugs.

"I'm just visiting India," I tell the hostess. "This is my first time at a dance bar. Where do I sit?"

"You may sit closer to the dance floor if you like, so you can see better, but it doesn't matter. If you have currency, the dancers will come to you."

She smiles and swishes away.

I sit in a lounge chair, order a drink and watch the dancing girls. They're dressed in traditional *ghagra clolis*, navel-revealing skirts and colorful, low-cut blouses. Basically, they aren't vulgar or dirty.

Women fill the dance floor, but few of them can actually dance. Most only shake their hips. I've never seen anything like this.

Patrons are of all ages. They walk up to the women on the floor and toss paper rupees over their heads. The currency floats around them and flutters to the floor. Wide eyed, I watch them in amazement.

I can see it's not the same for every girl. The prettiest ones attract the most money. One of the employees walks toward my chair. I wonder what he wants.

"Is this your first time at a dance bar?"

I nod.

"How do you like it?" He stoops down beside my chair.

"It's different," I say.

"This is a friendly business." He flashes perfect white teeth as he gives me a phony smile. "We help support the poorer population and appreciate your helping us maintain a better standard of living for the less fortunate. Our average dancer makes about 500 rupees a day. That's 15,000 a month, and helps to feed their families. We thank you for your patronage, but please do not touch our dancers without their consent."

I assure him I won't be touching anyone.

"Some dance bars have rooms where the customer can take his chosen girl, but our dance bar does not encourage prostitution," the young man says. "However, if you have a need, we can direct you to another service."

"Thank you for all the information. Maybe another night," I say. At first I thought he was like a host, but now I think he's more like a marketing manager, although I'm not sure what he's selling.

He stands and gives me a slight nod before he walks away. I return my attention to the dance floor.

A middle aged, expensively-dressed man is seated a few feet away from me. He looks my way and says, "If you see a woman you like, you may walk up and sprinkle her with rupees."

Apparently, he had overheard my conversation with the young man who works here.

"There's no limit or minimum." He waggles his finger at me. "Showering is addictive."

One song ends and another begins, but the women continue to shake their hips.

"Holy Toledo." My hand clamps across my open mouth. It's Daniela. She has come out on the floor and moved into the center of the room. She's changed her clothes and is dancing in the darkness. Her soft, silky negligee is much skimpier than what most of the other women are wearing.

Her almost naked body is beautiful and she can definitely dance. She moves between the transparent sheers, and is the prettiest woman on the floor. Soon, a number of men are showering her with currency. She revels at the attention, winking and blowing kisses to the patrons as she sways to the music.

I don't understand why a woman with all her money would do this. She's gotta be on drugs.

All at once, she moves toward the customers sitting in the chairs. I think she has recognized me as the man who has been following her and is headed straight for me. I know she will make a scene. I panic and stand, preparing for a quick exit.

Instead, she shimmies along the edge of the dance floor until she comes to a cluster of well-dressed men. She stands in the middle of the group. I can't fully see who she is talking, to, but I can hear her loud mouth.

"I thought you'd be here. Does your girlfriend know you're at a dance bar tonight?" She does not wait for his answer. The crowd cheers as she spins back to the center of the room.

I see that Kadam is the man she was berating. He appears embarrassed and leaves the bar without looking back. Tonight would have been a disaster if he had noticed me.

I pay my tab and leave. I've had enough of Miss Daniela for one day.

On my way to the hotel, I call Jeff. Daniela giving medical supplies to the hospital didn't surprise him, but he was interested in the money she got in return.

He asks me to hold on while he puts his mobile on speaker.

"Don't put your phone on speaker. It echoes and I hear everything you say twice."

He tells me he needs to take notes about what I found out.

"How many hands does it take you to write?" I ask.

"What kind of currency was it?" Jeff asks.

"I don't know, but there was a lot."

"Did you take a photo?" Jeff asks.

"No."

"You're some detective. You get evidence dropped right in your lap, and you don't get any kind of proof."

"I was hiding in my car and could barely see what was happening. I couldn't have captured it on a camera or on my phone without them seeing me. Even if I did take a picture of her giving them medicine, even if she charged them money, that would only prove she's a caring person. If she got a look at me, it would have blown the whole case."

"That's true," he says meekly.

"Take your phone off speaker, or I'm gonna hang up." I wait to see what he does.

"Do you always get what you want?"

"That's better," I say. "I have some weird news. I followed Daniela to a dance bar and what a performance she put on. I was really amazed, but I think she only went there to aggravate Kadam. Have you ever talked to the NCB about the dance bars?" I ask.

"Yeah, a number of times, but they say the dance bars are government regulated and have a large hand in the economy. The city patrols the bars, but they're limited as to how much they can do without stepping on someone's toes."

"Bad-a-bing," I say. "That's a dead give-away. If someone can't be stepped on, then you can be sure that someone is getting paid off."

"Why are you so negative about cops?" Jeff asks.

"It could very well be the narcotic squad," I say. "Maybe they operate like the Belize police. They don't appear to answer to anyone and they don't even try to work with the U.S. DEA.

"So what do you think?" I ask Jeff.

"The bars say they're helping the poor," he says, "but the house keeps at least sixty percent of the take, plus whatever they can skim off the top. Still, they say they're not making much money."

"Maybe they're not. You think graft comes cheap? The bars that have sex rooms might have to pay a kickback when someone sends them business. Whether the bars are making money off the women or not, at least the women can make a few bucks without being forced to sell their bodies to feed their families. So they can't be all bad," I tell Jeff.

Jeff says, "The government demands the police check out the bars on a regular basis and make sure the women are provided a way to arrive home safely, but I've heard that many women have been raped. I know of one bar that's suspected of having something to do with a couple of female homicides. Still, the police department claims they have no suspects or leads in either case."

"I imagine it's a big job to cover all the bases. Maybe they do know what's going on. They might be getting a piece of the action just to assure the NCB that everything is on the up and up. Anyway, I just called to tell you I'm on my way in."

"You always take the side of the criminal."

"You have to think like the criminal or you'll never catch him. I'll be in the lobby at five in the morning." I say goodnight and cut the phone off.

When I walk into the hotel, Gus, the hack from Manhattan, is sitting in the lobby.

He stands. "I've been waiting for you." He hands me a note. "This is where you can find Kadam if you need him. Word on the street says he's on someone's shit list and won't be around long. I thought it might be important to you."

"That's nice of you to take the time, but he's of little interest to me." I tuck the note in my pocket.

"Doesn't matter to me," he says. "I finished work, had some free time, so I thought I'd give you a heads up." He tips his cap and heads for the door.

"Wait a minute," I say. "How did you know I was staying at this hotel?"

"That was easy. I just went to the bar at the Marriott. I described you, and asked the bartender if he'd heard about a silver merchant who might be staying at his hotel. He said he didn't know where you were staying, but you came into the bar several times in the last two days."

"Was the bartender's name Cano?" I ask.

"Yeah, that's the guy," Gus says. "He mentioned you were a big tipper. Bartenders don't forget guys who are generous. He said he would check his computer because he thought you had used your credit card."

"I didn't use my credit card at that bar," I say.

"While he was doing that, I checked with the dining room to see if you had eaten there. The hostess remembered you. She said you came in looking for a friend. She also said you had an eye for pretty women. At least I know I got the right guy."

"So now you believe you have me pegged, but you still didn't know my name."

"That's true. So I went back to the bar. Cano had found your Visa number. You had charged a drink on your card and then had it cancelled. He remembered you had done him a favor. The manager checked with his contact at Visa and discovered you used your visa as identification at *The Latit Mumbai.*"

"I didn't charge anything on the Visa at *The Latit Mumbai,* either."

"Anyway, I figure *The Latit Mumbai* is a pretty good guess, so I stopped by and talked to Amar he's the bell captain and a good friend of mine." Gus grins. "He says not too many big guys wear flowered *abaca* shirts and get in late every night. He calls the front desk and just like that we got a match."

"Are you lookin' for trouble?" I ask him.

"Hold on now," he says. "I came here as a favor to you."

"A favor, you say. I don't even know this Kadam." I stare him down. "You come here tellin' me what some broad says. You check out where I go, what I put on my credit card. Is that your kind of favor?"

Gus turns to leave. "I'm outta here," the gutsy cabbie says.

"No, wait. I wanna know what this is all about. Why is some woman I don't know talking about me?"

"She's a nice lady. She didn't mean any harm. You got this all wrong. I figure you're from the states. You might not have friends over here. I was only being hospitable."

I take a good look at him. Hell, he's just a kid. He can't be much over thirty. "Hey, I'm sorry. I had a bad day. I guess I got carried away. I give him a light punch on the shoulder. "Fuhguddaboudit," I tell him.

He laughs. "Women look at things differently."

"They shouldn't assume," I say.

"Like that's gonna stop." He takes off his cap and fingers it nervously. "The way I understand it," Gus says. "You use your card for identification. It's on the bill. When you pay your bill with cash, the number drops off the bill automatically."

"That's what they tell you," I say. "I'm not so sure that's what happens." I look at Gus. He's smart, college educated and understands cyberspace. I might need him sometime.

"What really bugs me," the tough guy says. "You don't look like a Robert Anderson."

"I've heard that before, but it doesn't matter. Your parents give you a name when you're born and you're stuck with it for life." I laugh.

Gus leaves and I go up to my room. I think about how the savvy taxi driver found me. When Jeff hears this, he'll rip me up one side and down the other for being careless. Even though I don't want to listen to a lecture, I still call Jeff. Good, he doesn't answer. I guess he went to bed. I leave the message about Kadam on his phone.

I look at the clock. It's late and I'm a little high from that drink at the bar. I wonder what they put in that. I'm really too tired to talk to Angela. I'll be closer to Miami if I call her tomorrow from Canada.

CHAPTER NINETEEN
Vancouver, Canada

The government plane scheduled to go to Vancouver is filled with bureaucrats and there is no room for the three of us. We lose four hours trying to get another government flight, but none are available. Undeterred, Rajat calls reservations and purchases tickets on the next commercial jet going to Vancouver, which turns out to be an early evening flight.

He hangs up the phone. "Grab your gear. We got seats."

"Good." Jeff hurries out of the hotel and jumps into the driver's seat of my rental car. "We should take our recording equipment with us," he tells Rajat.

"We won't need it. Canadian officials prefer to handle the electronics themselves." Rajat climbs warily into the passenger seat.

"Are you sure?" Jeff asks.

"Yeah, I'm sure. Do you think I'd guess about something like that?" Rajat looks at me standing outside the car. "Are you going to get in?"

"Where are the keys?" Jeff asks.

"It's none of your business," I say.

"Oh, here they are—in the ignition," Jeff tells me. "Come on, jump in. It's late."

I'm waiting for him to get out of the driver's seat and he doesn't even notice.

Finally he says, "You don't mind if I drive, do you?"

"You wreck it, you pay for it."

"Didn't you buy insurance?" Jeff asks.

"I bought the bare minimum. I'm a good driver." I crawl into the back seat.

"What's Daniela's flight number?" Jeff asks me. "This number sounds familiar."

"I don't know." I want no part of the plan that Jeff and Rajat Singh have put together. If I'm going to get mixed up with criminals, I want to be the one in control of my destiny.

Jeff looks at me in the review mirror. "I gave you the information."

This conversation reminds me of a family vacation. We haven't even gotten off the ground and already we're disagreeing.

"You showed me the information, but then you kept it. I don't have a photographic memory." I hope I don't have to listen to this all the way to Canada.

"I'm sure I gave you the paper with her flight number on it." Jeff roots through a handful of papers while driving.

"What's the difference?" I say. We're gonna go anyway. I'm more worried about how I'm supposed to hide from this dame on the plane. She could have seen me at any given place while I was following her.

At the airport, Jeff checks the flight number and grabs the first person in authority that he can locate. He shows him our credentials and we are ushered through security and allowed to go directly to the plane, which is already in the boarding process. We stand in line with our boarding passes.

All of a sudden, Jeff locates Daniela's flight schedule. "I knew it," he says. "I never forget a number. This is Daniela's flight. It must have been delayed."

According to the man next to us, it was held up for an air conditioning problem.

"I hope it was fixed correctly and is able to cool the plane," Jeff says.

"You should be happy it was delayed or we still wouldn't have a plane." We move slowly toward our seats. "I'm surprised we're allowed to keep our weapons with us," I whisper.

"Don't look so smug," Jeff says. "If there are any terrorists on the plane, it has now become our responsibility to subdue them."

While we are stowing our bags in the overhead bin, Rajat's phone rings.

"Please turn your phone off," the airline attendant says." I'll let you know when you can turn it back on."

"Are you in love with that girl?" I ask Rajat.

"Nah, I just moved in with her so I'd have a place to stay. I never call her, but she calls me all the time. I don't tell her not to call because she pays all the bills. She's so jealous. I can't talk on the phone unless she knows who it is."

"Maybe you should get a place of your own."

"And pay rent? Forget that." He stretches his neck. "Have you seen Daniela?"

"No, she's probably busy. Fortunately, you and Jeff have never met Daniela because neither one of you could keep your mouth shut long enough to hide your ugly pusses," I mutter as I move along with the other passengers.

"What did you say?" Jeff asks.

"Nothing, I'm just admiring the beauty of this secret mission."

Luckily our seats are scattered. Jeff and Singh look like frightened owls, their big eyes searching every passenger who might meet their criteria of what a terrorist should look like. They'd make good extras in a movie scene about a plane crash.

We were told Daniela is working in first class, but I noticed she wasn't in the greeting group when we entered. She must be busy making drinks for her rich passengers. Later, I see her coming up the aisle, but she only comes part way to speak to another attendant, and then goes back to first class. Thank God she never goes anywhere near Jeff and Singh. They'd probably stop her to ask a question. I turn my head and look out the window. We're flying above the clouds and it's a beautiful night.

Rajat calls ahead to Canada's law enforcement and when we arrive the next morning, we are met by two men from the Serious Organized Crime Agency. A quiet gentleman named Theo, who sports a gray, chin strap beard, and a younger guy—fresh out of college—called Nathan are waiting for us. We start to follow them through the terminal.

I touch Jeff's arm and step into a men's room. Jeff follows me. I stop just inside the door.

"What's wrong?" he asks.

"I don't want to walk through the airport with these men. Some unscrupulous drug dealer might think I'm associated with law enforcement. Tell the agents I'll walk a short distance behind."

"What are you scared of?" Jeff asks.

"I'm not afraid, but if I happen to follow Daniela inside some place, I don't want a depraved drug smuggler with a .45 automatic waiting to blow my brains out."

"No one's gonna be watching for you," he says. "We're only going to a government office where SOCA is now located. This agency and several others are in the process of being combined into one force, so the organization is somewhat in limbo. We're obligated to get approval to do any investigating in Canada." Jeff shuffles his feet. "They're not sure which forms we need to use, so this may take awhile."

"You missed the point." I glare at him. "And why do we need approval to visit Canada? I thought the U.S. and Canada were buddy-buddy."

"Apparently you don't understand how protocol works." Jeff glares back.

"We're not questioning anyone. I'm just looking around to see if a girl is cheating on her fiancée. I'm not gonna arrest her. She won't even know I'm here."

"What about the drug smuggling?" Jeff asks.

"If I see anything that the DEA wants and I tell them, it's just hearsay. It's not legally binding. Once I get the information, it's up to the DEA to prove its validity. That's when you need approval."

"I can't do anything about it now," Jeff says. "There's paperwork that has to be filled out."

"There wouldn't be any paperwork if I had come alone. I'd just be a tourist."

"You'd be a tourist with a gun. They wouldn't let you on the plane." Jeff looks in the mirror and smoothes his hair.

"You wanna borrow my comb?" I swear, Jeff is turning out to be another Joe Gaetano.

We go to the parking lot and pile into Theo's car. When we leave the airport, we pass a sign that reads, *Vancouver 12 km.* It's not long before we arrive at the Canadian government office. We walk along a massive corridor until we reach the office we're looking for. Quite a few people mill around ahead of us. We're given a number and directed to sit. Instead Rajat, Theo and I go to the cafeteria for coffee while Jeff and Nathan wait for our number to be called.

Theo is a sociable fellow with a French accent and wayward gray hairs that protrude from his nose and ears. He smiles a lot and rocks a little when he talks.

"You come a long way to investigate a girl," Theo says.

"That's true," I say. "But she's special and plans to marry a good man. He's a little older than her, so he's not sure she's serious about the relationship."

"Ah," he nods. "The groom is jealous?"

"No, he's more like curious and cautious."

"You might only be looking for a promiscuous young lady, but anyone asking questions in Vancouver is seen as an intruder." Theo shakes his finger in my direction. "Be careful. Life has changed here. Vancouver used to be tolerant, but now marijuana nets more than six billion a year and is controlled by organized crime gangs. They do not like outsiders."

"All I want to do is look around. I won't ask any questions unless it's how to get from one place to another," I tell Theo.

"Sometimes it's just the area you ask about that makes them jumpy." He smiles. "The city might be a safer place for you than the outskirts."

"Why do you say that?" I ask.

"I tell you because it is not safe to be outside the city alone. Criminals now grow marijuana in unoccupied houses, barns and industrial buildings. When the crop is ready, sometimes another gang violently 'grow rip's' the place, by pulling the plants out of pots and stealing the harvest."

The aging man gently rubs his chin. "When this happens, whoever is tending the garden, or anyone else who is around is killed. Then it's up to the police, landlords and real estate agents to clean up the mess."

"That's interesting," I dead-pan.

"Our drug thieves are hardened criminals, and their numbers seem to double every year. I'll be happy to retire soon," he adds.

"How do they grow plants inside a building?"

"They use 1,000-watt light bulbs just like the tomato growers."

"Where does a person buy high-voltage light bulbs?" I ask.

"You can buy them in damn near any local store, but they're not cheap," Theo tells me. "We can't trace every light bulb sale to see where they're being used. Besides, I believe the store owners are in cahoots with the criminals. They know who buys them for tomatoes and who buys them for cannabis. I have even heard that store owners teach the new cannabis growers exactly how to use them."

"I didn't know that you could use high voltage lamps to grow plants."

"Tomato growers have been doing it for years. Canadian laws were never stringent about what was being grown, but now that drug cartels have moved in, the laws need to be changed to curb the criminal element. That's why we're merging some of our agencies. We need a better grip on the problem."

The Serious Organized Crime Agency turns out to be quite helpful. Before we left India, Jeff had phoned the agency and given them the name of the hotel where Daniela and the three of us would be staying. They have set up a recording system in Daniela's room at the Hyatt Regency.

"I noticed that almost everyone at the agency was speaking English." I tell Theo.

"That's almost a requirement in the police department, because of the influx of not only Americans, but because most of the European's also speak English. Even the Asian community can rattle off enough English to get what they want."

It's not long before we leave SOCA and go directly to our hotel.

A young electronic technician by the name of Liam has a room adjoining mine. He's assigned to stay with the telephone audio and video recording equipment. He tells us that we can hear any conversation going on in Daniela's suite and play it back later. We can also hear both sides of a telephone conversation on the hotel phone. The camera only covers the sitting room, but it's also the only way out.

The SOCA has placed a large screen in my suite. As usual, Daniela has a suite all to herself. Unless she has company, we don't expect to hear much in the way of conversation.

My room is next to Daniela's, and Jeff's is across the hall. Singh's room is next to the parking lot so he can see if she leaves the hotel—that is, if she rents a car. If she uses a cab, he'll have to take up reading in the lobby.

The equipment is already recording, and Daniela is talking to someone on her cell phone. I wonder why I can only hear her side of the conversation. I glance over at the technician.

"They're working on the mobile now," Liam says without my even posing the question. "I believe the call in progress is connected to India. She had her phone on speaker when a female answered. She asked the other woman where she was, and the woman said Mumbai, but then she turned the speaker off."

"Turn up the volume," I tell him.

"Sophia, are you still at your apartment?" Daniela asks before leaving the sitting room and going into the bedroom. We can still hear her, but we can't see her.

I wish she were talking on the hotel phone.

"Stop crying. I can't understand what you're saying," Daniela snaps.

She is amazingly quiet, so I don't know if the girl is crying or talking. I'm wondering if she has hung up. I look up on the screen, but no one is in the sitting room.

I hear a light knock on my door.

"Who's there?" I ask.

"Jeff."

Then I see Daniela on the screen leaving her bedroom and returning to the sitting room. She's still talking on her cell phone while she looks out the window.

When I open the door, Jeff and Singh come in. I touch the machine and point my finger toward my ear so they'll listen.

"Oh, my God! I can't believe you're still in India." Daniela says. "But you still have time to make tonight's flight."

For a minute Daniela is quiet.

"Daniela is talking to the woman from Columbia that she and Jorge were discussing when they had that terrible argument at Ramos' house," I tell Jeff.

"You know that stuff only stays in place for a day or two." Daniela says. "You need to take care of your responsibility." More silence. "Why didn't you tell me your car won't start? We can fix that. I'll call Kadam. He'll come over and take you to the airport." Daniela taps her fingers on the chair while she appears to be listening to the woman.

"We need to find out where this Sophia woman is before she does what Daniela wants her to do," I tell Jeff and Rajat. "We should get her out of India."

"If the NCB still has Kadam on their radar, they can pick him up and make him tell them where she is." I pull the note Gus gave me from my pocket. "He may have moved. If they don't know where he is, give them this address."

"They won't do that," Rajat says. "They're getting close to the big guy, If Kadam finds out he's being followed, it will ruin their case."

"Ruin their case? Are you telling me their case, if they even have one, is more important than the woman's life?"

"That woman's a mule. She hides drugs inside her body and transports them into the United States. She's part of the problem," Rajat tells me. "The bad part."

"What if she is being forced to do it?" I ask.

"She could have come to the police for protection," Singh says.

"Yeah and get herself killed quicker." I try to think of a solution.

"Focus, Nick. The reason we're here is to stop all this. We can't blow our cover now," Jeff says. "People who play with fire get burned. There's nothing we can do about it."

"Listen to me, Sophia." Daniela turns on her sweet side. "Stop crying and calm down. Nothing will go wrong. The plastic packets won't break and your stomach doesn't dissolve plastic. When you get back, we can talk."

Evidently, Daniela does not get the answer she wanted because her voice gets louder. "Don't tell me you're not going to Detroit. Of course you're going. It's your job. How do you intend to send money to your family without a job? I'll call Kadam. He'll take care of you."

I wait for Daniela's next reply, but instead her eyes open wide. Daniela loses patience and kicks the baseboard. "Didn't you take the birth control pills I sent?" She gets up from the sofa. "Why not?" She's quiet and seems to be listening to Sophia.

Daniela closes her eyes and takes a deep breath. She speaks softer. "Maybe it would be better if you wait until Kadam gets there." Again, there's silence.

"What do you mean you wanted a baby? I don't care if you're pregnant or not. I trusted you with packets worth two-hundred grand. If you want that baby to have a life, you'll do your job and take the next plane to Detroit, or you'll have more to worry about than being pregnant."

"Did she say pregnant?" I shout. "That does it."

"That does what?" Jeff asks.

"For crying out loud, we need to do something." I turn to Rajat.

He's on the phone talking to his girlfriend again.

"Tell that girl good-bye," I say. "If we get an address, you need to call the NCB in Mumbai and have the police pick her up so no one can get to her," I tell him. "If she's already swallowed the drugs, they may have to take her to a hospital."

"Take it easy, Nick," Jeff says. "We don't have an address or even a last name."

Abruptly, Daniela gets up and paces back and forth between the bedroom and the sitting room. Then she sits down sideways on a chair and crosses her legs.

"Nice gams," Rajat says.

I glare at him.

"Are you out of your mind?" Daniela shouts. "You don't just walk away from a job you've been paid to do." Daniela fans herself with a small magazine. "I'm sending Kadam to see that you get on that plane. Are you listening to me?"

All my life I've done things I've regretted. I don't care if it does interfere with India's drug case. This time I have a chance to change the outcome and save a woman's life. All I have to do now is find a way.

I don't know what the woman says next, but Daniela slams the phone against the heavy sideboard. We hear a loud crash. Daniela looks at the cell phone in disbelief.

"Oh, my God," she cries out. The phone is scattered on the floor in little pieces. Daniela's face scrunches. She crawls on the floor on her hands and knees picking up the black plastic and trying to put the broken phone back together, but there's no hope. The phone has completely cracked apart.

She's swinging her arms and screaming at the top of her lungs. We try to figure out what she is saying, but nothing she says makes any sense. Then Daniela goes into the bathroom and all we hear is cursing.

"Maybe now she'll use the hotel phone," Jeff says.

"I doubt it," Rajat says. "Maybe she'll look for a pay phone."

"You think she'll make a long-distance call about drugs with people standing close by." Jeff says. "No way."

We all sit and stare at the blank screen.

It's almost thirty minutes before she returns to the living room. She must have taken a shower because her hair is wet. Just as Jeff expected, she makes a call to Kadam. Maybe she'll tell him where to pick up Sophia. Before I can ask, the technician is already calling in for a trace on the line. I'm impressed.

When he answers, the first thing she says is "I'm on a hotel phone."

"Smart girl, but not smart enough," I tell Jeff.

"You need to pick up Sophia," Daniela tells Kadam. "She's freakin' out. She doesn't want to go to Detroit."

"That's not my problem." Kadam's voice comes over the speaker. "You brought her in. You're responsible for her."

I glance at Liam and hold my thumb up. He's doing a great job.

"Not anymore," Daniela spits back at Kadam. "You took over that obligation when you moved in with her."

"I heard she's pregnant, but I'm telling you right now, it's not my kid. I haven't even seen Sophia in over six months. Mehta made me move out. He's her point of contact now. Maybe there's something going on between the two of them."

"You expect me to believe that he sees anything in that idiot?" Daniela laughs.

"Call Samir. Check it out," he says.

"You know I'd never accuse him of that, besides right now that's not the problem. Samir promised delivery today. My shift got changed and I was a day late getting here. I picked up the packets late that night and delivered them the next morning to the couriers before noon. I thought everyone left India that day. I just found out that Sophia didn't go."

"Sounds like something she'd do." Kadam coughs. "Your plane was scheduled to get in early. Why didn't you make the delivery the night you got here?"

"Humph." For a moment, Daniela holds the hotel phone away from her ear. She takes a deep breath. "If you must know, after I lost a full day in the states the plane was again delayed and it got in late. I tried to call everyone from the plane, but the calls wouldn't go through. When I missed the connection time the bitches thought the deal was off, and they hightailed it for places unknown. It took me until noon the next day to find them. Hell, I didn't even get two hours sleep."

"Maybe you should reconsider my offer," Kadam says. "Then I'd help you."

"Are you smoking one of those big fat cigars?"

"Yep," he says.

"No wonder I can hardly understand what you're saying."

"I ain't said much," his words flounder.

"I want you to make her take care of business, and see that she gets on the plane," Daniela snaps.

"I understand what you're saying, but I can't go over Mehta's head. Besides, she won't listen to me. Someone else is telling her what to do. I think it's that guy from South America. Samir told me she's been flying home once a month and staying for a few days."

"What guy in South America?" Daniela asks.

"I don't know his name. I think he's from a place called Medellin."

Daniela's jaw drops. She reaches for a chair and sits down.

"I don't mind handling this situation," Kadam says. "However, you need to get approval from Mehta first because I've got a funny feeling about this. He hasn't been answering my calls. Something stinks."

Give him the address, I say over and over in my mind. I repeat my appeal again and again, hoping that somehow my pleading thoughts will travel to her subconscious. Of course they can't hear me and they never give the address.

"You're paranoid," she tells Kadam. "If Samir was upset about anything he would have told me. Do what I tell you or he'll really get pissed when Detroit calls him. You're lucky they called me first."

"The last guy Mehta refused to call back ended up dead," Kadam says. "I told you, I'm not gonna cross him."

"You're just lookin' for an excuse," Daniela tells him. "I'm tired, and I don't need this crap. Get your butt over there right now or I really will call Samir."

Kadam gives in. "It's too late to get an airline ticket for tonight. I'll call now and make a reservation for in the morning. I'll get a straight through flight. She'll be in Detroit at the same time as if she left tonight and had to change planes."

"Okay, if you're sure she'll be in Detroit tomorrow, I'll call and get them to agree to wait another day."

"I'm sure they'll agree," he says.

"Thanks Kadam, I owe you."

"You're damn right you do."

Daniela hangs up the phone but the recorder continues to spin slowly.

Singh looks at me. "Now do you see what we're up against?" He struts across the room with an air of importance. "A year ago, India's police force thought the Punjabi Mafia was less organized than many of the traditional crime families, but now they've adapted and tussle over turf for the lucrative drug trade."

"Your scenario doesn't play into what I'm looking for," I say. "The DEA thinks they know the man who is shipping drugs into the US. They asked me to get inside his organization, and I did. Instead of him wanting me to help him move drugs, he sent me here to check on his girlfriend. I'm not interested in the world's drug problems. I'm just looking to see if Daniela's cheating on him and whether Ramos has any drug connection in India that would be of interest to the DEA."

Rajat lights another cigarette off the butt before putting it out. "I just thought you'd like some background information," he says. "Vancouver has become a mecca for drugs. The city has many organized crime factions. Punjabi Mafia, Indo-Canadian Mafia and the Asian Mafia are the major players and the way law enforcement has been deteriorating, you don't always have someone watching your back."

"That's exactly why I like to work alone," I mumble.

"I understand your point, but people are being murdered just because they look like they might be a threat," Rajat says. "Every day someone dies and many are police officers."

I turn to Rajat. "You said you wanted to come along to help, so this is what I need done. Call the NCB now. Have them make up something to detain Kadam and hold him until we get back to India. He sounds scared to me. Have them offer him something to tell them where this Sophia is, then get her to safety."

Rajat hesitates. "They're not going to do that."

214

"Tell them the U.S. DEA has made the request," I say.

"Wait a minute," Jeff says. "You're not the DEA."

"The ambassador said I was in control of this venture and that I could do it my way without any interference." I turn to Rajat. "I'm running this show. Make the call."

Liam winks at me. "This is a direct line to India's NCB." The technician hands Rajat a headset.

I give Liam a high-five. I like this guy.

Rajat reluctantly makes the call and gets the ball rolling. "This plan is gonna backfire and I'm gonna get the blame."

"That's what rookies are for." I say.

"How many times do I have to tell you? I'm not a rookie. I've been a patrolman for ten years. I just got transferred to the NCB."

"Which, as far as drugs are concerned makes you a rookie."

"It's true that I haven't had a lot of experience with drugs, but—"

"I rest my case." I walk over to the recording machine. "Now let's get back to the problem at hand."

CHAPTER TWENTY

I doubt if Kadam will say anything to the cops about an American following him around and put himself under more suspicion. I guess it depends on how the NCB handles the questioning. With any luck, Kadam might not have put two and two together yet, but then maybe that's just wishful thinking.

"I need some air." Rajat leaves the room.

Daniela comes into her sitting room. She paces the floor and looks at her watch every few minutes. Several times, she puts her hand on the hotel phone, but walks away without making a call. Rajat returns smelling like cigarette smoke.

Time passes slowly. I pick at my cold room service breakfast, but mostly I drink coffee and wait.

"How long is it going to take before they pick up Kadam?" I ask Singh.

"The NCB notified me that they had already picked up Kadam and took him in for questioning on a bogus auto theft charge. They led him to believe they were detectives looking for a stolen car. A bureau detective is going to question him. I'm still waiting to hear if they've been able to convince Kadam to tell them the address where they can find Sophia."

"From now on, whenever you have any contact with the NCB I want to know about it immediately," I tell him.

"Okay," he says. "They haven't found out anything yet. I wasn't withholding pertinent information from you."

It's almost noon when Daniela picks up the hotel phone, again. We wait to see who she calls.

A female answers. "Felix's Vitamins and Nutriments."

"Let me speak to Felix," Daniela says.

"He's with a client. Maybe I can help you?"

"No, you cannot help me. I want to talk to Felix," Daniela snaps.

"May I tell him whose calling?"

"Daniela."

"And your last name?" the woman asks.

"Just tell him Daniela. He knows who I am."

"One moment please," she says. After a few seconds the woman comes back on the line. "Please hold. I'll transfer your call."

I hear one click, and then two seconds later a second click.

Liam says, "The woman has transferred the call from the downtown exchange center to the northern exchange center."

Soon we hear a man's voice. "Felix Bouchard," he says.

"Felix, darling," she purrs. "I'm in Vancouver."

"That's wonderful. I can't wait to see you."

"Come to the hotel now?" She plays with the phone cord, twisting the curly wire around her finger while she talks.

"Well, not right now. I'm in the middle of a meeting."

"I'll come there," she says.

"No, you can't come today. I'm having lunch with my wife."

"Cancel lunch. Tell her you have to entertain an important client and come to the hotel."

"Hey, babe." He slides into a persuasive demeanor. "It's not that easy. You know how it is. I don't want her to get suspicious."

"What's the difference?" Daniela huffs. "You're gonna divorce her anyway."

"That's true, but it won't be this year and I don't want to live in misery until my kids are grown."

"Your kids are only babies. It'll be years before they're grown."

"And until then, unless I get custody, I'm staying where I'm at. I thought you understood that."

"That's not what you told me. You said you loved me and wanted to be with me." She sinks into the wingback chair.

"And I do, but only if I get my kids. I don't want another man raising them. You promised to be patient. Give me a little time. I can work this out."

"Am I going to see you this trip?" she whines. "I'll only be here a couple of days."

"I'll be over tonight, but it will be late."

"How late?" she asks.

"I don't know. I have to see how things go today. I have an expensive shipment coming in late this afternoon."

She takes a different approach. "Please get someone to handle it." She begs.

"I need to do this myself," he says. "It's important."

Theo's ears perk up. "I need to notify SOCA. They've been trying to get concrete evidence on Bouchard for two years. This time they can catch him red-handed."

"Shh...I put my finger to my lips. "I wanna hear this."

"I'm coming over there right now," she says.

"Please, don't do that." His plea goes unnoticed.

"Do you love me?" she asks.

"Of course I do. I bought you a diamond ring, didn't I?"

"Does that mean you're coming to the hotel?"

"Listen to reason. I have a business to run."

There's a monumental pause and then Daniela says, "How would you like it if I called your wife and told her all about us?"

"Don't threaten me," he growls.

"It's not a threat. It's a promise."

Well, at least I now have evidence that shows her intent is to only marry Ramos for his money. After she gets what she wants, she will either divorce him or knock him off. By the time this guy is ready to leave his family, Ramos might already be broke or maybe dead.

Bouchard's voice softens. "I'll take you out to dinner."

She giggles. "That's better. See you at eight." She hangs up the phone. "I guess I straightened him out," she says to the walls.

When the call ends, I look at Theo. "What do you think of that?"

"It takes all kinds." Theo says. "I need to call the SOCA and let them know I'm on my way to see them."

"I'll go with you," Singh says.

"You have no jurisdiction here in Canada," Theo tells him.

"Wait a damn minute." Singh puts his hand on Theo's arm. "You wouldn't have this information if I hadn't asked the SOCA to set up the recording session."

"Save your complaining for someone else. I'm busy today." Theo looks at Nathan. "You stay here. If anything new happens on this case, let me know immediately."

"Yes, sir. I will." Nathan looks at the recording technician. "I'll stay close to Liam."

I glance at Theo, and then stare at the floor. I know he's right. He works for SOCA, and he has every right to do his job.

"Robert," Theo says. "Come with me."

Stunned, I look at Jeff.

"I'm on it," Jeff tells me. "I'll hang out with Nathan and Singh and keep in touch with you."

Theo and I go out the door and head for the SOCA. It's only a short drive. We arrive at the same complex we were at earlier, but we go into a different building.

When we arrive at the command post, Theo gets permission to speak with one of the high officials, Commander Leo St. Onge.

"*Bonjour*," the Frenchman says as we enter his office. He comes from behind his desk and embraces Theo, kissing him on each cheek. "It has been a long time since our paths have crossed. It's good to see you again, but what is this urgent information you have for me?" St. Onge gives me a disdained look, so Theo introduces me.

"This is Robert Anderson. He is a private investigator from the United States. His only concern is Daniela Diaz, a young lady who is planning to marrying a rich man in Belize. The groom has hired Mr. Anderson to acquire some personal information about the lady. I was assigned to accompany him during his visit to Canada, because—as I'm sure you know—she has been seen in the company of Felix Bouchard."

Leo St. Onge shakes my hand and returns to his chair behind the desk. Although there are two comfortable chairs for our convenience, we continue to stand in front of him.

"We have a covert listening device that the SOCA set up. It is running in Miss Diaz's hotel room and we overheard a conversation between Diaz and Bouchard," Theo tells him. "I do not know if this has anything to do with drugs or not, but he said he was unable to come to see her at the hotel because he was expecting an expensive shipment this afternoon that only he could accept."

"Are you suggesting that he has a shipment of drugs coming in?" St. Onge asks.

"I don't know. Mr. Anderson says he has reason to believe that Miss Diaz, who is an international airline stewardess, is more than just a friend of Felix Bouchard," Theo says. "We know trucks come and go all the time when he is not there. So I thought it strange that he would not put someone else in charge of the shipment rather than tell his lady friend he would see her later. That is my only motivation for coming here. The decision is up to you."

St. Onge's forehead wrinkles. "This is a tough call to make. The truck could be arriving as we speak."

"I have positioned a small detail to watch his place ever since we got the information and we are in constant contact," Theo says. "It has not yet arrived."

"Please be seated," the commander says. "Allow me to discuss this latest matter with the men who are working on this case. I'll be right back."

Theo gets nervous when twenty-five minutes go by.

I get a call from Singh. "How is it going?"

"We don't know yet. We're waiting for the commander to make a decision."

"Will you call me when he decides?" Singh asks

"Quit worrying. I'm not looking to make headlines. I'll make sure the NCB knows it was your idea to search and seize. Does that make you happy?"

"Well, it is the truth."

"I'm not positive, but it looks like we are going to go in. Don't call me anymore. I got more important things to think about." I end the call.

A few minutes later, St. Onge returns. "I apologize for taking so long. This is a grave move. My men are going to observe the situation from a distance and make their decision to advance based on what happens when the shipment arrives. Under the circumstances I have given my permission for you to go with them as observers if you care to do so."

I turn toward Theo. "Whadaya think?"

Theo nods.

"They'll move out in ten minutes. They're leaving from exit seven," he tells Theo.

Theo leads the way. We go out the door, down the steps, and through a long hallway that leads to exit seven. We rush through the door into the Ready Room and find about twenty men dressed similar to American S.W.A.T. team members.

One of the men advances toward us. "Are you Nick and Theo?

"My name is Robert Anderson." I extend my arm.

He shakes my hand. "I'm Captain Roy." He points across the room toward a guy. "My newest recruit saw you when you came in the front door. He says your name is Nick."

I glance to where he is pointing. It's the US FBI administrator, William Randolph Slovak who filled out my walking papers with the name Robert Anderson years ago.

"What's he doing in Canada?"

"He lives here now and works for us."

I can't believe it. I go halfway around the world to get away from my past, only to run into probably the one man who might recognize me in a mustache and beard.

The new recruit comes over and shakes my hand. "Nice to see you're on the right side of the law. The program has been good for you."

I don't know what to say. I hated Slovak's guts, still do, and now I'm gonna have to work with the son-of-a-bitch.

"How soon are we leaving?" Theo asks the captain.

"We're headed out right now."

Men are picking up their equipment and running outside to the trucks. The first three men are shouldering large shotguns.

I look at Theo. "What the hell are they going to do with those?"

"Those are breaching guns. When we have to get in quick, they can take down almost any door."

Guys with SMG's, like Ramos's men, jump into the second truck.

"What's with all the fire power?" I ask Theo. "I've never seen anything like this."

"You should recognize the guns." He laughs. "They're just bigger and more powerful than the machine guns the mob used to carry."

"Maybe I'll just hang around here until you get back," I tell Theo.

"Come on," he says. "Are you gonna let a little modern equipment make you miss all the fun? When we get back I'll have one of our men demonstrate that shotgun for you."

"That won't be necessary. I'm not into heavy artillery."

Theo grins. "This is not heavy artillery. Haven't you ever been in the military?"

"When I was eighteen the military was made up of volunteers. I guess I just didn't think about it. It's not that I don't appreciate what they do. Strange as it may seem, I was never really into guns. They've always just been a means to an end."

"Relax," he says. "These are a good bunch of youngsters. They're out cleaning up the streets every day. They have the best equipment money can buy." He urges me toward the first truck. "Watch your step." He points toward the men with weapons in front of us. "Their SMG's are air-cooled, magazine-fed and designed to fire pistol cartridges. They are one of the safest weapons around."

Theo and I pile into the first of two large armored trucks. Theo tells me that the men in our truck are carrying Heckler & Koch MP5's. He's proud of the Canadian Brotherhood. The two trucks travel almost bumper to bumper on a main highway, not fast, but at a steady pace. The trucks have dark windows that allow you to see out, but no one can see in. I watch the traffic as it goes by. Only a couple of small boys turn to look at the trucks. No one else seems to pay any attention.

Naturally, Slovak, the former US FBI employee, has settled into the seat next to mine. He appears to want to chat, but I keep my head turned toward Theo.

"Don't worry about your name," he whispers. "The only people who know your real name are me and the captain."

I turn and glare at him. "And Theo, and anyone else the three of you care to tell just to impress someone. This shows me just how secret the program really is."

"Don't hold a grudge. I was only doing my job. I guarantee not one of these men will ever mention it again."

"Look, Slovak, you're not in charge today, and I really don't want to talk to you, so don't bother me."

We arrive at an industrial park. It's full of every kind of building imaginable. When we reach a Quonset hut, the trucks stop. A sign on the front of the building reads "Johnson's Truck Repair Center." The door automatically opens, and we pull in.

"Well, isn't this convenient," I say.

"Yes, it is, and I'm no longer with the FBI. I'm just a member of this squad, so call me Bill," he says. "The hut was built here to be close to the building Felix Bouchard does business in. The SOCA has a phony business operating out of here just as a cover in case we need it. There is always room for our two trucks to pull in."

"Don't you think Bouchard is smart enough to have someone watching this building?" I ask Slovak.

"We bring these trucks here on a regular basis and we ignore his building. The repair shop has been here for five years, and we have never executed a raid, but we do have hidden cameras close to the ceiling, so we pretty much know what's going on at his place. They see these same trucks every day. I don't think they pay attention to them anymore."

As soon as the trucks stop, the men jump out. They exit through a side door and creep through thick foliage and stop at the edge of the clearing.

The men all wear high-powered binocular glasses to see exactly what's going on from a distance. The only noise is a fifteen mile-an-hour wind that's blowing in from the Pacific.

It's late in the day when a medium-sized truck pulls into Felix's parking lot. The roll-up door on the back of the truck goes up.

"Let me look through your high-powered glasses," I say to Theo.

The building is far enough away from the highway so that anyone who happens to pass by can't see into the back of the truck, but the high-powered binoculars allow the narcotic agents to see four men lurking inside. Each one is packing a weapon. Piled high behind the men are white brick-size packages.

The driver of the delivery truck goes to the door and pushes the buzzer. The door opens and Felix Bouchard is standing inside. He motions for the man to come in, and then closes the door. When the man comes back outside, he is carrying a black bag. He climbs into the driver's seat and lifts what appears to be a metal lid where the passenger seat usually is. The bag disappears from sight, and he closes the lid. It takes a minute, so we think he must be locking up some type of vault.

The huge garage door opens and the truck pulls inside. After the door closes, the SOCA men race across the highway. They force open a small door on the side of the building without the help of the breaching guns. Theo and I are right behind them. Theo motions for me to go around the outside of the building on the left side as he goes around to the back on the right side.

The building we have penetrated is much larger than I anticipated. I creep along, stooping so I can't be seen through a window, and pausing before I pass a doorway. Finally, I reach the end of the left side. I hear the faint sounds of the SOCA boys yelling for the drug dealers to hold up their hands. I guess that takes care of everything. Commander St. Onge will be celebrating tonight. I tuck my gun into the holster before I go around the back of the building to find Theo. When I turn the corner, I get clipped on the top of my head with what feels like a leather blackjack. I sink to the ground in a cloak of darkness.

CHAPTER TWENTY-ONE

Some time later, I open my eyes. I'm on the floor in the middle of a large warehouse.

"Who the hell are you?" a grizzly man asks.

I hesitate and pretend I'm still stunned. "I don't know."

"What are you doing on my property?" a different man asks.

I recognized him from the photo Theo had shown me while we were waiting in St. Onge's office. It was Felix Bouchard. "I don't know. Who are you? Where am I?"

"Don't play games with me. You came here with the SOCA."

"What's the SOCA?" I ask.

One of Felix's henchmen smacks me on the side of my head with the back of his hand.

My face slams against the cement. "I'm a silver dealer from The United States. I don't know what you're talking about."

Bouchard kicks me in the ribs. It takes my breath away, and my body doubles-up into a ball. I remember Agent Thompson telling me. "Sometimes you have to talk your way out of things." While I'm getting my breath back I think about a factory I'd noticed on the way to the Quonset hut. It wasn't close, but it's all I had.

"What are you doing here?" Bouchard asks.

"I don't know. I don't even know how I got here."

"You were outside my building, sneaking around. One of my employees dragged you inside."

"The last I remember, I took a cab to Vancouver Metal Importers. The cabbie left me off in front of a building and said it was just a short way down the road. I had just started walking when all these men came across the street and pushed me toward the front of the building. When they scattered apart and stopped shoving me around, I kept on going to get away from them."

"You're an American?" he asks

"Yes," I tell him.

"Then why do you have several sets of identification?"

So they went through my wallet. "It's a long story."

"I got time." He stands over me with a gun pointed at my head.

"When you travel around the world, it helps to have different sets of papers. I went to India to buy silver, and while I was there I became friends with a guy who came into the bar at the Marriot Hotel. When he found out I was coming to Vancouver he told me to look up Vancouver Metal Importers. He said I could get a good buy on gold and silver."

"Don't waste my time with lies. Vancouver Metal Importers doesn't sell gold and silver." Bouchard waves his gun in the air.

"I'm telling you the truth. The guy in India said his friend had previously owned gold and silver that's been melted down. He gave me the company name and address, but he didn't give me a name."

"I never saw any silver or gold at Vancouver Imports," Bouchard says.

"I don't doubt that. Previously owned gold and silver that's been melted down isn't gonna be sitting in a showcase."

"Don't get smart with me." His bleary eyes blink. "You say they're selling stolen property."

"That's not for me to say. I'm a dealer. I buy in one country and sell in another. I have no reason to question where the silver came from."

"What makes you think I'd believe a story like that?" He laughs.

"Please, Mr. ah. . .what's your name?"

"Everybody knows Felix Bouchard."

"Mr. Bouchard. I'm not from around here. I'm an American citizen."

"So how did you get mixed up with the drug authorities you came here with?"

"I'm telling you, I came to buy silver. I swear. I don't know anything about those men in the black suits. At first I thought they were after me."

"So how did you get to my place?"

"I told you. I came in a taxi. I gave the driver the address to Vancouver Metal Importers. He dropped me off on the highway in front of your place."

Felix pulls up a stool, sits down and holds the gun closer to my head. "Whadaya take me for, some kind of fool?"

"It's the truth. The cabbie told me to pay my fare and get out. He said Vancouver Metal Importers was just down the road."

"You would have had a hellava walk to the import company. It's damn near two kilometers from here. Why would a taxi driver tell you that?"

"I don't know. Right after he crossed the railroad tracks, he said he wasn't going any further. He said something about a neighborhood killing." I don't know where I got that thought. There probably haven't been any murders around here in years, and I'll end up trying to convince him that the cab driver was crazy.

"There's nothing wrong with this neighborhood," he says.

I thought he'd say that. Then he surprises me.

"It's the damn newspapers. They've told that same story a hundred times."

"What story?" I ask.

"A couple of old ladies were strangled in broad daylight in an alley down the street from here. The police said it was a serial killer. The local newspaper keeps bringing it up. It happened over a year ago, and people still don't want to go near that place."

Wow! What a reprieve. My brain starts wheeling and dealing.

"I'm not lying. I had just started walking to the metal company when a bunch of men rushed across the highway and damn near knocked me over. I had almost gotten away from their yelling and screaming when something hit my head."

He ignores my plea. "Cops are all alike. You can't trust any of them. Look what they did to you. They let you pay the price, and believe me, you will pay the price."

"I told you. I'm not a cop." I plead with him. "Do I look like a cop?

"Don't try to double talk me." Felix slurs his words.

"Look at the threads. Cops don't have the bread to buy this brand."

He looks me over, giving me a few seconds to think. Then he walks over to the table, picks up my wallet and looks through the cards.

"What's your real name?" he asks

"Robert Anderson. Look at my ID."

He holds up my international driver's license.

"And you say some drunk in a bar sent you to Vancouver Metals?"

"I didn't say he was a drunk. It was a nice hotel bar, filled with businessmen. He just gave me the company name. He said they often dealt with people from the United States."

"And exactly who is this businessman that sent you to Vancouver Metal?"

I think about his question. I have to give him a real name in case he decides to check it out. I know Kadam is in big trouble with the Punjabi Mafia. Hell, Bouchard might even know him, but no matter what Kadam says, he probably won't believe him. His name could be my ticket out of here.

"His name is Kadam," I say.

I begin to sweat. I don't think he's buying my story. Then he walks back to the table and tosses my wallet and cards toward me. The cards scatter on the floor.

"Leecho." He motions for one of his men to come close. "I remember a Kadam. He was with the Punjabi mob. Take this guy's guns and get the hell out of here. I want to talk to him alone."

Bouchard waits until his men leave and the door closes. "Do you want a drink?"

I nod. He pours two large shots of Canadian Club. My hands are tied together in front of me, so I pick up the glass with both hands. I take a large swallow and sit the glass gingerly on the floor.

"Maybe Kadam gave you something to bring to me."

"No, I told you before, I'm a silver dealer. I didn't bring you anything, but if you need something, I'll try to get it for you."

"What do you think a guy like you can do for me?" he asks.

I shrug. "Probably not much, but I'm sorry for this misunderstanding. I only came to Vancouver to buy silver. If you don't sell silver, then I'll leave and be out of your life. I don't want any trouble."

"I think you're lying through your teeth, and I'm going to get the truth out of you."

"Bottoms up," he says.

I watch as he downs the entire glass of liquor. I hear a cat meow. "Is that your cat?" I try to change his mood. "It must be hungry."

"Nah, it's a stray. It came in yesterday. I threw it out three times. It keeps sneaking back in."

Felix takes his gun out of the shoulder holster.

I shudder.

He aims the gun at the cat. "You lie to me and I'll kill you just as quick as I'd kill this cat." With that said, he shoots the cat. The bullet rips the cat apart.

Leecho opens the door. He's holding two pistols ready to fire. He stares at the dead cat.

Felix waves his gun at the man. "Go away."

The guy leaves, banging the door behind him.

"Nice shot," I say. "I couldn't have done better myself."

"You mean you couldn't have done as well." Felix burps.

"I suppose not, especially with my hands tied." Felix pours each of us another large shot. "How come you're totin' heat?"

"If your job was to buy precious metals and gems, wouldn't you carry a gun?"

"Yah." He nods. "Let's talk about this silver business. I want to get this straight. Are you telling me that the owner of Vancouver Metal Importers is a fence for stolen gold and silver?"

"He said they mostly dealt in silver that was why I was interested."

"I always wondered how that family could afford to drive a Mercedes. Tell me again about this silver business you're in. "

I wish now I had eaten more of the food in the hotel room. Booze gets to me on an empty stomach. "It's a funny thing. I've been dealing in silver for many years and no one ever questioned me, but since I've been to India and Canada I've run into a dozen men who want to know about it." I clear my throat.

"How'd you learn about silver?" Felix asks.

"I'm retired military." I swallow hard at the lie. "There wasn't any war going on, so I was able to travel all over the world." I'm glad Theo told me a little about his combat days. Bouchard just might start asking questions. "At first I started dabbling in silver as a hobby. I found out that there are people all over the world who will buy precious metals and gems without asking any questions as long as they are getting it at a good price. When I realized how much I could make I started traveling and in no time, I built a small fortune."

"What about you?" I ask. "What kind of business are you in?"

"Didn't you see the sign on the front of the building?" He frowns, but then he begins to talk. "I distribute vitamins all over the world. I don't make a lot of cash, but I do okay."

"The truth is, right after I got out of the cab, there was so much confusion, I didn't get a chance to look around. All I wanted to do was get out of the way of those guys in black jumpsuits."

He laughs and picks up his drink. "*Viva La France.*"

We toss back our heads and empty the glasses. I don't know exactly what I'm agreeing to, but he's laughing and that's a good sign.

"You got family?" he asks.

"Nope. I had a girlfriend once, but that didn't last long." I know this is a sore subject with him, so I decide to play the devil's advocate. "She always wanted something. No matter what I gave her, she wanted more. Finally, I had enough. I dumped her."

"You dumped her? How'd you do that?"

"I don't talk about it."

"You can tell me," he says.

"Let's just say I'm not the only guy she won't be bothering any more."

"Um, I like you." He tucks the gun back in the shoulder holster and unties my hands and feet.

I pick up my cards and wallet. He waits for me to lunge at him, but when he sat on the stool, I saw the bulge at his ankle. He has another weapon. Besides, his men are just on the other side of the door. I wouldn't get far even if I got a chance to grab his gun. I'd get off a poor shot and the three of them would drop me like a stuck pig.

"I know what you mean about women. I got this girl, and she knows how to please me. Don't misunderstand me, I like her a lot, but she causes me nothing but trouble." Bouchard spits toward the dead cat. "She reminds me of that cat. Always creeping into my brain, into my business, and now she's trying to sneak into my family."

"What are you gonna do about it?" I ask.

"Maybe Kadam sent you here for a reason even if he didn't know why. I believe that everything in life happens for a purpose." The way he correctly pronounces Kadam's name makes me think he really does know him, or at least knows about him.

He fills my glass and drains the rest of the booze into his.

"I think maybe you and me can do a little business."

"I don't believe in vitamins," I tell him.

"Vitamins and silver are for businessmen. This would be more like a favor to me. Even though I don't make a lot of money, I would pay well for this service." He tilts his head backward, and his chin sticks out. "This is very important to me."

He claims he doesn't have a lot of cash, but everything in this extravagant warehouse drips with expensive taste. I don't want to piss him off, but I also don't want to appear

231

overanxious to help him. Then he'd know for sure I was only kissing his ass to get my own butt out of here.

He waits a long time before he speaks to me again.

"You say you don't want to do this favor for me?" He stumbles over his words.

"I didn't say I was opposed to the favor. You haven't even told me what you want me to do."

"You know I could blow you away right now, and no one would ever know what happened to you?" He grins.

I think about all the people who have probably disappeared from this warehouse.

"Why would you put yourself in that position? You're a respected businessman. Looking at this building, I'd say you have a profitable establishment. It's hard to believe you would chance an arrest and the loss of your anonymity just to kill a man who has no interest in your vitamins—or this woman who causes you so much trouble."

"Ah, that's where you're wrong. I can see it in your eyes and hear it in your fancy words. You're contemplating the dollars you can make doing this tiny, little favor." Bouchard winks.

"Even if that were true, you're not obligated to do anything about the thoughts you might be having. The world will continue to turn regardless of your decision," I say.

"I don't care for theories. I like plain talk. I want to know what you can do for me."

"Then you must ask the question, plain and simple." My head throbs. I always get a headache when I drink without eating, or maybe it was that whack on the noggin'."

"How do I know I can trust you?" he asks.

"You don't. It would make more sense for you to have one of your trusted pals do this favor." I jerk my chin toward the closed door.

"Again, you're telling me no." He fumbles for his gun, but doesn't take it out of the holster.

"I did not say no. I am only trying to help you make up your mind."

He's getting drunker by the minute. If he falls asleep, I'm dead meat. I'll never get out of here. "I will do this favor for you, but you must be sober when we make the arrangements."

I'm amazed when he nods.

"If you let me leave today, I'll call you tomorrow and we will make arrangements to meet in a public place—two executives making a deal. You do not trust me to come back, and I do not trust you to pay me. If we never see each other again, what have we lost? Nothing," I say. "If we meet again, we both have a lot to gain. Let's see who breaks this promise."

"Do not have any doubt. We will meet again. My men will find you, no matter where you go."

I shrug. He asks me where I'm staying and I give him the only hotel name I can remember, besides the one I'm staying at.

"There's a hockey game at Roger's Arena," he says. "Come see the Canucks. They will show you how hockey is really played. I have box seats. Buy a cheap ticket and ask anyone where Felix Bouchard sits. They will show you the way. We will watch the game together and close this deal."

"Sounds good to me."

Leecho!" he calls out.

The door opens. Three muscular guys stand shoulder to shoulder. I'm surprised when Felix is able to stand and walk toward them. He whispers a few words, and they come over to where I am sitting. I don't know what is about to happen, but I don't think it will be good.

"Take Mr. Anderson to the Pinnacle Hotel, down by the waterfront." Felix unloads my guns. The bullets fall to the floor. "I don't want anything to happen to this silver dealer. You understand what I mean?"

The one called Leecho says something that sounds like it might be in French, but Bouchard waves him off.

I stand. "Thank you, Mr. Bouchard." I shake his hand. "I'll see you tomorrow,"

He doesn't answer. His strength is gone, and his arm is rubbery.

His men take me down a flight of stairs. When I try to look back, I'm shoved forward by a seedy-looking guy they call Dobbs. We go through a long tunnel, up another flight of stairs and come out about a block away in an old abandoned trailer. The windows are boarded up and a dog runs loose in the fenced-in yard. There's also an old car in the driveway.

We pile into the old heap. Leecho gets into the driver's seat, and I'm squashed in the backseat between Dobbs and a third guy they call Quirky.

Just the thought of sitting between these two thugs sobers me up. Dobbs has a raggedy beard, and the one they call Quirky, really is. They try to shove me back and forth between them, but there is not enough room, so I ignore them.

Quirky's eyeballs roll back in his head and all you can see is the white of his eyes. They take back roads, and we don't appear to be going toward the city. Leecho turns into a dirt road that has almost been taken over by the surrounding forest.

"Should we do it here?" Leecho says.

"This is as good a place as any," Quirky agrees.

"Wait a minute," I say. "Let's talk about this."

We pull off the road behind a patch of seven-foot-high bushes. Leecho, the driver, gets out of the car. I push and pull, but when I see Leecho's gun aimed at the back door, I let the two guys drag me out.

Leecho motions toward the ground. "Get down on you knees," he says. "Make your peace with the Lord. If you're a decent man, you're gonna see him soon."

"And if you're not," the quirky guy says. "You'll be a meetin' the devil."

They all laugh.

It's hard to maintain your dignity when you're on your knees begging. I raise my right arm slowly. "I'm a silver dealer. I have a lot of silver and Canadian cash. We can make a deal just between us. Bouchard will never know." I rattle on trying to make my point and save my life. "You won't have to dirty your hands—no chance of going to jail. Are you in?"

234

"Why should we make a deal when we can take it right out of your pockets?" Leecho asks.

"There's not much in my pockets, but there's a lot in the safe in my hotel room. Take me back there, and you can split a quarter million. Bouchard doesn't pay that kind of money."

"We tried that before. People promise and then they don't deliver and we do time in jail just for talkin' about it," the quirky one says.

Leecho looks at his friends. "Maybe this time it would be different."

Just when I think I'm getting somewhere, Quirky moves next to Leecho. "No more talk. Give me the gun. It's my turn to shoot." He grabs the gun and cocks the hammer.

I scream at Leecho. "Stop him! Think about the money! Stop him!"

Quirky pulls the trigger. There's a loud blast and I collapse on the ground.

CHAPTER TWENTY-TWO

I grasp my chest, feeling for blood. There's nothing, no bleeding, no pain. I'm alive. They begin to laugh hysterically.

"I told you he was scared. I win the bet. You guys pony-up."

Leecho and Quirky each hand Dobbs a fin. They put me back in the car. Again I'm sandwiched between two dysfunctional idiots in a moving vehicle driven by a reckless operator. None of them have any common sense, nor do they understand sound judgment. I might have considered taking on three guys even with guns, but three wackos with weapons and probably on drugs is a different story.

Warily, I look for an escape route, but even at forty-five miles an hour, jumping out could be deadly. The car is old and there are no automatic locks. I set my sights on the back-door handle. One quick move would open the door. After that, everything would depend on surprise, strength, and determination. My last thought is of Angela.

"We're almost there," Leecho shouts from the front seat.

My muscles tense. The back road makes a sharp turn and I see city lights in the distance. Ten minutes later, Leecho stops on the street a block away from the Pinnacle Harbour Front Hotel. They tell me to get out of the car. Then Leecho tosses my guns toward me. I catch the Glock, but my 442 drops on the pavement. As they pull away, I pick it up and stuff the small gun in my pocket and slide the Glock into the back of my jeans. I figure the thugs are parked somewhere close and are still watching, so I walk in the front door of the hotel.

The place is crowded, but no one seems to notice my torn shirt with blood on the sleeve where I wiped my face that had been scratched in the brush. I look out the back door. I don't see the car or any of the thugs, so I leave the hotel and hurry toward the cruise ship terminal. The dock is crowded, and I blend in with the tourists.

I look around, but I don't think anyone is following me. Nevertheless, I change direction and head for a crowd of people in front of the convention center. I go through the building and out the back door. A patio bar has drawn a large number of people.

I buy a cold drink and call my hotel room. Jeff's shaky voice answers the phone.

"Is Theo there?" I ask.

"Oh my God, it's Nick!" Jeff screams. "Quick, call Theo!" he shouts.

"Where's Theo? Why isn't he there with you?" I ask.

"He's out looking for you," Jeff says. "We thought you got caught by Felix's men. Captain Roy's squad looked everywhere for you. Where did you go?"

"I didn't *go* anywhere."

"Oh," Jeff says. "Just say yes or no," Jeff tells me.

He must think I'm unable able to talk.

"Stop," I say. "I'm okay. I'm at the Vancouver Convention Center. Tell Theo to pick me up at the back entrance."

"You want me to connect you to Theo?" Jeff asks.

"*No.*" I drag out my answer, so there will be no mistake. "Just have him pick me up ASAP at the back entrance, in an unmarked car."

Fifteen minutes later, I spot Theo. He's driving his personal car slowly through the maze of people who are jay walking across the street. I sprint to the curb and Theo stops to let me in.

"You look a little rough around the edges," he says. "What happened?"

I slide in next to him. "One of Felix's guys hit me on the head when I looked around the corner of the building."

"You know, you're supposed to peek first." He laughs.

"I did, that's when I got hit. Someone knew I was coming. I never saw the guy. He must have been standing on something because he clipped me on the top of my head and my lights went out."

"When I got to the end of the building, I looked for you, but no one was there." Theo keeps staring at me and runs over the curb. "Sorry," he says. "I'm just happy that Bouchard didn't kill you."

"It was touch and go there for a while, but I can take care of myself." That's easy to say now that I'm sitting safely in Theo's car.

"The right side of the building extends about sixty feet longer than the left. When I finally got to the back I noticed a set of steps on the left side of the building," Theo says. Whoever slammed you could've been standing up a few steps and you wouldn't have been able to see him. I went all the way around the building. I didn't see any sign of a scuffle and all the doors were locked."

"They must have taken me inside before you got there," I say. "Didn't anyone miss me?"

"Captain Roy thought you wandered off somewhere, so his men went looking for you, but I thought you must have found a way in and got caught."

"I wouldn't do something that stupid."

"Captain Roy wanted to get a search warrant and come in and get you, but I told him to wait and see if you could get out on your own."

"What? You made him wait to see if I could make it out on my own?" I stammer. "That lunatic might have killed me. Some friend you are."

"You got out, didn't you?"

"Yes, but no thanks to you," I say.

"You better thank me. If we had come back and burst through that door, you can bet he would have shot you and claimed he thought you were a burglar. It was bad enough that we accused him of dealing drugs. The only thing in that truck was vitamins."

Theo shakes his head. "They hadn't even started to unload the truck. It almost looked like they were waiting for us. We didn't have a search warrant, so Bouchard wouldn't let us go into the warehouse, but he let us in the garage to check the truck. All those white packages were filled with vitamins. There were no drugs."

"You're kiddin'. I'll bet St. Onge is pissed."

"I don't know. I haven't talked to him."

"I'm sorry I got you mixed-up in this mess," I tell him.

"You win some and you lose some." Theo smiles. "So, what happened at Bouchard's?"

"I woke up on the floor in the middle of a warehouse. Felix and some of his men were standing there looking at me. They questioned me, and I told them I was a silver dealer and that a guy I met in India named Kadam sent me there."

"Does he know Kadam?" Theo frowns.

"He didn't say, but he sent his men out of the room. We talked a long time about a lot of things. When the conversation turned to women, he told me he had a problem. He said he has this girlfriend who was giving him a lot of shit so he wants her taken permanently out of his life."

"I guess he's talking about Daniela?" Theo laughs.

"It appears to be that way. She seems to have a boyfriend close to every airport on her flight plan."

"Probably not every airport." Theo grins. "How did you get to the convention center?"

"Felix had three of his men take me to what he believed was my hotel."

I walked in the front door and straight out the back. When I saw a lot of people going in and out of the convention center, I decided it would be a better place to blend. That's when I called Jeff."

"Good thing you called when you did. Captain Roy had gotten a search warrant. We were going in at midnight."

I lean my head back and close my eyes. "I'm glad it's over."

"Now you can take a shower. You smell like a distillery," he says.

"Bouchard pumped me full of booze, and now I'm hungry."

"We'll be at the hotel in a few minutes. I'll call ahead and have Jeff order food."

When we arrive at the hotel, I go straight to my room, shower and put on clean clothes. When I come back into the sitting room everyone is waiting for me. The way they acted you'd think I'd been gone for a month.

I grab a plate of food and sit on the couch. "So what did I miss while I was gone?" I ask.

"I didn't want to say anything to anyone until you got back," Rajat says, "but after you and Theo left, the NCB sent me this video." He pulls out his phone and hands it to me.

"I don't know how to work this," I say. "Why didn't they just give you the information?"

Rajat takes his phone back, turns on the video, and sits it on the table so everyone can see. "You're gonna love this. It's almost like being there."

"Is that Kadam?" I point to the man on the screen.

"Yep." Rajat says. "He's coming out of the Marriot in Mumbai. He goes straight to his Cadillac." Rajat grins. "It's parked beyond the valet parking lot in the back. Not exactly hidden, but he's left his wheels behind a large dumpster in what looks like a No Parking zone." Rajat points to the narcs in plain clothes. "Those are National Control Bureau officers."

When Kadam gets close to his Caddy, the four officers emerge from behind several cars. One officer pulls a gun from his shoulder holster and snaps off the safety. The other three grab Kadam and strip him of a pistol and what looks like a small derringer. He struggles, but he's no match for the trained men.

"Who's taking this video?" Jeff asks.

"Roland," Rajat says. "He's a traffic cop, but he's a real good photographer and when he's not on duty he often helps other cops when they're in a questionable situation."

The officer in the video is holding a nine-millimeter. "Do you own this car," he says.

"Yes," Kadam snaps. "Is there a law against owning a car?"

Nathan and Liam crack up laughing.

"No, not if you're the owner. Do you have proper papers?" one of the narcs asks.

"Certainly, they're in my wallet." We hear Kadam say.

"I'm surprised he has a valid registration," Theo says.

The narcotics officer stands there holding out his hand.

"How do I know you're a real cop?"

"You'll know when we take you to jail."

While Kadam is looking for his papers, I ask, "What did Kadam say about being videoed?"

Rajat laughs. "They told me that Roland did it on his phone and Kadam was so busy arguing with the cops that he didn't seem to notice it right away."

We watch as Kadam pulls the certification from his wallet and thrusts it toward the officer holding the gun.

The officer takes the registration and slides it into his pocket. "Put him in the car," the Narc says.

When Kadam ask the cops why they're arresting him, the cop says, "We're not arresting you. We're only detaining you until we can determine if you are driving a stolen vehicle."

Kadam tries to delay the ride to the police station. "I can't leave my car parked here." Kadam argues, but the cop holding the gun gives Kadam a push toward the squad car.

"Take your hands off me." Kadam runs his hand over his jacket to smooth it.

"I've already called to have the car impounded," the officer says. "They're on their way."

Rajat points to Kadam's photo on his smart phone. "This is where he notices Roland taking his picture."

"What's he doing?" Kadam asks.

"He's taking your picture. Smile, you want to look good if this hits the six o'clock news," the cop says.

We see Kadam stick out his tongue. "Why are you letting him do this?" Kadam asks the cops.

We can't see Roland, but we hear him say. "They can't stop me. You know—freedom of the press."

"You can pick up your Caddy in the lot next to the Quora Jail," one narc says.

"Would you look at this," Nathan says.

Kadam is dancing around and waving his arms in front of the officers. "I have a driver's license and credit cards. I can prove I own this car."

Then the officer says, "Tell it to the Lieutenant at the station. We don't handle identity verification. We only take in the suspects."

"If those cops keep talking, Kadam is gonna catch on," I say. "He's gonna be yelling for a lawyer pretty soon, and then the cops will be in deep shit."

Kadam asks. "Suspected of what?"

They tell Kadam they were looking for a stolen car that matches his car's description, and they read him his rights.

"Shitty little patrol wagon." Kadam kicks a tire on the black Ford Escape.

"I don't think he knows they're from the narcotics squad," Jeff says.

The video suddenly ends. Rajat picks up his phone and touches a different app. It's a picture of Kadam at the local police station. Rajat runs his finger across the phone and the next still picture shows Kadam with an officer and the Chief of police.

"They told me the commander said he would hold him as long as he could, but they needed to get someone to question him ASAP." Rajat laughs.

"So what have they done since then?" I ask.

"I don't know. I haven't heard from anyone." Rajat puts his phone in his pocket.

CHAPTER TWENTY-THREE

It's already past midnight, but while I eat, Theo and I watch a rerun of what Daniela did this evening. Everyone else has gone to the bar. She's dressed in a flowing outfit and Liam tells us her dinner date was a no-show. Even worse—he didn't even call.

Daniela makes several calls to Kadam, but he doesn't answer. His mobile phone is no doubt locked up with the rest of his personal belongings while he's being held at the local jail.

"Rajat told me Kadam was arrested for auto theft and consequently is now being held for possession of drugs found in his car," I tell Theo.

"When did they find the drugs?" Theo asks.

"I don't know. Maybe there weren't any."

"Oh, boy. I don't like the sound of this," Theo says.

"It's India's problem. You don't have to worry about it."

We watch while Daniela places a number of calls to Samir, Sophia, and Felix. Liam tells us that no one called back and nothing else happened.

"I'm gonna fast forward through this blank area," Liam says.

I finish my dinner while Liam moves the recording ahead.

Then we see Daniela coming back into the livingroom. She has on a hotel robe. She's carrying a drink and a small bottle of pills. She drops onto the couch and turns on the television. She takes a couple of the pills, sips her drink and puts the medicine bottle into her pocket. When she finishes her drink, she turns off the television, goes into the bedroom and the lights go out.

"That's the last we saw of the woman this evening, Liam says. "Now we're on real time. Jeff relieved me a while ago and I got a couple of hours sleep. I'll stay here tonight. I have an alert signal set if anything moves in her sitting room, or if there is any noise made in the suite. If I doze off, the system will beep and it will wake me up."

"You're doing a fine job," I tell him.

Theo stands. "I gotta run. I need to get some sleep, too. I'll pick up Nathan and we'll see you early in the morning." He shakes my hand and leaves.

CHAPTER TWENTY-FOUR

The next day, Daniela takes a cab, and Rajat is assigned to follow her. The rest of us settle for room service breakfast and talk about the case. I call Rajat to see what is going on.

"Not much," he says. "I followed her to Felix's business. It appears that today is a Canadian holiday. Everything is closed, including Felix's Vitamin and Mineral Company. Then she went to a phone store, but that business was also closed. I do not know where we are going now, but I am still following her."

"Great, keep up the good work. I'll call you later," I tell him and hang up.

It's not long before Daniela's hotel phone rings. Of course we can't answer it, and she's not there. It finally stops ringing.

"Who do you think that was?" Nathan asks.

"It was probably a wrong number," Jeff says. "I didn't hear them leave a message."

"The number printed out on the hotel register," the technician says. "I called it into SOCA. It's billed to Garden Pharmacy. It's a local drug store in Mumbai."

"Hmm, that's interesting," Nathan says.

In the afternoon, Daniela returns to the hotel and goes into the bedroom, but there is no sign of Rajat.

"He must be outside talking on the phone to his girlfriend," Jeff says.

They all laugh.

"When did that light come on?" Liam asks. "It wasn't on a few minutes ago."

"What light?" I ask.

"The message light on the lady's phone is blinking," Liam says. "It wasn't lit up a few minutes ago."

They all look at each other.

"Remember there was a call earlier, but no one left a message," Nathan says.

On the screen, we see Daniela coming out of the bedroom. She has changed into the hotel robe. When she notices the light, she hurries to the phone and listens to the message.

We hear a female's recorded voice say, "Sophia's gonna talk."

Daniela drops the receiver onto the cradle. Her shoulders droop as she stares at the phone. She takes a deep breath and picks up the receiver and dials a number.

A recorded voice answers. "Lunickbox Pharmaceutical Company. If you know the extension number, you may dial it at anytime."

She presses four buttons. The call goes directly to voice mail and we hear a second recording. "You have reached the voice mail box of," there's a pause and then we hear a male voice say his name. "Nikhil Harran. Please leave a message."

After the beep, Daniela says. "We have a snitch. She's the one you call Pretty Baby. Take care of this now."

I look at Theo. "Are you thinking what I'm thinking?"

"Yep. It sounds like they're going to take Sophia out."

I walk over and stare out the window. "I wonder why we haven't heard from the NCB. By now he must have told the NCB where Sophia lives. If there is a leak, whoever it is must have found out that Kadam is in jail. They probably thought that if Kadam squealed Sophia will talk, too. That same person might have been the one who warned Daniela."

"We can suppose all night, but that won't keep Sophia alive." Jeff says.

"Call Rajat," I tell Jeff.

Rajat's phone goes straight to voice mail.

"Something's wrong. Send him a text. Keep trying to reach him."

Liam bursts into the conversation. "I talked to the phone company. They had some issues this morning with the voice mail system. They say the problem has now been corrected."

"If she only got one phone call, the phone company might have had more problems than just the voice mail," I say. "Maybe NCB couldn't get through to us."

"Could be," Liam mumbles.

I ask him to get someone in command at the NCB in Mumbai.

"What are you gonna do now?" Jeff asks.

"I'm gonna try to prevent a murder."

"The NCB is already taking care of that," Jeff tells me.

Liam holds up a head-set. "Robert, I have an officer on the line. It's the best I could do."

I put on the headset and talk to the officer. "Listen. This is important." I explain the problem about Sophia.

The officer tells me they already sent men to that address and the woman wouldn't let them in. He claims that they have to get a warrant issued before they can go in.

"The hit man could be on his way now. You have to go in and get her out," I say.

The officer asks me to hold on. He wants to check with his commander.

"Who are you talking to?" Jeff asks me.

"An imbecile."

"She's a criminal. Jeff shakes his head. "Let the NCB worry about her."

The officer comes back on the line. He says they have two officers on duty outside the apartment until they can get the woman out, but to be on the safe side, he says he'll pass my information on to them.

"Will you personally see that this is done?" I ask.

He tells me to hold on. He says his commander wants to talk to me. The next voice I hear is an irate boss. He asks for my name.

I explain who I am and why I am calling. I tell him about the anonymous message that was left for Daniela and where the call originated from. Then I ask him if Kadam gave the NCB any helpful information on the drug trafficking and most importantly did he give them an address to find Sophia.

He tells me yes, he got a little information, and that he understands my concern, but not to worry. He says he has everything under control. He has no intention of letting anyone kill his star witness. Then I get the real scoop. He adds, they have to wait until they can get Kadam asylum in another country before they can move forward.

"Did you get the address where Sophia is staying"

"We have a couple of men out there with her now. I gave this information to your man, Rajat Singh earlier in the day." He says good-bye and before I can say anything else he hangs up.

"Well, at least we know the NCB has Sophia." I tell Jeff.

Ten minutes later Rajat walks in the door.

"Where have you been?" I ask him.

"Doing my job. I followed Daniela clear to her room. I assumed you saw her come in. Then I went back outside for a smoke. You got a problem with that?" Rajat says.

"Did the NCB call you and tell you that Kadam cracked?" Jeff asks Rajat.

"No, but if he did that's good news," Rajat says.

"That's what I told him." Jeff sneers. "But Nick wants to make something out of it."

Singh pulls his phone from his pocket. "Oops. My phone is turned off. I do not know how that happened." He listens to his voice mail. "Oh, yes. They left a message."

"NCB said they talked to you," I tell him.

"They didn't talk to me."

"Rajat," I say. "I want you to call the NCB and see if you can find out what is going on. They don't like talking to me. Daniela got a message that Sophia was going to talk to the NCB. It came from the Garden Pharmacy. See if they can find out who made that call to Daniela."

"Garden Pharmacy," Jeff repeats out loud. "Isn't that where you said your girlfriend works?" He asks Rajat.

"She changed jobs. She hasn't worked there in over a month." Rajat walks to the window and looks outside.

"You just told me that a couple days ago," Jeff says.

"I had forgotten she changed stores." The testy Singh walks toward the small refrigerator. "I'm thirsty. As soon as I drink this juice, I'll get right on it."

Jeff might be playing it cool, or he might be dense as a brick wall, but Rajat's story is crap. I turn to Rajat, but before I can question him, I see Daniela reach for the phone. She makes a call to Ramos and tells him that she hasn't been feeling well and plans to come home.

"Being here will make you better," he says. "When will you arrive?"

"I haven't made any arrangements yet. I'll call you later with the details. I want to spend some time with you."

"That will be nice," he casually adds, "I miss you."

"That doesn't make a lot of sense," I tell Jeff. "He says he misses her, but he doesn't sound excited to me. He doesn't have the enthusiasm he usually has."

"You're upset about the NCB not calling us and now you're reading far too much into how Ramos feels about her coming home. He might just be tired." Jeff sighs.

While I'm talking to Jeff, Rajat lights a cigarette and picks up the bottle of juice. "I'm going outside." he bangs the door on his way out.

I ignore him, and look back at Jeff. "Why are you always judging me? I went into a critical zone, got knocked around, and made an inroad for the DEA in India and Canada. I could've been killed."

"What brought this up? That's just the life of a DEA agent. Get over it. Everything doesn't turn out perfect."

"I don't see you out there putting everything on the line."

"We all have a job to do. I do mine, you do yours."

"You know how easy it would be for me not to like you?"

"We'll be friends again when you need me," Jeff says. "Besides, I never get invited to hockey games and nobody ever confuses me with a hit man."

"Don't forget, I still have to meet with Felix tonight,"

"You'll be wearing a wire, and you'll have protection. As soon as Bouchard commits to the plan, Vancouver's SOCA will move in, grab him and charge him with intent to kill Daniela Diaz," Jeff tells me.

I can't believe Jeff is so naïve. "And by the way, I'm not wearing a wire. I'm using a mini recorder."

Jeff laughs. "You can't do that. Bouchard will spot a recorder in a hot second."

"I figure he'll be looking for a wire. I'm wearing a thin shirt so he can check it out. When he doesn't find anything, he's not likely to look below my belt line," I tell Jeff.

Jeff shakes his head. "Using a mini recorder isn't DEA approved."

"We do it my way or I don't do it at all. I want the DEA to notify Vancouver that Theo has the recorded evidence that connects Bouchard to the murder of Daniela Diaz. It can't be given to the police until after Daniela gets on her flight back to India and we get her and Sophia on a plane to Belize. Then Theo can give the SOCA the tape and they can arrest Bouchard."

"So now who's being crazy? How are you gonna hide a recorder?" Jeff asks. You won't get away with that. In fact, you'll be damn lucky if we get you out of Vancouver alive. Besides, I don't think the Canadian authorities will go for it."

I turn to Theo. "Can we get this show on the road?"

"I have several recorders in my car." Theo says. "One is relatively small. I think we can make it fit. We won't arrest him tonight, but backup will only be fifty feet away if you need them."

I think about that part. There'll be a lot of fans at the stadium. It'll be hard for the police to get through the crowd. I might be taking a big chance.

"You may like India's Agent Rajat Singh, but I don't trust him," I tell Jeff. "When he comes back inside, I'm going to question him about his girlfriend."

"I'll see you later." Jeff says. "I'm going to my room to change clothes.

When he leaves. I take a shower and get dressed while Theo sets up the miniature recorder. Theo tapes the recorder to my skin. He says he's worried about me and I probably should be, too.

I tell Theo, "Jeff called and said that Rajat let him know that he called the Garden Pharmacy. Supposedly, the pharmacist told Rajat that the only available phone at the pharmacy is behind the pharmacy window, and that he and his assistant said no one else used the phone today."

"Whose idea was it to have Rajat call the pharmacy?" Theo asks.

"I don't know."

"It sounds to me like someone is trying to set up an alibi."

"I think your right," I tell Theo.

Jeff walks in the door, "What's going on?"

"We're making plans for tonight," I say.

"I could have one of the detectives hang out close to Bouchard's box. He could be dressed in a Canucks jersey. No one will notice him," Jeff says.

"Not tonight! This guy's no novice. He'd recognize a cop no matter what he had on. If we don't provoke him he won't kill the operative, at least not until after the job is over."

"You can't be sure of that, Theo says. "What if he frisks you and finds the recorder?"

"I doubt he will be looking for a two-inch recorder. Besides, I don't think he will do that. We're gonna be with a lot of other people and he doesn't want anyone to know what he's doing. I'll just go along with him and play it cool."

"I hope you understand the chance you're taking," Theo says.

"If he has any idea of knocking me off, it will be after I do the job. That's when I'll need protection. My life and my paycheck will be ridin' on a narrow rail."

"Even if tonight goes well, don't make plans for anything you want to do in India just yet. We have to see how India wants to handle this," Jeff says.

"If we have to wait to see what India's politicians want to do, the FBI will say the NCB did all the work and the DEA will probably renege on my bonus."

"Don't you ever do anything just because it's the right thing to do?" Jeff says.

"If India's government tries to round up the group before we lock up Daniela, she could easily slip away. Then Ramos will blame me and Felix would be off the hook, too."

"Excuse me," Jeff says. "I thought you had seen the light and hoped you had turned over a new leaf."

"Don't get so sanctimonious. I haven't noticed you refusing any of the funds that regularly drop into your account."

"That's different." Jeff mumbles and walks to the other side of the room.

I guess he doesn't like a dose of his own medicine. I'm not really angry with him. He does a lot for me. I just like to bug him once in a while.

"Come on, Jeff." I cuff him on the shoulder. "I was only jokin'."

"One of these days," Jeff shakes his fist at me.

About an hour before game time, I leave for Rogers Arena and arrive fifteen minutes before face-off. I buy a cheap ticket, but head for the box-seats. Right before I reach my destination, I get stopped by an usher. He asks to see my ticket and I explain that I have been invited to watch the game with Felix Bouchard.

"Sure you were." He laughs. "Turn around and go back to your seat. There aren't any no-shows up front for this match-up. The Canucks are playing the Chicago Blackhawks."

"Mr. Bouchard and I do business together. He's expecting me."

"Andy." The usher calls to a kid selling hot dogs. "Put down those wieners and see if Felix is expecting—what did you say your name was?"

"Robert," I tell him.

"Ask Mr. Bouchard if he's expecting a guy named Robert?"

The kid puts down the hot dog case and takes off. He's back in a shot with a beautiful young lady.

"Right this way, Robert." The woman gives the usher a scornful look, takes my hand and pulls me along.

When we get to the box, I see a group of middle-aged men and several sexy young women. They're all wearing royal blue shirts, have a drink in their hand and are talking and laughing.

"Robert!" Felix shouts when I arrive. "So glad you could make it."

He introduces me to the men, most of whom seem to be called Luke.

"Sit, we'll talk at the end of the first period." He points to the seat next to him.

I nod and ease my frame into the seat. The recorder is just below the small roll of fat that hangs over my belt. This is the first time I can remember being happy to have the extra weight.

"Are you a vitamin distributor?" Luke asks.

"No, we're silver dealers." Felix answers for me.

"Silver! When did you get into silver?" a second Luke asks Felix.

"Five years ago. Not that it's any of your damn business."

Both of the Luke's take a seat in the back row of the box. Felix calls to one of the cocktail waitresses who is serving drinks to the patrons in the box-seats.

"Order whatever you want," he tells me. "She'll put it on my tab. I take good care of my friends."

I order a beer.

Felix punches my arm. "You gettin' a little too old to cut the hard stuff?"

Not wanting to cause a problem, I laugh. "I just want to keep a cool head in this hot game."

He laughs with me.

The skaters line up on the hash marks to face-off. It's not long before I realize the players are rougher than I had ever thought of them being. The Canucks score first.

"Keep your eye on this guy." Felix claps his hands and points to the player that hit the puck past the goalie. He'll score again. He holds 'the old hat trick' record."

I have no idea what he is talking about, but I applaud with him.

A short time later, there is what looks like a free-for-all on the ice. Only one of the Vancouver players, who deliberately struck an opposing player in the groin with his hockey stick, is sent to the penalty box for three minutes. Felix and most of the crowd boo the referee.

"That wasn't a major penalty. He barely touched the guy," Felix says to one of the Luke's.

I nod, despite the fact that the guy who was "barely touched" was hurting so bad he had to be helped off the ice.

At the end of the first period, Felix and I leave his friends. We weave our way through hundreds of fans to the other side of the stadium. Bouchard finds an empty corner so we can talk. I glance around, but don't see anyone milling close to us. We're too far away from any officer who might be able to help me.

"Who are you looking for?" Bouchard glares at me.

"I thought you might have changed your mind and arranged to have one of your illiterate thugs beat the hell out of me. This isn't exactly an everyday job."

"Nah, I wouldn't do that. A deal's a deal. Right?"

"That's right."

He puts his arm around my shoulder and slowly runs his hand down the back of my silk shirt. I know he's feeling for a thin wire. Theo was right when he said we had to get the recorder below my belt.

"What are you lookin' for?" I ask.

"I thought you might be wearing a wire," he says.

I open the first few buttons on my shirt. "Wanna look?"

"Nah, I trust you." Bouchard smiles when he doesn't find anything. "You say you dumped your last girlfriend. Did it break your heart?"

"Nah."

"Did she ever come back?"

"No."

"Did you have any repercussions from your breakup?" He continues to pry.

"Nope." I keep my answers short.

Bouchard puts his hand on my shoulder. "You do realize I want her iced? I don't ever want to see this broad again."

"Yep, I got it covered."

"You don't talk much." He takes his hand away.

I look him straight in the eye. "Are you asking me for details?"

"Not so long as she is gone for good. I really don't care how." He looks away.

"Well, then, all we need to discuss is the identity of the party involved, where I can find her, and the compensation."

"I appreciate your direct response, and I'm ready to do business." He gives me the information. "Here's a present for you." He hands me a royal blue bag with the printed name Canucks in gold lettering. "It's a bottle of scotch. Hold it on your lap. Half the contract money is under the bottle." He hands it to me just as casually as he would hand me a Blackhawk's shirt that no one else wanted.

We work our way back to our seats to finish watching the game. The second period begins and Bouchard punches me in the arm. "Did you see that deke my guy made? He faked that Blackhawk right out of the crease."

"Is he the skater that scored?"

"Nah, he's on defense. He has more apples than any other player in the league."

"Apples?" I squint.

He waves his arm. "Yeah apples, you know, assists."

"He came on board with the Canucks last year," the first Luke says "Felix thought he was a duster."

"A duster?" I frown.

They all look at me.

"I don't watch much hockey," I say.

After Bouchard laughs, they all laugh. "You're okay, buddy. Not everybody likes hockey, but if you lived in Vancouver, you just naturally become a fan."

"Yeah, last year that guy never got off the bench, but look at him now." The second Luke grins from ear to ear.

"Pay no attention to Luke," Felix tells me. "He's always running his mouth."

I shrug.

At the end of the second period they're all talking about the game, but since I don't know much about hockey, I don't join in.

Bouchard turns to me. "I know you're not interested in the game. You don't have to stay if you don't want to. You can leave now and miss the heavy traffic."

"That might be a good idea," I say.

"We'll work out the last details of that silver deal later," he says for Luke's benefit.

"Okay." I stand and shake his hand.

When I leave the stadium, I have a new deal and half the price of the job. Of course, I doubt very much if I will ever see the rest of the cash, and most likely, I won't be allowed to keep any of this incriminating evidence.

The major problem is how do I pull off this job without killing anyone, including myself, and still salvage a life with Angela.

CHAPTER TWENTY-FIVE

I'm on my way back to the hotel from the arena when I get a text from Jeff. The recording team working at the hotel is making progress. They've sent a portion of the audio-video that confirms Daniela dialing and speaking to Kadam on his mobile about forcing Sophia to deliver the drugs to Detroit.

The tape had more than enough evidence to charge Kadam with running drugs from India to Belize if he does not cooperate, so his attorney advised him to cop a plea for a lesser crime to get a lighter sentence.

I see the light at the end of the tunnel and I'm anxious to get this recording machine off my belly. It won't be long before Angela and I can be back together. However, when I walk into my suite, everybody has a long face.

"What's the matter" I ask. "Kadam's gonna cooperate. We should be celebrating."

Jeff is the first to answer. "The NCB is thinking of issuing warrants for all the people they have on their list who are involved in this drug cartel before there's a leak and they all disappear. I don't think the two cops guarding Sophia will be able to stop the mob and without her, the NCB won't have much of a case.

"It is just a bump in the road. They'll get the documents and go into the apartment and get her out. It just takes a little time," Rajat says.

"Yeah, time enough for Daniela, Samir, or some high ups in the Punjabi Mob to get rid of Sophia, and then the whole case goes down the drain," Jeff says.

"I don't think they'll issue warrants for the others until they get Sophia out of the apartment and into a safe place," I say.

The Dealer

"If there is a leak, we're screwed." Jeff walks over to the window. "The judge is in court today. He claims he can't have the warrant ready until ten o'clock in the morning."

"Are you suggesting that the NCB should break the law?" I ask Jeff.

"Well, someone has to do something," Jeff says.

"We'll just have to wait," I say. "With Daniela miles away from India and no cell phone, maybe the news won't travel so fast."

"There are other phones she can use and the stores will be open tomorrow. She'll get a new phone," Jeff says. "Why did you agree to do this job for Bouchard anyway? It has nothing to do with what we came for."

"Are you crazy? I'm not doing a job for Bouchard. That was just a set up."

"I didn't think you would, but he offered a lot of cash." he says. "I just don't like being here in Vancouver, not knowing where or when Bouchard's thugs might show up."

"I'm doing this to help Theo."

"You should have let Theo catch his own criminals."

"Do you agree that Theo has helped us out a lot, and we wouldn't even be this far without him?" I wait for Jeff's answer.

"Yes, but we can't spend government money doing another country's job."

"He went out on a limb to help us. We caused Vancouver's crime agency a lot of problems and they gave me information on Daniela I needed for Ramos."

"You're turning this all around," Jeff sputters.

"I felt certain that Bouchard would check for a wire and he did, but of course he didn't find one because thanks to Theo the mini recorder was well below my waist.

"Obviously, he was more concerned that I might say something in front of his friends, and he also didn't have the nerve to ask me to unzip my pants. He was more nervous than I was. Twice he whispered to me that I should wait until we were alone to discuss our deal, even though I hadn't mentioned it."

"By the time you arrived at the arena, he probably had already consumed a large amount of booze. That's why he didn't give you a thorough frisk." Jeff says.

"Maybe? I returned the mini recorder to Theo, so he could set up the groundwork to turn over the information to Vancouver's SOCA. They haven't been able to connect Bouchard to drug trafficking, but they feel certain they can win this case for the attempted murder of Daniela and put him in jail for a long time," I tell Jeff.

A few minutes later Theo comes in. "I'm glad your back," he says. "I'm sorry to give you bad news. We don't want to compromise your identity, but Canada wants you to sign a statement. Hopefully, you will not have to appear in court, but we won't know until it happens."

I nod, but I'm thinking that no way in hell will I ever set foot in Canada again for any reason whatsoever. Theo tells me Canada will not want to bring legal action against Daniela that they feel they can't win. Bouchard was the actual trafficker. She only gave him information.

"If the DEA tries to take Daniela to Belize or the United States to press charges, India's government will not likely comply." Theo frowns. "They will insist on enforcing the law and bringing legal proceedings against her in India, and I can't blame them. They have been focusing on this particular group for almost a year."

"We can't let that happen," Jeff says. "The United States is the country that tracked her down."

Theo turns to Jeff. "Arresting Daniela now and taking her to the U.S. or Belize would alert everyone operating in India and Vancouver. They would scatter and the drugs would move on other routes using different criminals. You must share the information with the NCB. They will start by charging them with using a mule to make this particular delivery to Detroit. Right now, we do not have all the evidence to charge the rest of the members of the drug cell, but we are very close. Now that we have the nucleus, we know where and how they operate. In short order India and Vancouver will be able to arrest the entire group."

After a few minutes, Jeff concurs with Theo, but I disagree with his assessment.

I turn to Jeff. "I thought you told me that we were here to handle drug trafficking through Belize and into the United States. That adds up to Daniela."

"I never said that," Jeff says.

"What?" I ask.

"Well, maybe I did, but that was before. This project has somehow gotten out of hand. It's bigger than we expected and we need to stay within India's laws. We got what we came for. That's the important thing."

"And what do you think I should do? If Bouchard finds out Daniela is alive he'll be out looking for me. The one thing I don't want to do is deal with his three goons. Especially, Leecho."

"We'll figure something out," Jeff says. "If all goes well, Daniela will be headed back to India on her job in first class and the NCB promised to be at the airport to pick her up. If they give her enough years in jail, maybe Bouchard will be satisfied."

"Don't count on that." I turn to Theo. "Meanwhile, our only way back to India is on the same flight that Daniela is working, so we have to turn this case over to Vancouver and catch our return flight to India."

"The one thing we have to make sure of is that we don't step on anyone's toes," Jeff says.

"Oh, so once again this is a political task. Why wasn't I told this before now?"

"When the DEA works with outsiders, information gets passed out on a need to know basis. It's not personal. That's just the way the system works." Jeff holds the palms of his hands up to me.

I glare at him.

"Stop and think about this," he says. "Don't go postal on me."

"Stop it," Theo snaps. "Let's cross one bridge at a time."

I'm livid, but Jeff and I thank Theo for his help and say our good-byes. I tell Theo I'll keep in touch, but he's no dummy.

"The only way I'll see you is if the law drags you back," Theo says. "That is, if they can find you."

CHAPTER TWENTY-SIX
Flying back to India

Jeff hands out our return airline tickets for India. It doesn't take me long to get packed, but Jeff has paperwork he needs to complete and fax to Belize, so I use the extra time to call Angela.

I dial the number and lay the phone on the bed.

"Hi sweetie," she says when our phones connect. "I was just thinking about you."

"I hope it was good thoughts." I zip my back pack.

"Very good thoughts," she says. "I finished my quilt and I want to go home."

"What if I told you that I have things pretty well wrapped up here and that I'll be home soon?"

"Do you mean that, or are you telling me that to make me feel good and then later change your story?"

"Well, I'm not positive, but the odds are good. I'm probably looking at a week before I fly into Miami and we can take that long flight home together."

"That would be terrific. I'm beginning to think I've overstayed my welcome."

"Why? Are you and Helen not getting along?"

"No, we're fine, but she has this friend who shared an apartment with a buddy and the buddy moved out. Apparently, he couldn't afford the place by himself, so he moved in permanently with Helen. It's a good thing. They've been dating off and on for some time. Helen's happy."

"Is he giving you a bad time? I'll have a nice talk with him. You won't have any more problems."

"It's nothing like that. It's just that I think it would be nice if they could be alone and I feel like I'm in the way. They both said I should stay. I told them I have a room at the condo, but they insisted I spend the last few days with them."

"I'll be there just as soon as I can, but right now I have to go out. Hold on a minute.

"Okay, I'm back," I say.

"What happened?" she asks.

"I dropped my Air Canada ticket and it slid under the bed." Oh, why did I tell her that?

"Are you in Canada?"

"No, well yes, but I'm leaving."

"Leaving for where?"

"Leaving to come home," I say.

"You're coming now?" she asks.

"No, not now, but soon."

"Where are you going now?"

I don't want to lie, but I don't want to say India. "I'm just going back to where I was staying before. So what are your mother and father doing these days?"

"They're doing the same things I told you about before and why are you trying to change the subject?"

"I'm not trying to keep anything from you. It's just the same old business, nothing new, and nothing you'd be interested in."

"Liar."

"Okay, you got me. I'm going to India."

"India! What are you gonna do there?"

I knew she was gonna ask that. "Let's talk about this when I see you."

"Is it that dangerous?" she asks.

"No, it's not dangerous. It's just the military. They think everything's a secret."

"Okay, but when you left, you said you weren't going to do anything dangerous. I don't want anything to happen to you."

"Don't worry, darling. I'm not wearing a uniform, I'm not in a war zone and I'm not fighting an enemy." At least not the usual kind of enemy.

"You promise?"

I cross my fingers. "I promise."

I tell her I love her and we hang up. If I had stayed on the phone, she would have found a way to get more information out of me.

Jeff calls and says he's ready to leave for the airport. Fortunately for us, Daniela has been with the airline for a number of years and retains her position as First Class Attendant. Rajat is a little skittish because he has passed Daniela in the hotel hall twice. Once again, we get scattered seats in coach, and Rajat takes the one closest to the back of the plane.

CHAPTER TWENTY-SEVEN

After a long flight, we disembark around 9 a.m. and stop for coffee and a croissant sandwich at the airport Starbucks while we plan our strategy for the day.

I see a woman in a flowered dress scurrying toward the exit that leads to the taxi line. I point toward the woman. "Is that Daniela?"

"It sure is," Jeff shouts.

We chase after her. The lady jumps in the taxi and the cab pulls away from the curb. The next two cabs in line are full of people and baggage is being loaded into the trunks.

Jeff is ahead of me, waving his arms as he tries to stop the taxi driver, but I memorize the cab number.

"Do you still have the telephone number and passcode in your smart phone that we used before we went to Canada?" I ask Rajat.

"Yes." Rajat searches his pockets for his mobile.

"Did you leave it on the plane?" I ask.

"No, it is here. I just have to find it," Rajat says.

Jeff jogs back to where we are standing. He's out of breath.

"What happened to the NCB?" I ask Jeff. "You told me Rajat called ahead and they said they would be waiting at the gate to pick her up. So where are they?"

"I don't know," he says.

"How could they miss her?" It seems to take forever before Rajat's NCB contact answers his mobile phone.

He gets the information and looks sheepishly at me. "They said she must have changed from her uniform to street clothes on the plane and slipped off with other passengers."

"That's not an answer. That's an excuse," I tell him.

However, the NCB has evidently been able to contact the dispatcher of the cab company that Daniela is riding in and they give them her destination address. The NCB passes the address on to Rajat.

"Come on. Let's grab a cab," I say. "I don't want to lose her."

"The NCB is sending a patrolman to takes us to our objective," Rajat says.

"They're gonna do what?" I ask.

"He will take us to where Daniela went." Rajat puts his phone back in his pocket. "They said they have a guy in the area. He will be here in a few minutes. His name is Officer Charak. It is best that we have an officer of the law with us."

I watch a cab pull away. "We could've been on our way."

A few minutes later, the patrolman has his flashing lights on when he pulls up to the curb and Rajat, Jeff and I jump in.

"Where to?" Charak asks.

Rajat tells the patrolman the street name and the cop makes a U-turn in the middle of busy traffic.

I guess the cabbie couldn't have done that. "Twenty-four hundred," I call out.

We go several blocks.

"What was that number again?" Charak is cutting in and out between the cars.

After Rajat rattles off the number, he says. "When I spoke with the NCB, I told them why we needed the address. They said it is the same address that two officers had been sent to earlier in the day. They said she wouldn't let them in, without a search warrant, but the officers were trying to talk her into opening the door.

"She might not even be there because if the men got inside her apartment, they're plan was to take her into custody for her own safety," Rajat says.

I tell Rajat that maybe she wasn't part of the cartel, that she might have been forced to participate.

"I thought you wanted to prove she was guilty." Rajat tosses a cigarette out the window.

"All I wanted to do was find out the truth."

We come to a traffic jam and Charak puts on his siren. He uses half of the sidewalk to get passed the traffic.

"Turn your siren and flashing lights off a couple of blocks before we get there," I tell him.

It's not far to the place we're looking for. It's a busy neighborhood with people milling around everywhere. Children play on the sidewalks, but there is no sign of Daniela or the cab she came in. She must have gone into the apartment building.

"Park the squad car away from the building," I tell the officer.

The patrol car goes past the building and turns into an alley. We all jump out and hurry back to the apartment. Two small boys are playing a ball and stick game on the sidewalk. I step between them and they stop and look up at me.

"Did you see a pretty lady with long black hair go in the door a few minutes ago?" I ask.

One boy nods. I motion for the boys to play their game further down the street. They look at the cop and immediately skedaddle.

We take the elevator to the third floor, get off, and tiptoe toward apartment 305. The door is open, and a large suitcase is standing just outside the door. Jeff and Rajat go inside. I linger in the hallway to check out the building exits and hear the click, clack of high-heeled shoes going down the back cement stairs. I run down the hallway to the staircase and peer over the railing. I see a woman at the bottom of the stairs in a flowered dress. It's gotta be Daniela.

"Stop. Police!" I shout, but she ignores me and runs down the hallway. I run down the stairs and hear a door slam, followed by a loud blast of what sounds like gun fire. The sound echoes through the stairwell, and it's difficult to tell exactly where the noise came from.

At the bottom of the steps, I stop and glance down the hallway. The light above the elevator indicates that it's on the third floor. For a moment I think she might have gone back upstairs. I look at the entrance to the building. I figure I better take a look outside before I check out the third floor. Not knowing what might be outside I take out my gun before cracking the door. I'm stunned. Daniela is spread awkwardly on the front steps of the building.

I feel my stomach flip-flop. Even though, I have had many bad thoughts about her, I could not have shot her and I didn't want her to get hurt.

The patrolman who brought us here is stooping next to her. For a moment, I think he might have shot her, but his gun is tightly holstered.

I hurry out the doorway and kneel next to him. I feel for some sign of life, but there is nothing. Her body is still warm, but there is no pulse. Bright red blood pools on the wide steps. I take off my shirt and pack it tightly against the large hole where the bullet exited.

A small group of people are standing on the sidewalk staring at the ghastly scene.

"I called for backup," the officer says. "The hospital is just a block away."

Shrill sirens wail and red lights dance on the windows of the building when an ambulance screeches to a stop. Technicians grab their gear and race toward Daniela. One of the technicians tosses my bloody shirt aside and packs ice where the bullet came out of her body.

They work feverishly, but in the end, there is nothing they can do. It's horrible to think that a beautiful young girl who had everything to live for has been mercilessly killed.

This will be brutal news for Ramos. It'll be hard for me to explain how this all happened. He loves Daniela so much he would do anything for her and probably did. I think he knew she was dealing drugs. He just didn't want to believe it.

I step into the sunlight.

"Up there!" Officer Charak points. "The shooter was on the roof of the building across the street. He had a rifle."

People continue to gather.

"Were you able to get off a shot?" I ask.

"No, he was on the top of the roof, next to the chimney. I had no chance. As soon as he made the shot, he disappeared behind the smokestack and I assume he went down the backside of the building."

"That's a really steep roof. He must have had a ladder. Maybe someone saw him," I say.

"When I reported the assault, I gave the dispatcher the coordinates of the building the assassin used," Charak's voice quivers.

I return my gun to the pants holster. My hand is covered with sticky blood.

Time stands still. The crowd gawks at me like they're expecting me to do something, but there's nothing I can do.

Rajat and Jeff come out the front door.

"What happened?" Jeff asks.

Rajat looks at the blood on my hands. "Step back," he says to me. He holds his gun leveled straight at my chest.

Three patrol cars arrive at the scene. Five police officers and a detective in a tan dress shirt instantly surround the four of us. Officer Charak uses his handkerchief to wipe the sweat from his brow.

Rajat shows the detective his badge.

"Are you from the NCB?" they ask.

"Yes," Rajat says. "You need to take his gun." Rajat points to me.

"What's the matter with you? I didn't shoot her," I say.

"That is what all killers say," Rajat says.

"Wait a minute," Officer Charak speaks up.

Rajat shoves Charak out of his way. "This is Robert Anderson. He's a hired killer. Is that not right, Agent Blackwell?"

Jeff's mouth is hanging open, but he doesn't say anything.

One officer draws his gun and steps toward Rajat. "Put away your weapon," he says.

Rajat holsters his pistol.

Then the officer asks, "Is this the guy who shot the lady?"

"Yes, sir," Rajat says. "He's a hit man. He had a contract to kill her."

Another officer grabs my arms, pulls them behind me, and clamps on a set of handcuffs.

I pull away from him, but now my arms are pinned behind me. "I didn't kill this woman," I tell him.

Rajat tries to shove me, but I don't budge.

The detective steps between me and Rajat. "I'm telling you right now. Anymore outbreaks and I'm taking you all for a ride."

Officer Charak, who sports the same type of badge as the five cops, works his way into the circle of police officers. He points his finger at me. "This man did not shoot the woman."

Rajat is livid. He turns to Jeff. "Tell them, Blackwell. Tell the officers he had a contract to kill this woman. Her boyfriend paid him to kill her."

One of the patrolmen pushes Rajat backward. "You wanna go to jail?"

Rajat stands down.

Jeff looks at me. "He had a contract, but I didn't see him shoot her."

"Jeff, this is no time to hold a grudge. You know I didn't shoot Daniela. Tell the cops."

"You two also wanna go for a ride?" the same pushy officer asks.

We all glare at each other.

"Nobody talks unless I ask a question," the detective says.

I don't bring it to their attention, but while we're playing games, the real shooter is getting away.

Charak speaks to the patrol officers. "Two Americans and one *adhikaaree*."

They all grin.

"I am not a rookie. I was just transferred to the NCB," Rajat tells the Mumbai police officers.

"Tape his mouth," one of the officers says.

The detective shakes his head. "What happened here tonight, Charak?" He appears to know the cop that drove us here.

"I was working on the eastside when I got a call from the dispatcher. She told me to pick up these three guys and bring them to this address. She also said two detectives from NCB were already here at apartment 305, with a lady who had called for police protection. I drove these gentlemen to this address, parked the patrol car and walked with them to the front of the building. They went inside and I waited for them to come back."

"And then what happened?" the detective asks.

"While I was waiting, the lady came out of the front entrance of the building and she was shot. I looked around and spotted the shooter up on the roof of the building across the street."

"Did you see a gun?" the detective asks.

"Yes, he had a rifle," Charak says.

"What happened after that?" the detective continues his questioning.

"The shooter disappeared and I called for an ambulance and police backup," Charak says. "That's when Mr. Anderson came out of the building. He tied his shirt around the wound to help stop the bleeding. A few minutes later, the ambulance arrived. The other two men came out of the building and right after that, you guys pulled up."

The detective looks at the three of us. "Do you all agree with Officer Charak's story?" he asks.

"Yes," I say.

Jeff and Rajat nod their heads, even though Rajat is still glaring at me.

The detective and three of the officers step a few feet away and whisper to each other. While they discuss the situation, another officer tells the crowd to move on, but most of them disregard his request. The last patrolman yellow tapes the crime scene and writes down our names and addresses before removing my handcuffs.

The detective gives us permission to leave the premises. He pulls Charak aside and says, "Go back to your patrol unit. We'll handle the incident."

"I need to talk to the woman and the NCB in apartment 305 before I leave," I tell the detective.

"They have already left the building from the back exit," he says. "We were notified by the NCB to let them leave quietly."

Rajat calls the NCB, but they tell him that Sophia is under heavy guard. No one is being permitted to talk to her. I barely acknowledge Rajat's existence. I can't wait to get out of this so-called FBI situation. I will never agree to help anyone again, I say for the fourth or fifth time.

The place is quiet. Several people stop and ask the officers what happened, but most just look and move on. Daniela's covered body and the white chalk mark surrounding her is all that is left on the steps. Several reporters have arrived and are taking pictures from outside the yellow tape line. A little late in my opinion, but the officers are now talking about looking for the killer and seeing if there were any witnesses.

We're stranded without a car, so Jeff decides to call a cab. "Let's call that cab driver you met," Jeff says.

"I don't have his number," I tell him.

"I have it on my speed dial." Jeff says.

Before I can object, Jeff dials Gus's number. Jeff tells Gus where we are and he says he'll arrive in fifteen minutes.

"It may not be a good idea to say anything about the case in front of Gus," I tell Jeff.

"Why not? You said he told you he knows all about Mumbai. He may help find her killer."

"He could be good friends with the mob or a drug dealer. I don't know him," I say.

"You're right." Jeff is quick to agree. "Let's not talk about any of this on the way back to the airport. All that worrying about how you were gonna make it look like you made the hit was for nothing. Bouchard got his wish and you don't have to kill Daniela."

"Don't forget. When we get back, you owe me an apology," I tell Jeff.

"For what? I only told the cops the truth."

"Thanks a bunch, dude. First chance I get, I'll return the favor."

"I doubt you'll get that chance." Jeff laughs. "So what do you think happened here?"

"Maybe Bouchard didn't trust me and had one of his goons do the job," I say. "Here comes the cab. Zip your mouth."

The cab pulls up in front of the building. "Hey, Robert. You came back."

"Hi," I say. "It's nice to see you again."

"What brings you and your friends to this part of town?" he asks. "There's no silver that I know of around here."

Jeff climbs into the back seat of the cab and Rajat tells him to move over.

"Where do you think you're going?" I ask Rajat.

"Back to the airport," he says. "I left my car there and I have to pick up my luggage."

"You're not going in this cab. Get your own. I never want to see you again."

"Let him ride, Nick," Jeff says. "We all have to pick up our luggage. It's all over now. Let's not stir up trouble."

I glare, but I don't answer.

Rajat gets in the cab.

"The *Chhatrapati Shivaji*," Jeff says to the cabbie.

I sit up front with Gus. He's stretching his neck toward the murder scene. "Hey, this is the address where that girl was killed. I just heard it on the news. Did you see what happened?"

"No, we don't know anything about it. We were just here visiting friends," Jeff says.

"You were visiting friends in this apartment building?"

"We were in the building next door," Jeff says.

"You were standing in front of an apartment house decorated with yellow crime tape stretched halfway across the building. Three patrol cars are parked on the sidewalk, and a group of pedestrians are craning their necks to see what's going on, and you don't ask anyone what happened?"

"Jeff meant we're not from here and didn't want to get involved," I say.

"Did your friends beat you up and steal your shirt?" He laughs.

"Give a break, Gus. We can't talk about it."

"I understand," he glances back at Jeff. "Look in that bag on the floor, there's a black T-shirt mixed in there. I carry an extra in case I spill something on me. It's not much, but it's better than walking into an airport with no shirt on."

"Thanks," I say. "Give me your address and I'll return it.

"Nah, it's old. Not worth the postage to send it back."

The cabbie looks in his rearview mirror at Rajat. "Is that cop with you, Robert? Maybe you better drop him off wherever you found him. He isn't anything but trouble. He could get you killed."

"He's okay." I say. "He's with me."

"Then you have questionable friends. The people who live around here are drug dealers, junkies, or criminals. If you don't believe me, ask that cop in the back seat, not that he's any better."

"I appreciate your concern," I tell Gus. "But the business we had here is finished. We won't be back."

"I'm sure glad to hear that," he says. "If your friend had told me this cop was with you, I wouldn't have come to pick you up. I don't normally pick-up or deliver from this area."

A few minutes later, we're back at the airport. Jeff and Rajat jump out of the cab and head for the luggage carousel.

I give Gus a crisp hundred-dollar bill. "It's a birthday gift. Take care of that baby that's on the way. I probably won't ever see you again." I pull the T-shirt over my head. It's a little tight but it's okay.

"You never can tell. Things don't always turn out the way we want them to. If you need me, I'm as close as your phone."

We shake hands and the Buick lumbers away from the curb. I'm glad this is over.

When I catch up with Jeff and Rajat, I see they have found all our luggage.

"I wonder if Bouchard will hear about Daniela, or if he'll think you shot her," Jeff says.

"Probably not." Rajat quips. "He's long gone. I just spoke with NCB. They told me that Vancouver's Criminal Justice Division had already picked Bouchard up and booked him for attempted murder."

I hear what Rajat is telling Jeff, but I don't look at him.

"They weren't supposed to do that," Jeff says. "Will they change the charge to first degree murder when they find out she's dead?"

"I don't know, but as soon as Robert signed the papers they had a judge issue the order. They picked up Bouchard and padlocked his business," Rajat says.

"At least you got half the price for killing Daniela," Jeff tells me. "You can take me out to dinner."

"I wish. Vancouver's Seriously Organized Crime Agency lifted that little bundle of evidence just as soon as I signed the affidavit."

Rajat turns away and walks toward his car. A patrol car screeches to a stop a few feet from Rajat and two officers jump out.

"Hi, guys. What's all the commotion?" Rajat asks.

"You," one of them answers.

They handcuff him and read him his rights.

Jeff hurries over to where they're standing. "What's going on?"

"We're arresting Rajat. He's an informer for the Punjabi Mob. We already have his girlfriend in custody."

"I'm not an informer!" Rajat reaches his cuffed wrists out to Jeff. "Tell them this is all a mistake. I didn't know she was doing that. We talked about the case, but I thought she was just interested in what I did. She told me she loved me. I swear I didn't know."

"That's enough fellow, get in the car."

"I want a lawyer," Rajat says.

"Tell it to the judge," the other officer says.

The patrol car drives away.

Jeff and I leave the airport.

"What do you make of that?" Jeff asks.

"I told you about that guy from day one. If you're gonna stay in this line of work, you need to become a better judge of character."

"I guess you were right all along," he says.

"Gas, ass, or grass, nothing's free." I tell him.

CHAPTER TWENTY-EIGHT
Belize

When Jeff and I arrive in Belize, Jon, the ambassador's driver, picks us up at the airport and takes us to the embassy. Jon keeps the partition closed and doesn't talk to us. I get the feeling that something is very wrong. We meet with Ambassador Logan. He had been following our itinerary, which Jeff had provided from beginning to end.

Jeff goes into Cox's office to file the needed reports and I sit in a chair in front of Logan's desk.

Logan leans back in his chair. "Most of the FBI and the DEA have gone back to the states. They acquired the information they needed to secure their position in Washington. The American people are joyful that the FBI and the DEA are doing their job and that the drugs that flowed from Belize through Mexico and into the United States have been stopped."

"Is that the good news?" I ask.

"It's much more complicated than you might imagine." Logan frowns. "Drugs are here to stay, my friend. The only thing that has changed is getting to know the new carriers. Belize's economical difficulties remain the same. No matter what else is happening, the politicians must nourish the tourist trade and provide a stable and safe city for the native people who live here."

"Are you telling me that risking my life didn't change anything?"

Logan shrugs.

"How come you told me that doing this job was for the good of the nation?"

"That was all true. When people read that their country has a government working to cure any problem, it makes them feel safe and secure.

I snort.

"Listen to this." Logan turns to an international radio station.

The station is in the middle of broadcast regarding a Punjabi Mafia's drug related murder in Mumbai. "A major drug bust by the U.S. DEA of a cartel that was run by members of the Punjabi mob from India, Belize, and possibly Canada has been broken up" the announcer says".

"The American news stations have been running the same story all day," Logan says. That was the U.S. Administration's intent and it came out better than they expected."

"Someday we'll have a government that really cares about the American people, instead of lining their own pockets, no matter what harm they cause." Logan tells me.

"That's not gonna happen," I say.

"You never know," Logan says. "It could be sooner than you think."

"Well, until then, I'm gonna get myself a gun, even if I have to break the law. Right now I need to be able to protect myself and my wife. I'm not interested in the world's problems." I contemplate my morning meeting with Ramos. "I'm more concerned with how I'm going to tell Ramos that I may have caused Daniela's death?"

"I wouldn't worry about it," Logan quips.

"That's because you don't have to do it."

He shrugs. "Cox is handling the paperwork. He said your last paycheck and bonus will be deposited to your account on file."

There doesn't seem to be anymore to say, so I stand.

"I want to thank you for everything you have done for your country," the ambassador says. "Jon will take you to Ramos's tomorrow morning. Ramos is expecting you around 10:00 am. My driver will wait for you and bring you back to the embassy."

"I don't want to inconvenience you. I can drive my own car."

"When we realized your stay was extended, the rental was returned. By the way, I would like to ask you for a personal favor."

Naturally, I tell him I would be glad to help, even though I'm disgusted with all the political involvement. None of this is Logan's fault. However, I'm prepared to say no if he expects me to continue working with the government.

"Do you remember the young boy the people called Willy Wiggle?"

"Yes, I do."

"He's staying here at the embassy. We took him in shortly after you left for India. We found out he was born with an ear defect. His father was a sailor on a cargo ship, and after Willy was born, his father never returned. Not long ago, his mother died and he has been living on his own for several months with the help of neighbors."

"I'm so sorry to hear that." I shift my weight.

"My wife and I have decided to adopt him. He appears to be quite happy with the idea. We recently found out that he can have an operation to fix his hearing problem."

"That's good," I say.

"If you are going back to Miami to pick up your girlfriend, I thought you might accompany him on the plane. I hesitate to send him alone."

The request takes me by surprise. It's not what I expected.

"It would be my pleasure." For the first time in weeks I break out in a smile of true happiness.

I shake his hand and we say good-bye. The next morning, Jon is waiting in the limo at the embassy gate.

"Did you have a nice trip?"

"Yes, I learned a lot, saw more than I expected and I'm glad to be back."

Today, Jon drives slowly, so it takes a while to get to the mansion. Ramos is waiting outside on the patio. Jon walks toward the back door. He wants to say hello to Rosie. I make my way to the patio.

Ramos stands and shakes my hand. I'm wondering how to approach the subject of his girlfriend.

"Good to see you back." He pauses. "The airline called this morning and told me about Daniela's unfortunate accident."

I want to tell him that it was no mishap, but I only say, "I'm so sorry, my friend, I wanted to tell you in person."

"I will miss her," he says. "Deedee is far too young to comprehend what happened to her mother. However, I am sure I will be in a better state of mind when the time comes to explain Daniela's death."

"Is your daughter here?"

"No, she went into town with her tutor, Miss Wright. They are ordering a Steinway at the music store. I want Deedee to have artistic training to go with her studies."

I'd have thought he would have been more upset by Daniela's fate. He had led me to believe that she was all he ever wanted. I'm a little confused. Should I tell him what she was doing in her off hours, or should I pretend she was a saint and let him live out his life in peace? Again, Ramos makes it easy for me.

"I do not need your report. What good is it to me now that she is gone? Life has a way of changing your objectives and we learn to live with whatever life deals us."

"I understand," I say. "You do not need to pay the balance of our agreement. Your loss is already too great."

"Don't be foolish. I always pay my debts. This is why I have so many friends and business acquaintances. I always keep my word. Honesty will take you many places during your lifetime, and it will make you successful."

I do not argue with him. I like the good life, and now that I have Angela, I want to travel. That leaves little or no time to make a living. I guess I'm lucky to have my wages and bonus from the DEA, and Ramos has staked me to a bundle that will last for quite a while.

What I need to do is go back to dealing cards. That's what I'm good at. Only from now on, I'm gonna have a legal job. We haven't touched any of Angela's 401K, even though she has frequently offered. I tell her we'll save it for a rainy day, or maybe she'll need it in her old age after I'm gone.

Ramos and I sit on the patio and talk about Belize and how happy he is to be spending his final years in such a pleasant atmosphere.

His cell phone rings, and he plucks it from the table. "Please excuse me," he says. "I must take this call. I'll be right back."

"Hello, Jorge. Thank you for returning my call," he says as he leaves the patio and walks to the far end of the yard to the gazebo.

I reach into my pocket for my own phone to see if I have missed any calls, and find the listening device Jeff gave me when we were in India. It had worked well for me there so I turn it on and put it in my ear.

"Are you there, Jorge? I thought I heard your phone click off."

"I can hear you. Can you hear me?" Jorge says.

"Ah." I smile. He has turned on the speaker. Now I can hear both sides of the conversation.

"Yes," Ramos tells him.

"I didn't know if I should call you at home." Jorge hesitates.

"Jon says that the intercepting equipment was dismantled last night and most of the American FBI and DEA have left the country."

"How did everything go? Did the private investigator you hired get the information you wanted?" Jorge asks.

"As it turns out, I do not need any information," Ramos says. "This time your sister went too far. She threatened our top contact in Canada. She also accused Kadam of getting Sophia pregnant. Thank goodness Kadam was allowed to contact our attorney before he ratted on two Punjabi associates. The attorney gave him the names of the two expendables who are going to take the fall for this small inconvenience. When Sophia got scared she went to the NCB. They are allowing her to go back to Colombia."

"Do you think Sophia will talk?" Jorge sounds really worried.

"She told the NCB she was forced into it, and that she only knew Daniela. They are not interested in Sophia."

"What do you want me to do?" he asks.

"Nothing. Edwardo will take care of that situation when Sophia returns to Columbia. When Sophia did not listen to Daniela, she lost her functionality. I was upset when Daniela went outside our pocket and hired her contact at Lunickbox Pharmaceutical to take out Sophia. I want you to learn from this. You can't make snap judgments."

"You do know Eduardo has been seeing Sophia on a regular basis?" Jorge says.

"Eduardo is an animal. He will find another compatible partner. My only hope for Deedee is that his genes do not permeate her life."

"Wow, I never thought Daniela would go that far. She lives in a fantasy world. She thinks she can control every man she meets with sex," Jorge says. "How is Daniela going to handle my taking over the business?"

"I'm sorry to tell you, but Daniela made the ultimate sacrifice." Ramos takes a deep breath. "When she found out that Sophia had called the police for protection, she tried to intercept the meeting, but she was too late. The NCB was already there. Daniela tried to sneak away from the building, but her own executioner mistook her for Sophia and shot her."

"Oh my God," Jorge says. "Is she gonna be okay?"

"I'm afraid not," Ramos says softly. "She died before the ambulance could get her to the hospital."

There is a long silence.

"The question is, are *you* going to be okay?"

Jorge hesitates. "Yes," he says. "I'll be fine."

"I'll see that you have sufficient time for a proper mourning period," Ramos says.

"Will we be changing any procedures?"

"I don't think so, but if a change is necessary, I will let you know," Ramos says. "There will be a short hiatus before we do any business. This will give you time to upgrade the shipping of the produce we spoke about while you were here. I want you to be ready to take over the shipping of the health supplements. Right now, I have other matters to attend to, and I need to end our conversation."

"I understand," Jorge says.

I'm absolutely amazed. They're talking about Jorge's sister, and the woman Ramos wanted to marry. No one is crying or even sounding sad. It's business as usual. I didn't even like the woman, yet I felt something when her life was so violently interrupted.

When Ramos finishes his call, he walks back to where I'm standing. The hearing device is back in my pocket, and I pretend to be checking my email. I guess Ambassador Logan knows what he is talking about. Drugs are here to stay.

Ramos lifts the lid from a vegetable basket. He picks up a money bag from inside and hands it to me. I glance at the currency inside.

"There is no need to count it. It's all there. You earned it fair and square. I must admit, you are some kind of dealer. I'm glad our paths have crossed. We never know what the future will bring. Maybe you will come back to Belize when you truly retire. You are always welcome in my home."

"Thank you," I say. I don't tell him that Belize is not on my list of favorites. "I have to go now. I need to close my account at Alliance Bank. I'm hoping to wire this cash to my Swiss account.

He holds his finger up. "One minute," he says and goes inside the house. When he comes out he hands me a card. "Ask for Senior Esposito, show him the card. He will transfer your funds."

Jon returns from his walk and I tell him I'm ready to leave.

Ramos and I say our good-byes. We make no future plans. We both know we'll never see each other again.

On our way back, I ask Jon to stop at the bank. As I get out of the Limo to go into the bank, I see the card only has a company name and telephone number. Then I notice a tiny mark in the corner of the card. The same mark that was on the card that the bar tender in India gave me.

That's strange, or is it?

CHAPTER TWENTY-NINE
Miami, Florida, USA

It's Monday, and when I spoke with Angela a couple of days ago, I told her if I could make plane reservations, I would fly in sometime today. Mrs. Logan is coming to the Miami International Airport to pick up me and Willy. She has also agreed to drop me off at Helen's. It will be a nice surprise for Angela and she won't have to drive through all the traffic. She said Helen was eager to meet me.

When Willy and I arrive, I call Mrs. Logan. She is waiting in the cell phone parking lot, and drives to the passenger pick up location in front of baggage claim.

She and Willy have been talking on the phone ever since the Logan's agreed to adopt him, but when we get in the car he becomes shy and chooses to sit in the back seat with me.

"It's okay," she tells me. "We have a whole lifetime to get acquainted—don't we Willy?"

He smiles, but doesn't say anything. She has brought him a present. She hands it to me to give to him. He takes the mechanical building set, but doesn't say anything.

I give her Helen's address.

She smiles. "That's only a short distance from our house."

I thank her when she drops me off, and tell Willy good-bye, but he won't let go of my hand. When I say Mrs. Logan is going to take him to her house, tears mist his eyes.

Willy understands what I am saying and he has known for some time that he is coming here to live with a new family He points to the heavy traffic, holds his hand over his eyes and hunches his shoulders.

"It'll be okay." I coax him to sit up front with Mrs. Logan. "She will take care of you. You will have your own room, she will cook food for you every day, and she is going to buy you a new bike."

Again, he shrugs.

I reach into my pocket and hand him twenty-five dollars. He grasps the money tightly and his eyes sparkle.

"That will tide you over until she can cook for you."

He smiles and sways back and forth.

"He's used to being on his own," I tell Mrs. Logan. "He needs a little money in his pocket to feel secure."

She reaches for her purse.

"No, no, he has enough for now." I close the car door.

I see the tears in his eyes. Willy waves as they drive away. I don't blame him for being upset. He's lost a father and a mother and now he's with a stranger in a foreign land.

I pick up my bag and walk to the front door. I wonder if the Logans know about Willy's drug problem.

Helen is standing in the doorway. "Nick? What are you doing here?"

"How did you know I was Nick?" I ask.

"Who else would arrive on Monday with luggage? Come here, Muffy." She picks up her cat. "I want you to meet Mr. Nick."

I grin and touch my finger to my lips. "I want to surprise Angela."

"She's not here. She went to meet you." Helen says.

"She didn't know what airline or what time I would get here."

"Oh, she didn't go to the airport."

I never know what Angela is gonna do. "Where'd she go?"

"When the FBI called, they said they would pick her up and take her to you. I took the day off so I could help her pack because they gave such short notice."

"Agent Cox," I mutter. "I'm gonna kill him."

Helen holds the door open. "Please, come inside. An FBI man picked her up early this morning. She must be somewhere close by."

I take out my cell phone and call Angela. Her mobile must be turned off because it goes straight to her mailbox. I tap my speed dial list and call Agent Cox. I'm glad I haven't taken the time to delete the number. He doesn't answer. I leave a message.

Then I call Jeff. I breathe a sigh of relief when he answers.

"Jeff. I just arrived in Miami. When I came to pick up Angela, her roommate told me the FBI came and took her to meet me. Where is Cox and what the hell is going on?"

"Nothing that I know of," Jeff says. "Let me walk over to Logan's office. Cox is in there saying good-bye to Donald right now."

I tap my foot, impatiently waiting for Jeff to find Cox. Helen is looking at me oddly.

"It's just a miscommunication," she says. "Please don't be upset. If she's with the FBI, I'm sure she is in good hands."

"You don't know them like I do." Sweat is pouring off my forehead.

Jeff comes back on the line. "Both Logan and Cox say they don't have any idea why the FBI would pick her up. Cox says he never told anyone but Logan that you had a girlfriend, and Logan says he never told anyone. They say they don't have her address and that they don't even know her last name."

"I've already wasted too much time. I'm calling the FBI office here in Miami right now," I tell Jeff.

"That's the right thing to do," Jeff replies.

"Who are you to tell what the right thing to do is?" I say.

"Hold on, Nick. I know you're upset. Cox and I are the last guys here. We're catching a plane in two hours. I'll call you when we get there."

"This better be straightened out long before you get here."

Helen hands me an index card. "I looked up the number for the FBI, but all I could find was the national telephone number, so I called it. They gave me a local number here in Miami."

"Thanks." I take the card.

"Nick, I'm really sorry."

"It's not your fault. It's the stupid job I did. I never should have taken it. Who knows what this government agency is doing? If anything happens to her, I'm gonna call the President. He needs to know what's going on in this country."

"How about a scotch and water? It'll settle your nerves," she says.

I nod and dial the number on the index card. I get an agent's mailbox and leave a message.

"I'm sure this is just an inconvenience. As soon as she finds out that you're not coming to wherever she went, she'll call you."

"You're right. I just worry about her," I say, but a thousand scenarios run through my mind. Such as, maybe Ramos figured a girlfriend for a girlfriend was fair.

She pours my drink. "That's only natural." Helen looks at me and smiles.

I take a sip and let it trickle down my throat. Helen opens a can of Coke and sits on the couch across from me. Neither one of us says anything. I think she's worried, too.

All at once, I have an idea. "Maybe she went to the condo to say good-bye to her parents." I dial her mother's cell phone number.

"Now why didn't I think of that?" Helen goes into the kitchen.

"Della." I try to sound casual. "Is Angela there with you?"

"No, darling, we said our good-bye's last night. She called this morning and said she was on her way to meet you. I was glad to hear that you were coming home. I imagine you're exhausted from running all over the world."

"I'm fine. Did she say where she was meeting me?"

"No she didn't. Don't you know where she was going to meet you?" I hear the apprehension in her voice.

"Well, yes, but—"

"Hold on a minute," she says. "Let me ask Emory. He spoke with her longer than I did. She may have told him."

I wait, knowing that if he doesn't know, I have just opened a whole new can of worms, and her parents will be frantic until we hear from her.

"Nick, dear. He says she didn't tell him. He wants to know where you are?"

"I'm at Helen's. I tried to call her, but she didn't answer her phone. I left her a message, but I haven't heard back yet."

"You need to text her. She usually looks at her texts. She doesn't always check her phone messages."

"I'll do that." I say good-bye before she can question me any further. I don't want to upset Della and Emory, and I don't want them to know how long she has been missing.

Helen returns from the kitchen. I guess she heard the phone conversation. "That's not good news," she says. "Maybe you should try to call the FBI again."

Just as I lean my head back against the chair to think about what I need to say to the FBI, my Samsung rings. It looks like the number is from somewhere out of the country. It's probably the FBI returning my call. "Hello."

"Nick?" a male voice says.

"Who's calling?" I reply.

"Never mind who's calling," the man says.

"Who wants to know?" I repeat.

"Do you want to know who's calling, or do you want to see your girlfriend again?"

I think my heart has stopped beating, but actually I'm holding my breath. I try to speak, but nothing comes out.

"I think you get the picture. Let's try this again. Is this Nick?"

"Yes."

"That's better. I have a message for you from Felix Bouchard. It appears that you have double crossed the wrong guy, but he's willing to give you a second chance. You're to contact Vancouver's Criminal Justice Division and tell them the recording you and he made was a fake. A joke recorded at a party. That no money was ever paid to you, and that you knew it was a joke and that he never intended to have you kill Daniela Diaz. When they release Bouchard, we'll let your pretty little Angela go."

"Who is this?" I turn up the volume and put my phone on speaker. I try to hear some background noise I might recognize. All I can hear is the clickety-clack of a moving railroad car.

Helen comes back into the room. "What's the matter, Nick? You're as white as a ghost."

I place my finger to my lips for her to be quiet.

"Where is Angela? What have you done with her?" I hold the phone close to my ear. What is that cadence in the distance? Maybe a drum, no it's an auctioneer. I change the phone to the other ear, but the sound has stopped. "Fuck!" I'm not sure what that cadence was.

"The three of us are taking real good care of her," the caller says.

"What three?" I ask.

"You remember us. We took real good care of you, too." He performs his hideous laugh.

I gasp when I realize that Angela is being held hostage by Bouchard's mentally ill perverts.

"If you hurt her, you'll pay with your life," I say.

"Get this message straight. You're the one who holds her life in your hands. You will determine whether she lives or dies." I recognize the voice. His words flow loud and clear from my smart phone.

He's right. I remember him well. He's big, husky Leecho. "I know who you are," I growl.

"Bouchard trusted you, but I wanted to kill you. I knew as soon as you opened your big mouth that you were trouble," he says. "When they came to arrest him, I told him he should have shot you the day we caught you sneakin' around. Then he wouldn't have had this problem."

Again, he laughs hysterically.

Helen sinks into the couch. She can tell by my voice that Angela is in big trouble. "Oh dear God," she whispers.

"You got forty-eight hours. After you sign the legal papers and Bouchard gets sprung, I'll call you and tell you where to pick up Angela. If Bouchard gets put in the pen, then Angela gets put in the river. You got that?"

"Wait a minute. I'm not even in the same country. You know how slow the law is. I can't do that in forty-eight hours."

"Then I suggest you start working on it right away."

My fist slams the wooden end-table, and my drink spills on the marble floor.

I can see Helen is ready to yell or scream. I jump up and put my hand over her mouth. She struggles but I hold on tight. My phone is on the table, but I swear I hear the faint sound of a church bell. It's probably my imagination.

The guy hangs up and my phone turns off.

I let go of Helen and tell her "I'm sorry."

She's crying. I put my arms around her and she sobs.

"I didn't mean to hurt you."

"Why did you do that?" Her eyes blaze.

"It was Leecho. I couldn't let him know I was with anyone. It would have put your life in danger."

"Who's Leecho?" she asks.

"He's a thug that works for a really bad drug dealer who I helped put in jail."

"Does this Leecho have Angela?" she asks.

"Yes. He's holding her hostage. If I don't agree to help him, he might harm Angela. He's using her to get freedom for his boss."

"I think we should call the police. They will know how to handle this." Helen wipes her eyes.

I pull myself together. "Don't talk about this to anyone," I tell Helen. "I'll take care of it."

"How are you gonna do that?" she asks

"I don't know yet. This guy, Leecho, is unstable, and bringing in the police is a sure way to get Angela killed." I can see that Helen has no faith in me. I place a call to Theo.

CHAPTER THIRTY

Theo answers his phone. "Hi, guy. Did you make it home okay?" He laughs "I didn't think I'd be hearing from you so soon."

"I need your help," I tell him.

"Don't tell me you got another deal in Canada? You know I don't approve of this kind of thing. Before you drag me into another one of your get rich schemes, tell me about your trip home."

"Stop joking around," I say. "This is no scheme. Bouchard's goons have my girlfriend. Leecho says if his boss goes to prison, he's gonna kill her. He says Bouchard wants me to rescind all that information I gave the SOCA."

"I don't know if you can do that without committing perjury and going to jail," he says. "And anything I can do for you won't matter. You're gonna have to go a lot higher than me."

"I understand, but I'm in Miami and I can't leave. Even if rescinding is doable, I still have to find out where Bouchard's gang is holding Angela and go in after her. Leecho only gave me forty-eight hours."

"I see what you mean," Theo says.

"What if you get a phony set of papers made up?" I ask Theo. "You show them to Bouchard and send them to his guy here in Miami. Maybe he'll let her go. Then we can renege on the deal."

"I knew you'd have a deal in there somewhere," he says.

"It's worth a try," I say. "In the meantime, I'll work on finding out where she is.

Call me back as soon as you have any information," I say.

"I'm on my way. I'll see what I can do." Theo says good-bye.

When I hang up, I hear Helen talking on the phone. "Hold on, Della." Helen looks at the floor.

"You told them?" I say.

"Yes, I had too. They're really upset, especially her dad. They want me to come and stay with them at the condo until this is settled. They're worried that there will be trouble here at my house. Frankly, I'm scared, too, so I'm going to take them up on the offer."

"That's a good idea."

Helen returns to her conversation with Della and soon hangs up. "Will you wait until I pack a few things to take with me?"

"Yes. I have a few calls to make. I'm really dreading one call, but I can't see any other way out. I don't know anyone else who might have a security clearance."

Helen goes into the bedroom and her cat comes over and rubs against my feet. The cat purrs, and an image of Gaetano's head appears where the cat's face should be. I point my index finger like it was a gun at Gaetano's ugly face, and wonder if Bouchard saw my face on the cat he shot. Sweet little Muffy swats my pant leg, hisses, then struts out of the room.

I put in a call to Joe Gaetano.

"Chief Investigator's Office, Joseph Gaetano speaking."

"I'm surprised you don't have a secretary or an administrator answering your phone," I tell him.

He's quiet for a moment. "My secretary is out to lunch. How may I help you?"

"I see you're all business. Not like the old days when you didn't have your shit together."

"Who is this?" he demands.

"It's your old buddy, Nick. I just called to thank you for the recommendation you gave me. We caught the drug smugglers and I got all the credit. I always thought you didn't care much for me, but I guess the years have seasoned you." I laugh to break his hostile attitude. "I understand you got a big promotion. I'm proud of you." I spread the sugar on thick. "We're a couple of Hoboken kids that did well in spite of how we were raised."

"Ah. . .Nick. . . you ole son-of-a-gun. It's good. . . to hear. . . from you," he stammers.

I know I've caught him off guard and I want to get the information I need before the idiot has time to think about what he's doing.

"How are you?" he asks.

"I'm fine. I'm employed by the federal government now. I'm an FBI agent."

"Wow. How'd you manage that?"

"Part of it was your recommendation. I'm out on the road with a senior agent right now, and we just got a cell phone call from a guy who the agent thinks is a serial killer. We need an address or at least a close location of where the call originated."

"You're with a senior FBI agent chasing a serial killer?"

"Yes, but for some strange reason we can't get our call to go through our tracking system. I don't know if the problem is on our end or the agency's side. We're afraid if we don't pick the killer up now, he might leave town and who knows when we'll get another chance like this."

"That's true," Joe says.

"But if your position doesn't allow you to have secret clearance information, I'll understand why you can't help me." I wait to see if he takes the bait.

"A man in my position has to be entitled," he says. "I have a secret security clearance."

"I knew I could count on you. You always were a good detective."

"Well, thanks, Nick. I like to set a good example."

I almost choke. Some people never change.

"Hold on a minute," he says.

"Okay," I say. Then I hear a click.

I'm afraid he might have cut me off, but then he comes back on the line. He gets information from me about the cell phone call I received from my fictitious serial killer.

"Hold on again," Joe says.

Again, I hear the click.

"Are you there?" Joe says.

I say yes, and some guy says, "this is Roger."

"I think I did this wrong," Joe says. "Hold on again."

When I hear the next click, I stay quiet.

"Are you there, Roger?" Joe says.

"Yes," Roger says. I wait quietly while they talk. Joe gives Roger all the information that I had just given Gaetano.

"This is not something I normally do." Roger says. "In fact, I'm not sure I can do it. I'll have to get help from my buddy in Ohio. Are you sure your friend is FBI?"

"Yes, I'm positive. This is an urgent request in order to catch a serial killer."

"We're kinda busy today," Roger tells Joe. "I need a little time."

I hear one more click and Joe's back on line with me. I guess he had accidently used his three-way button.

"This is going to take a while. I'll call you when I get the information."

I wanted to know now before Joe had time to think about it, but since the guy that's getting the information for him was a little reluctant to do it. I don't think Joe will be bragging to anyone about how he was able to find out Leecho's location. "Okay, I'll wait for your call."

"It's good to talk to you, Nick," he says.

"Likewise." I hang up.

Helen comes out of her room with a good size suitcase.

"How long do you plan on staying at the condo?" I ask.

"I'm staying with them until Angela comes home. They need me." She hands me a key. "This opens the front and the back door. You can stay in Angela's room. It's the first door on your right. Turn the air-conditioner down if you leave the house and leave a light on in the living room in case you don't come home at night."

I nod.

"I've made you a list," she says. "Including my cell phone number."

"Would you like me to follow you over to Angela's condo to make sure you get there safely?"

"No, I'll phone you when I get to Della's. I have to call my friend, too. He also wants to know I'm safe. He's gonna stay at a motel for a few days until we see what happens. Don't get any blood on my carpet."

I laugh.

"I'm not joking," she says. "Call me right away if you hear from her."

"I will, and you do the same. Try not to say too much to her parents."

"You know you're asking the impossible. Her father will rant and rave until you get her back home. The main reason I'm going is to be with Della. She said she needs me. You can use my computer. Angela set up the guest register. You can use her rental car. The keys are on her dresser."

"Thanks, Helen. You're a big help."

CHAPTER THIRTY-ONE

It's not long before Theo calls back. "Phony papers are not going to work. Bouchard has an attorney. He gave me his papers to fax to you."

"I have no choice." I say.

"This is perjury, Nick. You really need to think about what you're getting into."

"Are you kidding me? You know these people. They're brain sick. They have no respect for human life. Leecho gave me an ultimatum, and so far he's refused to negotiate the time period. Just send the papers to me." I read off Helen's fax number to him. "We'll argue the perjury rules another day. If I expect to see Angela alive again, I have to play by Bouchard's rules."

"That doesn't sound like you," Theo says.

"Well, I don't feel like me either. I've never had so much to lose, and my confidence level is being stretched to the limit," I say. "See what you can find out about Leecho. Maybe he has something in his past we can use. See if he has a family. I need something to counteract this attack and get me more time."

"I'll get right on it," Theo says. "Do you want me to fly down there?"

"You couldn't get here in time. I've got to do something now."

"I understand," he says.

"No, you really don't. I've been with these men. I was scared to death when I thought they were going to kill me."

"We're gonna resolve this. Don't worry." Theo tells me.

I try to control my mind, but I can't think straight. "I have no idea what she might be going through. Who knows what they may be doing to her."

Theo clears his throat. "Maybe you should bring in the police."

"Like you did for me," I say.

"That was different."

"No it wasn't. You were right. Bouchard would have shot me, and if I make a mistake, Leecho will kill Angela and get rid of her body just like he got rid of the expendables who worked for Bouchard. We're not dealing with ordinary people."

"I'll send the papers," Theo tells me.

"Keep your phone close. I want to be in constant touch with you."

"I'll be here whenever you need me," Theo says.

I play the telephone conversation with Leecho over and over in my mind. There was definitely a clickety-clack of train wheels, so he has to be close to a useable train track. If he's close by for me to pick up Angela, he must be somewhere in Dade or Broward County. And there are only two main railroads on the east coast of Florida that I know of. I also heard what sounded like an auction, and maybe the ringing of a distant church bell.

While I'm raiding Helen's refrigerator, my phone rings. It's Theo. I tell him that I have signed the papers and returned them to him.

"I was just calling to say I got them," he says.

"Leecho didn't call me until ten o'clock, so I have until late tomorrow before my time is up. Don't give the papers to Bouchard until it's close to forty-eight hours."

"You have my word," Theo says. "I didn't find an address on Leecho, but his real name is Greely Potash. So now you know why they call him Leecho. The phone number you gave me is listed to Felix's Vitamins and Nutriments."

"That's not a surprise," I tell Theo. "I'm waiting on a call from Joe Gaetano. He's a New Jersey detective who has connections with a person who can use satellites to triangulate where a call was originated from. I'll call you back."

As soon as I hang up, my phone rings.

"I got the information for you," Joe says. "The person using the phone called from an area in Fort Lauderdale. He gives me an approximate address. I checked the location and I found a

Day's Inn and an IHOP. They also called several numbers in Canada."

"That's great," I tell him.

"Are you still in the states?" he asks.

I'm not sure what I should tell him. "Yes, but I'm leaving tomorrow morning."

"I don't suppose you could get me a position with the FBI?" he asks.

"I don't think I could, but I know Agent Cox can," I tell him. "As a matter of fact, Agent Cox has a high opinion of you."

"You don't say? He seems like s very smart man," Joe says.

"Oh, he is. I think you and him would get along just great. He's out of the country this week, but call him next week. I'll put in a good word for you."

"Thanks, Nick. I always said you were a great friend."

"No problem."

I hang up and delete the call. I hope I never have to call that asshole again.

I look in the newspaper and on the computer for auctions, but nothing is listed for that area. Maybe I was mistaken. Maybe it wasn't an auctioneer.

I lie down on the bed, and close my eyes. "Hang in there, baby. I'm coming to get you." Then I add. "Please don't let anything happen to Angela. Please, please, please. I'll get a job. No more card dealing. No more deals. I promise." I jump when I feel Angela's hand slide down my arm, like she always does in the middle of the night. I open my eyes. Was I praying? I look around the room. There's nobody in the room but me. I look at the other side of the bed. No one is there.

I'm tired, but except for the few minutes I dozed off, sleep eludes me. I'm up before dawn. I get dressed and go into Helen's kitchen. I find tea, hot chocolate, sodas, water and juice, but no coffee.

I drive north from Dade to Broward County. I stop for coffee in Fort Lauderdale. My stomach growls and I end up eating breakfast. After eating, I spy a Sports Authority a few stores away, and I look through the store until I find a thin black windbreaker with a hood. There's webbing under the arm pits and across the back so maybe it won't be too hot.

I stop in the church parking lot on Sunrise Boulevard. The house next door to the church is old, empty and there's a piece of demolition equipment parked in the driveway. Old junk piled high at the curb, is waiting to be picked up by the city. I guess the house is gonna be torn down.

Before I get out of the car, I put on my new jacket and pull the hood over my head. If by chance this is the right area, Leecho might be hanging out close by.

I walk casually over to the curb. Bingo! There's a printed HOUSE AUCTION sign that's been ripped in half and stuffed in a box with old newspapers. The date on the sign is yesterday. I get back in the car. This might be the right place. I wonder how long it will take before a train comes by.

I drive across the street to the Day's Inn and park Angela's white Chevy rental. I sit there looking at the rear of the three-story hotel. There's a back door, but it probably requires a room card to gain access.

While I'm sitting there, I get a call from DEA Agent Jeff Blackwell. He says that after he and FBI Agent Walter Cox had completed their assignment in Belize, they flew home together to Florida.

"We just got here," he says. "How's everything going?"

"Not great, but I have a little information. I may have found the area where he made the call from. There's a Day's Inn, but I don't know if Bouchard's men are here, or if they have Angela with them."

"What's the address?" he asks.

I give him the name and address of the hotel. "It's on Sunrise Boulevard, right next to the railroad crossing. There's a church on one side of the street, and there's an old vacant house beside it," I tell him. "The hotel is across the street next to IHOP. I'm not even sure this is where she is, but I don't have any other leads. Leecho might have just made the call from here." I give Leecho's real name and his Canadian phone number to Jeff.

"I'm driving Angela's rental car. It's a 2007 white Chevy. I'm parked behind the hotel," I tell him.

"We're just leaving the airport. We'll connect with you as soon as we can get there." Jeff hangs up.

It'll take those guys at least an hour to get here from the Miami airport. I need to get in that back door and I'm sure it has a solid lock on it. I have to take a chance. I get out of the car and go in the front door to get a room.

"Will the room key let me in the back door?" I ask.

"Yes, sir," the lady at the front desk says. "Luggage carts are sitting right inside the door, if you care to bring your suitcases in that way." She hands me my key.

I go back out the front door and hear the far-off sound of a train. When the train gets closer, the engineer uses the whistle to warn drivers that it's crossing the major highway. The clickety-clack is loud and clear. If the auctioneer had been in front of the house I would have been able to hear him shouting out the bids. The church is old and doesn't look like it is being used anymore, but there is a new church further down the block that has a high bell tower. Even without hearing it, I feel certain it could be heard from here even during a train crossing. I don't want to put too much stock in this place because it doesn't look like an area where someone would hold a person hostage, but I have nothing else to go on.

CHAPTER THIRTY-TWO

I go back to Angela's car to wait for Jeff and Agent Cox. Time is going by, and I'm getting nervous. Even If I give Bouchard what he wants, I still have no guarantee that he'll keep his word and release Angela. I think of how quick Bouchard decided to get rid of Daniela. He might do the same with Angela.

I reach up and touch the little silver cross that Angela always has in the car she's driving. It sparkles in the sunlight. She even hung it in my car when we went out together. A warm feeling flows through me when I think about her. I can't wait any longer. I need to call in the police now.

I blink when I see two guys coming out the back door of the hotel. It's Leecho and Dobbs. I slouch in the car seat. They leave the hotel and walk over to IHOP. They must be going to eat lunch.

Now it won't be one against three. I'll have plenty of time. This is my chance. I can't wait for the agents. I have to go in now while there's only one guy inside. I pull the car up close to the hotel. If she's there, we will have to get out quick before Leecho and Dobbs come back. I go in through the front entrance and walk up to the desk. I'm happy to see a different desk clerk.

I flash my room card. "I'm with the Greely Potash group. They gave me my key, but I forgot my room number." I laugh.

Without even a second glance or a question, he taps a few keys on his computer and says room 125. I must look terrible because he thinks I'm one of them.

Then I hear a couple of shots. My heart beats faster. I've waited to long, I'm shaking all over. I run to room 125 and knock on the door.

"Sit down. Put your hands behind you." I hear a man's voice say.

I bang on the door again.

"Who's there?" the same voice asks.

"It's Leecho. I forgot my key," I say in a deep growl.

There's a loud crash of glass.

"Open the damn door!" I shout

"Okay. okay," the voice says.

It's gotta be Quirky. Who else would be in there?

The door opens slowly. I give it a shove and it hits Quirky in the head.

"Damn." He stumbles backwards. The only person in the room is Quirky, and the only thing he has on is a pair of trousers. No shoes, no shirt, no belt and his zipper is down.

I charge in and give him a hard shove up against the wall. "Where's Angela?" He tumbles and crouches close to the floor.

Angela's suitcase has been opened and dumped on the floor in the middle of the room, Oh my God. What have they done to her. A broken chair lies next to the window. The window is splintered, but there is no hole to get out of the room. I run to the window. Angela is nowhere in sight. I look in the empty bathroom and then I spy the door to the adjoining room is slightly open. Maybe she went out that way.

I start for the door, but Quirky has grabbed his shoes and shirt and is headed out of the room. I tackle him, and we tussle on the floor. He's easy to subdue. I hit him with a hard right, and he lays still.

I turn around and bump into a sharp left hook just above my nose. Blood gushes and streams into my eye.

"Felix might give you a second chance, but not me," Leecho says.

"I already faxed the papers back to Theo. He's taking them to Bouchard's attorney," I tell him.

"Do you think I'd believe that?" Leecho grunts.

"Call Bouchard," I say. "He probably already has the papers."

Evidently the guys left their guns in the room when they went to get something to eat or Leecho wouldn't have bothered to fight me. I reach for my gun, but he's quick. He sticks his foot between mine, and we go down. We wrestle on the floor. We roll over the suitcase and slam into the dresser. He twists my arm behind me while he reaches for the dresser drawer. Dobbs is headed for the other side of the room. He opens the small drawer in the night stand.

Leecho gives my arm another twist and the pain shoots up my neck and into my head.

There's a loud blast of gunfire and a bullet explodes against the dresser. Dobbs drops his Glock and puts his hands in the air.

I blink. I can only see out of one eye, but I'm sure it's Angela and she's brandishing a pistol.

"Don't just stand there, Dobbs. Take that gun away from the bitch before she gets lucky." Another shot rips through the air and passes inches from Leecho's head.

"Shoot her!" he yells at Dobbs.

"I can't shoot a woman," Dobbs says.

"Then take her friggin' gun." Leecho screams again.

"Back out of here," I tell Angela. "Don't do anything foolish."

"She's not backing out of anywhere." Leecho says.

Somehow Leecho stretched far enough to reach his gun, but I have his arm bent and his weapon is pointed toward the dresser.

"Don't worry, Dobbs. I got my gun leveled right at his head." Leecho lies." She's a poor shot. Take her pistol."

I gasp when Dobbs walks around the bed toward Angela.

"Better not try that." DEA agent Jeff Blackwell comes into the room and steps between Angela and Dobbs.

"So she's got a back up. Big deal, it's still two to one, our favor." The crazed Leecho laughs again.

"Three to two! Drop the guns." FBI agent Walter Adonis Cox III has never looked so good to me. I could kiss the son of a bitch.

Leecho lets go of my arm and drops his gun. Dobbs hands his Saturday night special to Jeff.

I still have questions. "How'd you guy's get here so quick?" I pull away from Leecho and stand.

"It's only a short drive." Cox says.

"From Miami? You're kidding. It always takes me at least an hour in traffic."

"We never fly into Miami." Jeff says. "We live in Broward County. We flew into Fort Lauderdale."

"How'd you know to come to this room?"

"We followed the gun shots. We knew you had it under control." Jeff clamps handcuffs on all three criminals.

"Don't encourage him," Cox says. "He already thinks he's God's gift."

"Well, I think he is." Angela puts her bloody arm around me.

I love her so much.

Cox checks out the broken chair by the window, then turns to Angela. "You broke this window with a chair?"

"Not exactly, I shot it twice before I tried to shove the chair through, but it wouldn't give. I cut my arm on a piece of glass before I realized Quirky was putting his clothes on and had left the adjoining room door unlocked."

Quirky wakes up and looks around. "I told them we shouldn't have come here," Quirky says. "Every time we go to a hotel, we end up in jail. What happened this time?"

"You tell us," Leecho says. "We came back because we heard the shots. We thought you were in trouble. How did the woman get loose?"

Quirky cocks his head to one side. "The pretty woman promised me a kiss."

"And a person should always comply with the deal." Angela walks over and gives Quirky a big kiss, right on the lips.

Cox and Jeff laugh and I glare at them.

Jeff puts his hand on my arm. "Look, we got this under control. I'll call Theo and tell him to shred those legal papers and keep Broussard locked up. We'll handle the rest of this. You and your girlfriend can take-off.

I shake their hands. "Good job, guys. I owe you."

"Maybe we'll take you up on that," Cox says.

Angela gives me one of her looks, like she's saying—never again.

On our way to the emergency room, I ask Angela, why did you agree to kiss Quirky? He's so disgusting. Look what they did to your suitcase."

"No, I did that," she says. "I was all packed when they came to pick me up. I guess they never thought that I would have a gun in my suitcase, because they never looked. I was in such a hurry when I packed that I didn't remember where it was, so I just dumped it on the floor and the gun fell out"

"Was it loaded?" I ask

"Yes, but the safety was on."

"Do you realize that the safety could have been knocked off when the gun hit the floor?"

"I didn't have time to think about that." Her lower lip quivers.

"I'm glad Jeff and Cox got here before you got another shot off."

"I wasn't going to shoot again. I was out of bullets."

"Where are the rest of the bullets?" I blurt out.

"I used them to practice. The gun didn't come with extra bullets. I had a hard-enough time convincing the salesman to fill the clip." Then she winks. "Lean over here, darling," she says. She takes a handkerchief from her pocket and pats the blood from my eye.

"I have a couple of more questions," I say.

"And what would you like to know?" she asks.

"To start with, who gave you the gun?"

"No one, silly. Helen took me to a little gun shop close to where she works. Dad told her you tended to be a little crazy, so she thought I might need it."

"When did you learn to shoot a gun?"

"Well," she says in her special way. "Remember me telling you that when I was a little girl my parents spent the winters in Miami? And one day they took me to visit my Uncle Morris Crockett who lived in Broward County, in what was then a little western town named Davie.

"He was the one who was related to Davy Crockett, right?"

"Yeah, he's the one." She smiles and her eyes twinkle.

"You told me he taught you a lot about politics. Did he also teach you to shoot a gun?"

"Let's just say, he tried." She stops and grins. "And when we have children you can tell them the rest of our story."

"Children! When did we decide to have kids?"

THE END

Made in the USA
Lexington, KY
13 April 2019